Bound Away

VIRGINIA AND THE WESTWARD MOVEMENT

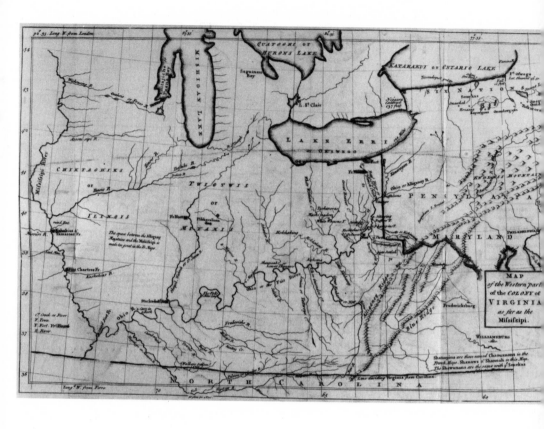

Bound Away

VIRGINIA AND THE

WESTWARD MOVEMENT

David Hackett Fischer and James C. Kelly

University Press of Virginia
Charlottesville and London

The University Press of Virginia
©2000 by the Virginia Historical Society and David Hackett Fischer
Printed in the United States of America

First published in 2000

∞The paper used in this publication meets the minimum requirements
of the American National Standard for Information Sciences—Permanence of
Paper for Printed Library Materials, ANSI Z39.48-1984.

Frontispiece: *Map of the Western Parts of the Colony of Virginia, as Far as
the Missisipi,* in *The Journal of Major George Washington* (London, 1754).
(Virginia Historical Society)

Jacket and cover art: *Fairview Inn or Three Mile House on Old Frederick Road* (detail),
by Thomas Ruckle, c. 1829. (Maryland Historical Society, Baltimore)

Library of Congress Cataloging-in-Publication Data

    Fischer, David Hackett, 1935–
      Bound away : Virginia and the westward movement / David Hackett
    Fischer and James C. Kelly.
         p.   cm.
      "This book began as a catalog for an exhibition, at the Virginia
    Historical Society, to mark the centenary of Frederick Jackson
    Turner's thesis on 'the significance of the frontier in American
    history'"—Pref.
      Includes bibliographical references (p.   ) and index.
      ISBN 0-8139-1773-5 (cloth : alk. paper). —ISBN 0-8139-1774-3
    (pbk. : alk. paper)
      1. Virginia— History—Colonial period, ca. 1600–1775.
    2. Virginia—History—1775–1865. 3. Virginia—Population—History.
    4. Migration, Internal—Virginia—History. 5. Migration, Internal—
    United States—History. 6. Frontier thesis. 7. United States—
    Territorial expansion—History. 8. Frontier and pioneer life—
    Virginia. 9. Frontier and pioneer life—United States. I. Kelly,
    James C., 1949– . II. Virginia Historical Society. III. Title.
    F229.F534 2000
    975.5'02—dc21   99-30766
                                   CIP

Contents

Illustrations

Foreword

THE MOVE WEST always began with a decision. For Nelson and Polly Bryan, the decision was months, maybe years in the making. Whatever their reasoning, in the spring of 1818 they prepared for a fateful journey. The particulars of why they were taking such an important step are not known. Family records indicate that Nelson Bryan had been born near Winchester, Virginia, shortly after the American Revolution. He had married Polly Petty in 1806, and in the next twelve years the couple produced six children, who in 1818 ranged in age from eleven years to only a few months old. The Bryans probably made their living on a farm. In 1818, however, powerful forces tugged or pushed the family westward. Were they unhappy with their lot in Virginia, or were they drawn by frequent reports of cheap, rich land and unlimited opportunities in "the West"? We can only speculate.

When the time came to leave, Nelson and Polly Bryan more than likely packed up as much as they could in a wagon or two, bade tearful good-byes to family and friends, and then headed down the great emigrant highway with their six children, never to return to Virginia. As they traveled south through the Shenandoah Valley, they would have met scores of other families who had made the same decision. All along the way, they would have seen gangs of slaves being transported for sale at high prices in the Deep South. They may have encountered a sheriff looking for an escaped murderer who had headed west to start a new life.

Some six weeks into their journey, they crossed into Tennessee. Days later at Knoxville, they would have headed due west. In a week or so they probably climbed up the great Cumberland Plateau at Crab Orchard, following a primitive road that had been used by tens of thousands of immigrants for more than forty years and by Cherokee Indians for longer than anyone could remember. As they sat around the campfire at night, the children, no doubt, were spooked by the thought of ghosts and Indians lurking in the heavily forested hills.

Several days later, some two months after leaving home, the Bryan family would have rolled their wagon down the highlands into a land of rich alluvial soil, limestone outcroppings, and wide stream bottoms in Middle Tennessee. About eight miles south of the little town of Lebanon in Wilson County, just east of Nashville, they halted at the Round Lick of Spring Creek, their journey ended. Why did they stop? Several Virginia families had moved there in the previous decade, and as was often the case in the history of the westward movement, one may have sent regular communications to their friends in the Old Dominion. The Bryans simply may have been following the advice of an old friend who had relayed the virtues of the land around Spring Creek.

Nelson and Polly Bryan came to Spring Creek to stay, but most of their children and their children's children picked up where they left off and continued the great folk migration. Their offspring moved to Missouri, Texas, and California, continuing a cycle of family moves that had begun in Scotland and northern Ireland centuries before. One of their great-grandsons (my grandfather) was born and raised on the farm in Spring Creek, but as a young man he moved to a white-collar job in another county. There he met a young woman whose maternal line had come to Tennessee from Virginia three generations earlier. When they married in 1905, two old Virginia family lines merged. And again repeating the cycle, their children and their children's children grew up and left home to seek opportunities elsewhere. Ironically, opportunity drew me and my family to Virginia twelve years ago, bringing full circle the move my great, great, great-grandfather made from the Old Dominion 182 years ago.

The story of my family is one that could be repeated in only slightly altered form by every American. If there is any constant in American history, it is that we are a nation of movers. Most of us know or have a sense of when our ancestors came to America. For those people who have studied their family histories in depth, it quickly becomes evident that once their forebears got here, they and their offspring rarely stayed in the same place. All American families have been participants in part or all of the three great migrations in our history—from elsewhere to America, then from east to west, and finally from country to city. Demographers have even identified a fourth migratory trend in the last half century—from city to suburb. These great migrations have had a profound effect in shaping the course of American history.

This book examines in detail one of those great migrations and how it profoundly affected one state. In doing so, it tells an often-neglected part of Virginia history. By the time of American independence, Virginia was the wealthiest, most populous, and most politically influential element of the infant nation. Yet within the next seventy-five years, the Old Dominion declined dramatically. Virginia in the mid–nineteenth century was far less influential in the councils of the nation than it had been a few decades earlier. From the preeminent place it had occupied since the colonial period, the Old Dominion slipped almost suddenly into a secondary role. Why? The emigration of nearly a million Virginians to the Deep South and West not only drained the state of population and capital; it also siphoned off thousands of able sons and daughters whose energy, vigor, talent, and leadership Virginia could ill afford to lose. Virginia's great loss proved to be the great gain of scores of states to the south and west.

For some 300,000 Virginians, the decision to move west was out of their hands. Although we tend to think of the westward movement as a white phenomenon, about a third involved in the process were black. Indeed, many African Americans living today in Kentucky, Tennessee, Alabama, and Texas can, like Alex Haley, trace their roots to the Old Dominion. As historian Kenneth Stampp has observed, "Among the antebellum southerners who left the impoverished lands of the [East] for the fresh lands of the southwest—among those who cut down the forest, grubbed the stumps, cleared the cane brakes, drained the swamps, and broke the virgin soil—were negro slaves as well as white pioneers."

The subject covered in *Bound Away* is large and complex. The book has a definite point of view that is open to challenge, and not everyone who goes through it will agree with it. We welcome this controversy, because we intentionally made the exhibit on which it is based intellectually provocative.

Today, many Americans are "bound away," seeking new opportunities no less so than did the flood of people who left Virginia in the early nineteenth century. If anything, this book tries to dispel the myth of modern mobility. One quickly sees that people moving in and out of neighborhoods, from one state to another, or from one job opportunity to another are merely a continuation of a phenomenon that was set in motion centuries ago. And if the last four hundred years are any indication, Virginians and their fellow Americans will remain in motion for generations to come.

This book had its roots in the most ambitious and successful exhibition ever mounted at the Virginia Historical Society. We are grateful to the University Press of Virginia for undertaking to ensure that the splendid research and interpretation of David Hackett Fischer and James C. Kelly are widely disseminated.

Charles F. Bryan, Jr.
Director
Virginia Historical Society

Preface

THIS BOOK BEGAN as a catalog for an exhibition, at the Virginia Historical Society, to mark the centenary of Frederick Jackson Turner's thesis on "the significance of the frontier in American history." Our purpose was to have another look at that subject, in a manner different from that of Turner himself. The original frontier thesis studied the westward movement in terms of its destination. We decided to approach it in terms of its origins.

The title of the exhibition came from an old folk song called "Shenandoah." Many readers will remember its chorus: "Away! I'm bound away!" Those words, which travelers sang as they crossed the western rivers, summarize several themes that we have found in their experience—themes in some ways opposite to those of Frederick Jackson Turner himself.

Turner's frontier thesis was about the transformation of ideas and institutions at the edge of settlement. Our story is about continuity in the midst of change and the power of cultural persistence in the westward movement. It is also about the interplay of contingency and determinism in a large historical process. Unlike Turner, whose idea of a frontier developed in his native Wisconsin, our story is about a southern migration in which some people moved freely to the West and others traveled in chains.

In all of these ways, we believe that Americans who moved west to the frontier were truly "bound away." For us, those two words capture the complexity of their historical condition more accurately than did the frontier thesis itself.

Historians differ from one another not merely in their answers but more profoundly in their organizing questions. The genius of the Turner thesis was its success in spawning so many questions and so many different meanings of the word *frontier*. In historical usage Turner's frontier has referred variously to a specific place, a particular process, a zone of interaction, a cultural myth, and a general historical problem.

During the early twentieth century, most writings on the subject were about the frontier as a place—the American West. The Turner thesis was used to frame the descriptive history of a distinctive region. Later, a second set of questions centered on the frontier as a process—not the West but the westward movement, which was understood as the expansion of a hegemonic Anglo-American culture in the New World.

A very different set of questions were taken up by the "new western historians" who worked in the last quarter of the twentieth century. Some of them rejected the centrality of Anglo-American culture in the United States and tried to reconstruct the idea of the frontier as a "zone of interaction" between different cultural groups.

Other "new western historians" were Marxists, heavily materialist and deeply alienated from American institutions. For them, the idea of a frontier appeared to be a form of "false consciousness," far removed from the reality of western history. Turner's frontier became for them a cultural myth which shaped the self-identity of a corrupt capitalist culture.

We wish to offer neither a critique of their work nor an apology for our own. Suffice to say that we see things differently. We believe that Turner's frontier was not primarily a myth but something that actually happened in the world. We also think that it was not, in the fashionable sense, a "zone of interaction" between cultures but a place where one culture rapidly established a hegemony which persists to this day.

Further, we believe that the importance of this subject transcends its reference to a specific place (the American West) and a particular process (the westward movement in the United States). The frontier also can be studied in more general terms as part of a large historical problem about culture and environment, continuity and change, and how things came to be.

The frontier in this sense embraces not merely the English-speaking cultures that established a hegemony in North America but the expansion of Aztec cultures in Mexico, Bantu societies in southern Africa, Germanic and Celtic tribes in Europe, Chinese civilization in Asia, Polynesians in the Pacific, Vikings in Scandinavia, Slavic nations in eastern Europe, and Islamic religion in the Middle East, to name only a few. Turner's frontier thesis deserves to be studied as part of a world historical problem.

Bound Away

VIRGINIA AND THE WESTWARD MOVEMENT

Introduction

ON A HOT CHICAGO DAY, July 12, 1893, a great crowd gathered in the gleaming pavilions of the World's Columbian Exposition to celebrate the 400th anniversary of the European discovery of America. In the course of the afternoon, the crowd divided in a symbolic way. Many spectators moved eastward to the shore of Lake Michigan and watched the arrival of a replica Viking ship from Europe. Others went in the opposite direction and attended a performance of Buffalo Bill's American Wild West Show.

In the evening a third group traveled uptown to the Art Institute of Chicago, where a special meeting of the American Historical Association tried to find a deeper meaning for the day. The program had been organized by Johns Hopkins professor Herbert Baxter Adams, dean of America's new historical profession. It reflected his strong interest in the European origins of American culture. The sweltering audience sat patiently through learned papers on popular risings in medieval England, Jefferson and the social compact, the relation of history to politics, and as a concession to local scholars, early lead mining in Illinois and Wisconsin.[1]

The last scholar on the program was Adams's former student Frederick Jackson Turner, thirty-one years old, an instructor at the University of Wisconsin. Turner rose to his feet and delivered a challenge to his teacher in a paper called "The Significance of the Frontier in American History." He summarized his thesis in a sentence: "The existence of an area of free land, its continuous recession, and the advance of American settlement westward, explain American development."[2]

By "frontier," Turner meant an area of "free land." Drawing heavily on the work of Italian social scientist Achille Loria, he argued that "so long as free land exists, the opportunity for a competency exists, and economic power

1. An announcement by the U.S. Census Bureau in 1891 that it could no longer find the line of a western frontier on its maps inspired Frederick Jackson Turner to write his paper on "The Significance of the Frontier in American History."

secures political power." On the basis of this assumption, Turner concluded that "the frontier is productive of individualism" and that "frontier individualism has from the beginning promoted democracy." In that way he argued that the free land of the American frontier created a nation of free people.[3]

Turner also suggested that the frontier might be understood in another sense, as the "meeting point between savagery and civilization." This zone, he argued, was the area of the "most rapid and effective Americanization," a place where different groups mixed and merged into the "composite nationality" of the United States.[4]

The audience at the Art Institute was not much interested in the young man's ideas. It had been a long day, and one scholar remembered afterward that the room responded with "bored indifference" to a "young instructor from a backwater college." There were no questions and no discussion. A reporter who covered the meeting showed more interest in the early lead mines of Illinois than in the frontier thesis.[5]

Five months later Turner tried again. He gave his paper at the State Historical Society of Wisconsin and published it in the proceedings of the American Historical Association. When it first appeared in print, many scholars did not understand it. One took it to be a thesis "about the state and its geographic origins." Another contemptuously called its author "a very provincial type of historian."[6]

Readers who were not professional historians responded in a different way. Journalist Talcott Williams in Philadelphia praised the paper as "the most informative and illuminating contribution to American history I have read in recent years." Theodore Roosevelt wrote Turner a letter of congratulations for "striking some first class ideas." Woodrow Wilson took an interest in the young man and paid him the sincerest compliment by borrowing his ideas.[7] Praise was soon matched by criticism. A controversy began, and has continued to our own time. The problem at its center is the subject of this book.[8]

Framing the Inquiry: Germ Theory and Frontier Thesis

At The Johns Hopkins University, Herbert Baxter Adams and his colleagues had developed what Turner contemptuously called the "germ theory of politics." This was not a single idea but a cluster of conceptual models. One version held that America's free institutions developed from European "germs" that had been carried from the forests of ancient Germany to medieval

Britain and thence to modern America. Other versions argued more broadly for the persistence of old cultures in a new environment.[9] The frontier thesis revised these ideas without rejecting them altogether. Turner argued that the American environment in which the European germs were planted was at least as important as the germs themselves.

On the question of validity in these ideas, historians have divided into different camps. Like the crowds at the Columbian Exposition, one group of scholars turned eastward toward the traffic from Europe; another group went the other way and watched the Wild West show. Some of Turner's disciples (mostly in the West) restated the frontier thesis in terms stronger even than those of the master himself.[10] Several of his critics (mainly on the eastern seaboard) insisted that the frontier thesis was literal nonsense in its own terms. In 1945 Carlton J. H. Hayes challenged the frontier historians by posing a simple question, "The American Frontier—Frontier of What?" Hayes insisted that Turner's American frontier was the cutting edge of European culture in the New World.[11]

Problems of Culture and Environment, Continuity and Change

At the center of this controversy is a set of larger questions about culture and environment as determinants of historical change. The germ theorists believed that cultural imperatives were more powerful than environmental forces. This approach found one of its most coherent expressions in a model of cultural geography developed by German scholar August Meitzen in the late nineteenth century. Called the *Altlandschaft* ("old country") theory, this school held that "the first permanent occupants of an area will influence all subsequent occupants and therefore have a lasting settlement effect."[12]

Opposed to this model is the Turnerian idea that in North America at least, the physical environment radically transformed the culture that was carried into it. "At the frontier," Turner wrote, "the bonds of custom are broken and unrestraint is triumphant." He believed that "each frontier did indeed furnish a new field of opportunity, a gate of escape from the bondage of the past. . . . scorn of older society, impatience of its restraints and its ideas, and indifference to its lessons, have accompanied the frontier."[13]

This is a question not only about culture and environment but also about continuity and change. Germ theorists, some of them at least, put heavy

2. Turner's teacher Herbert Baxter Adams was a leading proponent of the "germ theory," which held that American institutions grew from the seed of European, especially Teutonic, culture. The frontier thesis was a counterargument to this idea.

stress on themes of cultural persistence. The frontier thesis, in most of its versions, was a model of cultural transformation.

How are we to resolve these questions? At the outset it should be clear that any viable answer must take the form of a mediating model. Even so, the problem of balance and proportion remains very much in doubt.

Also doubtful is the question of linkage among its various parts. Culture, environment, continuity, and change can be combined many different ways. The germ theory combines culture with continuity; the frontier thesis links environment and change. But one might also consider an association between environment and continuity or between culture and change. There are many possible permutations, which can only be assessed by close study and careful research. Otherwise, the problem of the frontier and American culture begins to resemble Oscar Wilde's question about whether "fogs caused the English mentality, or the English mentality caused fogs."[14]

Another issue is the relationship of determinisms in general to processes of choice and contingency. At the outset it should be clear that determinants of westward movement always operated upon individual choices, such as the decision of Nelson and Polly Bryan to move their family west from Virginia to Tennessee. That choice was followed by others, when their children and grandchildren decided to move to Missouri, Texas, and California. America's westward movement was a web of choices: where to go, when to leave, and whether to stay or move again. For America's cultural history some of the most important choices were about what to take along or leave behind.

The Material Problem: Free Land

Yet another set of problems has emerged in controversies among scholars who disputed Turner's understanding of the environment itself, and especially the effect of what he called "free land." At the same moment when Turner argued that free land caused the growth of American democracy, it is interesting to discover that the greatest of Russian historians, V. O. Kliuchevsky, used precisely the same cause to explain an opposite effect.

For Turner the central question of American history was to explain the growth of freedom and democracy. His answer was free land. For Kliuchevsky, the central problem in Russian history was to explain the growth of serfdom and autocracy. His answer was also free land.

3. The great Russian historian V. O. Kliuchevsky believed that "free land" led to unfree labor in systems of serfdom and slavery throughout the world.

Kliuchevsky believed that an abundance of free land in eastern Europe created a problem for owners of great estates. The availability of land threatened to draw off their workforce. To hold their laborers, landowners bound their workers to the land through the institution of serfdom.

The European scholar H. J. Nieboer went further than Kliuchevsky. He argued that the same cause operated wherever land was abundant to create serfdom in eastern Europe, latifundia systems in Latin America, and race slavery in the United States.

The difference between these schools of interpretation could not be more dramatic. While Turner believed that free land created a democracy of freehold farmers, Kliuchevsky and Nieboer took the opposite stand: they held that free land led to unfree systems of serfdom and slavery. The two European historians cited the American South as a classic example.[15]

Kliuchevsky and Turner appear to have written in ignorance of one another, but in the twentieth century other scholars began to compare their works. One who did so was Evsey Domar, a Russian historian who taught in America. Domar sided with Kliuchevsky and Nieboer. He dismissed Turner's North American case as a minor anomaly—hardly a satisfactory solution for North Americans. The question might be reopened, with special attention to those parts of America where freedom and slavery coexisted.[16]

The Migration Problem: The "M-Factor"

A third major problem centers on a cluster of questions about migration, which George W. Pierson called the "M-Factor" in American history. In the generations since Turner, social historians have tended to become less interested in the frontier and more attentive to migration as a determinant of cultural development in the history of the United States. They have studied the structure of the migration process, the characteristics of migrants (such as gender, class, age, family status), the effect of migration on cultural continuity and change, and also the decision to move. Many of the effects that Turner assigned to the frontier have been attributed by other scholars to migration. The same questions that have been addressed to the frontier might be asked about migration to, within, and from various parts of America.[17]

Also important here is the question of the effect of emigration on the society that the migrants left behind. Followers of Frederick Jackson Turner, more than Turner himself, believed that the frontier functioned as a social "safety valve" for the East, releasing pressures that might have increased class conflict. Critics of Turner have strongly disagreed. This problem has been discussed at length, mainly by reference to the northern states. Less attention has been given to the effect of emigration in the American South. Was the frontier a safety valve for slavery? Did it give the South's peculiar institution a longer lease on life? Here is a hard question for Turnerians. If the answer is no, then the safety valve mechanism itself is called into question; if the answer is yes, then the idea that the frontier fostered freedom and democracy is undercut.[18]

The Cultural Problem: Unity and Pluralism

Yet another problem has risen from Turner's concept of the frontier as a place of "rapid and effective Americanization," a zone for assimilation and the growth of "composite nationality." Many historians today understand the main lines of American history in a very different way—not in terms of growing assimilation and "Americanization" but of growing diversity and pluralism. This problem poses another set of questions about the westward movement. Did it make Americans one people? Did it reinforce our differences? Did the dynamics of unity and diversity change through time and vary through space? Here again, study of particular parts of the westward movement has much to teach us.

All of these issues are directly connected to a larger ethical problem that lies at the heart of American history. Like most historians of his generation, Frederick Jackson Turner assumed that the central problem of American history was to explain the determinants of a voluntary society—an open system that tended to become increasingly democratic in its politics, capitalist in its economy, libertarian in its laws, individualist in its society, and pluralist in its culture.

Colleagues who disagreed with him on the significance of the frontier shared that same concern. Even as they rejected his answer, they accepted his central question. Most American historical writing has been an attempt to explain the origin and stability of an open society—by reference to the American environment, or the culture that migrated there, or the process of migration, or some combination of these factors.

This remained the central question of American history until the late twentieth century, when it was challenged by a generation of scholars who came of age in the troubled years of Vietnam and Watergate. Their primary purpose was not to ask why the United States became an open society but why it was not more open. These historians of the Vietnam-Watergate generation rejected not merely the answers of Frederick Jackson Turner but also his organizing question. Some who called themselves "new western historians" rewrote the history of the American West as a story of environmental destruction, economic exploitation, social inequality, and cultural disintegration. A few went out of their way to avoid all mention of Turner—no easy task in western historiography. One called the frontier the "f-word" and tried without success to purge it from historical usage.[19]

The new western history appeared during the 1970s and 1980s. In the 1990s other scholars have turned away from it. One wonders what the future holds. Is the generation of Vietnam and Watergate an iconoclastic aberration in American historiography or a harbinger of things to come? Here is another question to keep in mind.[20]

A Problem of Method: Virginia as a Case Study

Supporters and opponents of the frontier thesis have tended to differ in methods as well as results. Those who favored Turner's ideas tended to support them by close study of the American West. Critics preferred to make comparative study of different frontiers in America and Europe. The problem itself calls for a combination of both methods: close study and comparative analysis through time and space.

Another difficulty in any sustained study of the frontier is the vast sweep of the problem. There were frontiers in many nations and every era of world history. Even within the United States there were frontiers in different regions and successive westward movements within the same region. It is necessary to frame the problem in large general terms but to study it with careful attention to particularities of time and space.

The difficulty of studying the problem is further compounded by a revolution in historical scholarship during the century after Turner presented his thesis. In 1893 history was conceived mainly as the study of past politics. Turner himself did not wish to be constrained within those limits and broadened his discipline into the study of social and ecological processes. The frontier thesis was an early precursor of the new social history that came to dominate academic scholarship in the mid–twentieth century.

A century later yet another kind of history is developing. It calls itself cultural history and brings together both the old political history and the new social history. It studies large structures and processes, but with reference to particular events and individual people. The new cultural history thinks of people not as objects of deterministic processes but as agents who are actively engaged in choices that make a difference in the world.

All of these trends have greatly improved the study of history, but they add heavy burdens to any project such as this. How are we to find a way forward? This inquiry seeks a solution by examining the westward movement in its relation to Virginia—only one of America's fifty states, but one that was once much larger than its present size. It offers a special opportunity in the length of its history, which spans four centuries of the American experience. The purpose of this work is to examine only Virginia's part in the westward movement but to do so in the largest possible terms. We consider successive westward movements from Europe and Africa to Virginia, then the westward movement that happened within Virginia, and finally the westward movement from Virginia to the Mississippi Valley and beyond.

This inquiry is organized in that spirit—a study of people who made a difference in the large historical process that we remember as the westward movement. It seeks to combine an interest in structure and process with a concern for individual choices. It aspires to a history in which individuals were not merely pawns of historical forces but agents and even architects of historical events.

The inquiry has its own perspective, but it invites readers to make their own judgments, free from the constraints of academic orthodoxy on all sides of the question. It aspires to an American history that addresses large questions without filiopietism on the one hand or iconoclasm on the other.

This is, indeed, a very serious question for anyone who cares about American history. Some have wearied of it and have complained of the long debate about the Turner thesis as a "dance of the scholastic angels." It is not so. The issues that Turner raised in 1893 cut deep into the grain of American culture. They are not merely academic questions and not only confined to the distant past. They gain new global meaning and importance with the events of every passing day.

1

Migration to Virginia

AMERICA'S WESTWARD MOVEMENT did not begin in America itself. It was part of a long historical process that started many centuries earlier. Much recent research has dissolved the simple Turnerian distinction between a moving frontier in America and a static society in Europe.

In England during the early modern era, ruling elites complained of the many migrants who flowed through their communities. This movement was not confined to a minority. In Buckinghamshire between 1573 and 1584, more than 80 percent of the population had moved at least once in their lives. That finding has been replicated for many English counties under the Tudors and Stuarts.[1]

On the winding roads of rural England, one might have met many different people on the move: landless younger sons of highborn families in quest of honor and fortune, pious pilgrims in hope of salvation, yeomen in search of land, laborers looking for work, seamen seeking a ship, orphans and beggars who wished to find food and shelter in a hostile world. Many of these people traveled great distances. One recent study has found that the poor made longer journeys than the rich. Nearly one-quarter of English vagrants traveled more than 100 miles at a time.[2]

Much of this movement was "subsistence migration," which arose from desperate need in an economy of scarcity, where land and work and food were in short supply. More of it was what British scholars call "betterment migration," driven by a strong Christian ethic of individual striving.

In many ways this British "betterment migration" was similar to the westward movement that developed later in America. Some of it flowed from densely settled regions to "marginal, mostly woodland and pastoral areas," such as the Forest of Whittlewood in Northamptonshire or the Forest of Arden in Warwickshire. David Hey observes that English laborers were "setting up homes on the edges of commons and uncultivated tracts of land in many parts of the country during the Tudor and Stuart Period." Two other students of English migration conclude, "Poorer folk were attracted to the woodlands by the relative freedom of open unregulated settlements." In early modern England this movement to the "edge of the unused" resembled migration to the American frontier.[3]

Most "betterment migration" led in a different direction—toward the seaport cities, and especially to London, which in the two centuries from 1550 to 1750 attracted a million English migrants from a nation of five million in 1650. Other large flows carried toward Bristol and smaller coastal towns. The stone quays of these English seaports were lined with bluff-bowed merchantmen outward bound to Europe, the Indies, and America. Those who sailed for the New World were merely continuing a process that had begun many years before.[4]

The cause and consequences of this incessant movement have been much debated by European historians. In general their conclusions are very different from those of American scholars about migration in the United States. Two British historians speak for many colleagues when they conclude that "migration had an ambivalent role in early modern England." Peter Clark and David Souden observe that such movement promoted urban growth and economic development but also worked "in opposition to those trends." They find that it "lubricated the machinery of the social system" but also caused serious social problems. Few scholars in Britain or Europe believe that the migration and resettlement of population caused an opening of society or promoted democracy, liberty, or equality, as Turner believed they did in North America.[5]

The First European Colonists

Whatever its cause and consequence, this English migration spread to America at an earlier date and in a different way than our histories teach us. From 1578 to 1625 more than thirty English-speaking settlements were planted in what is now the United States.[6] The textbooks commonly mention only three—Roanoke, Jamestown, and Plymouth. There were many others, and their origins were as diverse as the migratory movements of early modern Europe. Most began without fanfare and left only the faintest traces behind. Many were fishing stations, founded as early as the sixteenth century, perhaps earlier. Some were small farming settlements planted in the early seventeenth century by men who sought land of their own.

Beyond these collective efforts, single individuals also found their separate ways from Europe to America. The founders of Jamestown and Plymouth both discovered traces of Europeans who had been there before them. The Pilgrims found on Cape Cod a "place like a grave" and within it a skull with "fine yellow hair still on it," bound up with a needle, a knife, a "sailor's canvass cassock," and a pair of cloth breeches. Alongside were the bones of a child in a small bundle.[7]

The colonists of Jamestown made a similar discovery. In the interior of Virginia, about twenty miles from the present site of Richmond, they found a "Boy about the age of ten yeeres, which had a head of haire of a perfect yellow and a reasonable white skinne, which is a Miracle amongst all Savages."[8] In other parts of the Chesapeake region, they came upon other children with light chestnut hair and fair complexions, who might have been descended from the lost colonists of Roanoke or from shipwrecked seamen.

Long before the first major colonies were founded, more than a few anonymous English waifs and strays were wandering in the American wilderness. Their lonely presence reminds us that settlement of English-speaking America began as an extension of incessant migration in Europe. This was not primarily a corporate enterprise but a movement of individuals on their own errands to the New World. The founding of Virginia was part of this long process.

Inventing the Idea of Virginia: Gilbert, Ralegh, and Roanoke Colony

Virginia was an idea before it was a place—a "countrey fained by imagination," in Sir Humphrey Gilbert's haunting phrase.[9] It began as one of many American utopias that stirred powerfully in European minds. Some of these dream-colonies were religious visions. Others were secular images of prosperity and power. The original idea of Virginia included both of these notions, but mainly it was something else—a different sort of dream world that strongly appealed to adventurous young English gentlemen-at-arms, who thought of the New World as a field of honor. They also dreamed of gold and glory and Christian service. All of these ambitions were intertwined, but honor was what they lived and died for. This complex idea shaped the colony of Virginia as powerfully as any material pressures.

The idea of Virginia as a field of honor was developed by two highborn English adventurers who never actually settled in the land of their dreams. The first was Sir Humphrey Gilbert (1539?–1583). Like so many leaders to appear in our story, he was the penniless younger son of West Country gentry. Educated at Eton and Oxford, he lived by his wit and his sword, roaming the world in search of honor and riches. After trying his hand as a soldier of fortune in France, a colonizer in Ireland, and a pirate on the Spanish Main, he became one of the first to think of North America as a home for England's restless population and a field of honor for its younger sons. Queen

4. For Sir Humphrey Gilbert, Virginia was a "countrey fained by imagination," an idea before it was a place. One portrait of Gilbert is inscribed "SYR HUMPHREY GILBERT KNIGHT DROWNED IN THE DISCOVERIE OF VIRGINIA ANNO 1584."

Elizabeth I gave him a charter to settle any part of America not owned by another Christian monarch. He may have planted a small colony in 1578, and he tried again in 1583 with three ships and 260 people. His destination is not known, for he never reached it. While sailing south from Newfoundland along the coast of America, he lost one of his ships with all hands and was forced to turn back for supplies.

On the way home Sir Humphrey Gilbert gallantly traveled in his smaller vessel, which others feared to sail. In midocean he met high seas and heavy weather. Gilbert was last seen from the larger ship, sitting calmly in the face of mortal danger, reading a book that appears to have been Sir Thomas More's *Utopia*. He called out cheerfully to his friends across the raging water, "We are as neere to heaven by sea as by land," a paraphrase from More's work.[10] It proved to be a prophecy. That midnight, as his comrades watched anxiously from the other ship, the lights of Gilbert's little vessel suddenly disappeared. The death of this English gentleman, like his life and American adventures, was a vision of honor and Christian glory.

Gilbert's stepbrother, Sir Walter Ralegh, shared a similar dream. He also was a gentleman-at-arms, "from his infancie brought up and trained to martiall discipline, both by land and sea." Those who knew him wrote that he was driven by "double desire of honour . . . to attempt honourable actions worthie of honour."[11]

With his own royal charter in 1584, he sent a scouting voyage to explore the coast below the Chesapeake Bay, which on the strength of its glowing report he was the first to name Virginia, in honor of his sovereign Elizabeth I, the virgin queen. In 1585 Ralegh sent "gentlem[e]n of good worth with a competent number of soldiers," to establish a military base on Roanoke Island. As did many of his contemporaries, Ralegh thought of America as a savage and dangerous wilderness. Danger was one of its attractions. His purpose was exploration and conquest. Richard Hakluyt wrote of Ralegh's errand, "No greater glory can be handed down than to conquer the barbarian, to recall the savage and the pagan to civility, to draw the ignorant within the orbit of reason, and to fill with reverence for divinity the godless and the ungodly." This was one part of Ralegh's American dream. Another was to annoy the king of Spain, to find gold and rubies, and to discover a passage to the Indies.[12]

5. Sir Walter Ralegh, with the world in his hand. A friend wrote that he was driven by "double desire of honour . . . to attempt honourable actions worthie of honour."

Roanoke proved a poor field for Ralegh's dreams. His gentlemen and soldiers found little opportunity for deeds of honor on that sandy island. When Sir Francis Drake visited in 1586, the entire settlement boarded his ships and were happy to sail home.

In 1587 Ralegh tried again. This time he attempted to combine Gilbert's purposes with his own and decided to plant a self-sustaining colony of English families. Calling himself lord and governor in Virginia, he sent over Lieutenant Governor John White with 117 colonists—among them nine children and seventeen women—who began to come to terms with their new environment. They started to raise tobacco and harvested the first Anglo-American export crop—a supply of sassafras which was thought to be a wonder drug for syphilis. On August 18, 1587, White's daughter Ellinor White Dare gave birth to a girl who was named Virginia Dare in honor of the place and its patron.

Nine days later John White sailed home to barter his sassafras for more capital. He never saw his fellow colonists again. Before he could return, war broke out between Spain and England. When a relief voyage finally got through in 1590, it found the colony mysteriously abandoned. There was no sign of violence and only the uncertain word *Croatan,* carved in plain letters on a post.

The Lost Colony of Roanoke disappeared in a haze of historical romance, but the idea of Virginia survived and even flourished in English minds, all the more because of the mysterious fate of its creators. Inspired by these glorious disasters, by Sir Humphrey Gilbert's vision of America as an English home away from home, and Sir Walter Ralegh's dream of Virginia as a field of honor, others took up the idea with great and lasting consequences.

The Migration to Jamestown, 1607–25

After the death of Queen Elizabeth in 1603, her Scottish cousin James I made peace with Spain. Colonizing quickly revived, but in a new form. The quest for honor and glory by restless gentlemen adventurers was subjected to the economic discipline of a joint-stock company—an artifact of more importance in westward expansion than the caravel or Conestoga wagon. The joint-stock company was a powerful engine for the mobilization of energy and capital. As an instrument of larger human purposes, however, it was deeply flawed in ways that made a difference for the history of Virginia.

The Crown granted royal charters for the colonization of America to two Virginia companies. The Virginia Company of Plymouth received the right to settle between the 38th and 45th degrees of latitude—roughly the area between the Potomac River and what is now the Canadian border. The Virginia Company of London was granted the right to colonize anywhere between the 34th and 41st parallels, from Long Island to below Cape Hatteras.

The Virginia Company of Plymouth was a shaky operation. It founded in Maine a small colony called Sagadahoc that collapsed after the first New England winter. The Virginia Company of London was stronger and better funded. A large part of the English aristocracy invested in it, as did many

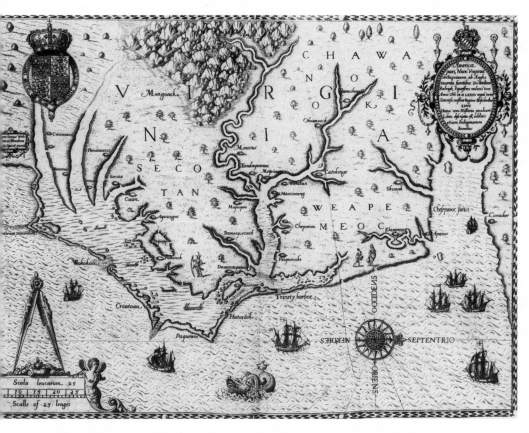

6. The first map of Virginia was published in 1590 by John White, artist for Ralegh's expedition. The Chesapeake Bay is at the right, and Roanoke Island is in the center, between the Outer Banks and the mainland of what is now North Carolina.

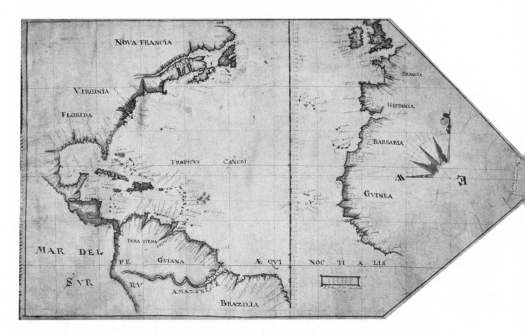

7. This manuscript map, used by the Virginia Company of London, 1607–9, is one
of the first to identify Cape Cod ("C. Kod"), where in 1620 the *Mayflower* settlers
made their American landfall. Probably the Pilgrims were not blown off course.
They were working within a larger idea of Virginia, the name at first given to
all English claims in North America.

merchants in the City of London. More money was raised in small sums by
a lottery. With this capital in hand, the Virginia Company of London sent
144 colonists in three ships, the *Susan Constant, Godspeed,* and *Discovery.* On
May 13, 1607, they came ashore twenty miles up the James River, on a peninsula that pleased them for its anchorage. "Our shippes doe lie so neere the
shoare that they are moored to the Trees in six fathom water," George Percy
reported.[13]

The anchorage was important because the English settlers thought of their
colony as a base for further exploration. Within a week one-armed Captain
Christopher Newport was searching for a passage to the South Sea. Sir Francis Drake had sailed the coast of California in 1579 and reported a range of
mountains not far from the sea. When the Indians of Virginia indicated that
mountains were to be found only a few days' march inland, the founders of
Jamestown leaped to the conclusion that the South Sea was no more than

ten days' journey distant. This hopeful idea was a long time dying. It appeared as late as 1651 in a map by Virginia Farrer, an Englishwoman whose family had a long association with Virginia.

On June 22 Captain Newport's ships sailed for England. Only about 104 colonists remained in Jamestown. The rest of the original 144 decided, wisely, to return home.[14] In the settlement of early America and the westward movement, there was often a large back-migration of this sort, followed by heavy traffic in both directions. This pattern had long appeared in Europe, where scholars found that every stream of migration had its counterstream. The

8. Virginia Farrer's map of Virginia (1651) shows the "Sea of China and the Indies," or Pacific Ocean, just beyond the Blue Ridge Mountains, a common belief that inspired many hopes and several expeditions. John Farrer, an investor in the colony, had named his daughter Virginia "so that speaking unto her, looking upon her, and hearing others call her by name, he might think upon both at once."

same thing happened in most American migrations. Reverse movement, and the two-way traffic that followed in its wake, meant that cultural communications continued between the fringe of settlement and its place of origin. In the early history of Virginia, this continuing exchange helped to shape the culture of the colony in its critical years.

The colonists who remained in Jamestown were an extraordinary group, very different from other English settlers in America. Most were called gentlemen—that is, men of "gentle" families, with coats of arms on register at the College of Heralds in London. They were recruited from a narrow elite who made up less than 10 percent of the English population in 1607, and yet they were 60 percent of Jamestown's founders. Another 20 percent were skilled workers of some sort; the remaining 20 percent were laborers and servants. A similar pattern appeared in the second and third voyages to Jamestown.

These settlers were all male. No woman lived among them. They were also very young and very English. The Virginia Company sent out a few foreign artisans in the first three voyages. German and Polish experts were hired to help in the manufacture of naval stores. Italian glass workers were also recruited to make beads for trade with the Indians. These settlers were so uncomfortable in the colony that one of the Poles joined the Indians, and the Italians cracked the glass furnace with a crowbar in a frantic effort to get home.[15]

The settlement called James Fort or Jamestown (pronounced *Jimston*) was deliberately planted close to the Indian settlements and fortified against attack. It proved safe enough in that regard but dangerous in another way. John Smith remembered that "our Tents were rotten and our Cabbins worse then nought." George Percy wrote later, "Our food was but a small Can of Barlie sod in water, to five men a day, our drinke cold water taken out of the River, which was at a floud verie salt, at a low tide full of slime and filth, which was the destruction of many of our men."

By July many were ill. In August they began to die of "bloody fluxes" and "fevers" and "swellings." Within three months these colonists had so polluted their immediate environment that they destroyed themselves in the process. By January 1608, when the first supply ships returned, 66 of the original 100 or 104 were dead. The rest, in the words of Captain John Smith, were "in such dispaire, as they would rather starve and rot with idlenes, then be persuaded to do any thing for their owne reliefe without constraint."[16]

NOVA BRITANNIA.

OFFERING MOST

Excellent fruites by Planting in
VIRGINIA.

Exciting all such as be well affected
to further the same.

LONDON
Printed for SAMVEL MACHAM, and are to be sold at
his Shop in Pauls Church-yard, at the
Signe of the Bul-head.
1 6 0 9.

9. This promotional pamphlet by Robert Johnson pleaded for colonists called "planters," as distinct from "adventurers," who were investors in England. Johnson extolled Virginia as an "earthly Paradice" at a time when Jamestown was a purgatory for its wretched inhabitants.

Captain John Smith, the self-made son of a Lincolnshire tenant farmer, had his own dream for Virginia. He wished to establish at Jamestown a more egalitarian social order based on widespread ownership of land. To that end he proposed a headright system which gave fifty acres to anyone who settled in the colony. Part of his scheme was adopted, but it did not work as he intended. Few landless emigrants could pay their passage to Virginia, except by engaging themselves as indentured servants—a practice that Smith deplored. His ideas were at odds with those of other leaders, who strongly opposed him.

In 1608 John Smith was arrested and sentenced to be hanged. He was saved only by the fortuitous arrival of Captain Christopher Newport with supplies and reinforcements. Smith devoted himself to exploring the Potomac and Rappahannock rivers. In an hour of need, he became president of Virginia and saved the colony by obtaining Indian corn in the winter of 1608–9. He continued in office until he was severely wounded in a gunpowder explosion and returned to England. His vision for the colony was rejected by the Virginia Company, and the headright system was used to reward large landowners instead of small proprietors. John Smith's dream of Virginia was a road not taken.[17]

After Smith left, conditions rapidly deteriorated and reached bottom in the terrible "starving time" that nearly destroyed the colony in 1609. Of 490 who were there at the time of Smith's departure, only 60 remained alive six months later. The rest died of hunger, disease, and oppression. This event marked the beginning of a disaster that continued more than a decade, in scenes of self-inflicted suffering on an epic scale.

In London the Virginia Company applied its wealth to replacing these human losses but not to removing their cause. Sir Edwin Sandys became treasurer of the Virginia Company in 1619 and urged every parish to send its poor to Virginia. He recruited homeless children from the streets of London and in three years sent over more than 3,500 settlers, twice as many as in the preceding ten years combined. Sandys succeeded only in supplying more work for the Grim Reaper, the true ruler of early Virginia. Mortality continued at catastrophic rates. Of 4,270 immigrants who had been sent by Sandys (or arrived earlier), only 1,240 were still living on Good Friday, March 22, 1622.

On that day the colony suffered another epic disaster. Powhatan's confederacy attacked Jamestown and tried to drive the English into the sea. The

ENGLANDS ✤ ABCONTRAFACTVR DES H. HAVBTMAN IOHAN SCHMIDTS ADMIRALN DES NEWEN

Æta 37.
A° 1616

Diß abbildung dein antlitz schawt, aber zwar
Welch zeigt Dein gabn vnd lob, gibt großern schein,
Dein Entdeckung vnd vberwindung klar
Der Wilden leudt, so durch Dir gezaemet sein
Schawn beßer Dein gemüdt, vnd bringn dir ehr,
Auffn kupfr. Jnwendig Du des goldts hast mehr.

10. Captain John Smith has suffered the vagaries of historiographical fortune, extolled by filiopietists as the savior of Virginia and condemned as a politically incorrect conquistador, an oppressor of native peoples, and an agent of neofeudalism.

Indians killed 347 settlers and nearly destroyed the colony. The Virginia Company tried yet again to revive it. Altogether, between 1607 and 1625 perhaps 8,500 colonists were sent to Jamestown. But at the end of that period only 1,218 remained. Of the others, many wisely fled at the earliest opportunity. Most succumbed to war, starvation, disease, and despair.

Who remained? By 1625 most of the gentlemen had disappeared. In a census taken that year, colonists with titles of respect such as "Sir" or "Mister" or "gentleman" had fallen from 60 percent of the population to merely 5 percent. Even this small proportion included "Mr." Argall Yeardley, who was four years of age, and "Mr." Francis Yeardley, who was barely one year old—a reminder that this was a hierarchical world of orders and estates in which rank was fixed at birth.[18]

In 1625 most Virginians were single males of humble rank. About half were servants. Nearly 60 percent had no kin in the colony. After two decades of settlement, only 8 percent were native born. Few of the population were young children. Only 17 percent were under the age of fifteen, and they were mostly immigrants too. Older people were even fewer. Barely 1 percent were in their mid-forties or older. Scarcely anyone survived even to middle age.

This was a masculine world, more like a mining camp or a military post than a settled society. In 1625 men outnumbered women seven to one. One might expect that most women in such a setting would have been quick to find husbands. Later in American history a steamboat that carried a cargo of single women up a western river was met by young men who shouted proposals of marriage from the shore through megaphones. But it was not so in early Virginia. Of a total of sixty-five women who were aged twenty or older in 1625, forty-three were not married. The majority were single not because they were newly arrived—thirty-nine had been in Virginia since 1622—but because thirty-four of them were bondservants for whom marriage was actively discouraged or forbidden outright.

There were many reasons why Virginia remained a colony of immigrants long after other colonial populations in America were native born. One factor was disease and the high death rate. Another was the gender ratio. Not the least important factor was a system of servitude which held many women in bondage. They were required to be housekeepers or field workers for the colony's small ruling elite—not wives or mothers.

In the first years of settlement, when Jamestown was the American frontier, most of the Turnerian processes applied in reverse. Freedom did not increase but actually diminished in Captain John Smith's system of forced labor (1608), in Lord De La Warr's forced settlements (1610), in Sir Thomas Dale's severe "Lawes Divine Morall and Martiall" (1611–12), and in the tyranny of Sir Samuel Argall (1617–18). For more than a decade, the colonists were forced into a system of compulsory labor that Edmund S. Morgan calls "semimilitary work gangs" in communal fields. Above them was an arbitrary government that operated under martial law, with brutal discipline, drumhead trials, and summary executions.

A New Regime for Virginia

The experiment with forced labor in communal fields proved to be yet another failure. In 1614 the colony began to shift from collective farms to private gardens. Individual settlers were allowed to farm three acres but had no private title to the land. By 1617 each free colonist was allowed 100 acres in fee simple and 50 acres more for every headright. Separate plantations

11. This obsolete sixteenth-century burgonet (a type of helmet) was excavated at Jordan's Point, Prince George's County. The Virginia Company sent out more than 2,000 helmets of which many were cast-off war surplus from the Tower of London.

began to spring up along the James River. The commercial farming of tobacco, introduced by John Rolfe in 1612, spread rapidly, and prices at first
were very high.

Here was a new period in the history of Virginia, an era of greater private ownership, but not in a Turnerian way. While tidewater Virginia was
still a frontier, it passed increasingly into the hands of a small, self-serving
immigrant elite. In 1625 half the colonists were servants, and half the servants
were owned by ten men.

These masters were not Virginia gentlemen. The richest of them was Abraham Peirsey, who ran the company store and sold provisions to other immigrants at three times the set price. His books always showed a loss, yet he
himself grew from "a verie poore man" to the richest leader in the colony,
with forty servants in 1625.

The next most affluent master, with thirty-six servants in 1625, was Governor George Yeardley, "a right worthie statesman for his own profit," as one
Virginian bitterly described him. Yeardley arrived with "nothing more valuable than a sword," made a fortune by "notable oppressions," looted the
colony, and went back to London with fourteen servants in livery.

Also in this elite was William Tucker, a ship's captain who won the company's commission to trade with the Indians. When the Pamunkey Indians
threatened his business, he invited 200 to a feast and murdered them all with
poisoned wine; those slow to die were beheaded.

Another large holder was Dr. John Pott, the company physician and acting governor for a short period, who enriched himself by "cuting out the
markes of other mens neate cattell and markinge them for himselfe with his
owne handes, whereby he hath gotten into a greate stock of cattell."[19]

These men bought and sold their servants without regard to English law.
Thomas Best in 1623 complained that his master "hath sold me for a £150
sterling like a damnd slave." A few brave souls challenged this elite and became its victims. When Richard Crocker complained that Peirsey "deal[t]
uppon nothing but extortion," the plaintiff had his ears nailed to the pillory.
Richard Barnes in 1624 was sentenced to have his arms broken and his
tongue bored through with an awl. He was made to run a gauntlet of forty
men and was butted by every one of them and then "kicked downe and
footed out of the fort."[20] Others were executed for lesser offenses.

Fresh supplies of servants were sent to Virginia. Many were young men.
Some were children collected on the streets of London—among them the

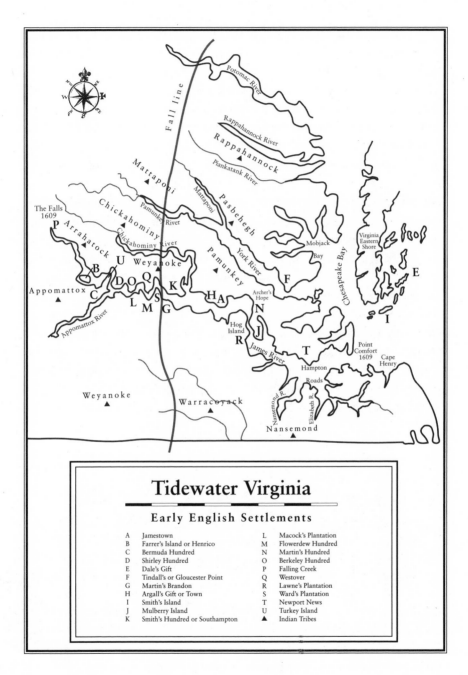

Tidewater Virginia

Early English Settlements

A	Jamestown	L	Macock's Plantation
B	Farrer's Island or Henrico	M	Flowerdew Hundred
C	Bermuda Hundred	N	Martin's Hundred
D	Shirley Hundred	O	Berkeley Hundred
E	Dale's Gift	P	Falling Creek
F	Tindall's or Gloucester Point	Q	Westover
G	Martin's Brandon	R	Lawne's Plantation
H	Argall's Gift or Town	S	Ward's Plantation
I	Smith's Island	T	Newport News
J	Mulberry Island	U	Turkey Island
K	Smith's Hundred or Southampton	▲	Indian Tribes

Duty boys, so called from the ship that brought them, who were sold into seven years' service for £10 a head. If they committed a crime, they were forced to serve another seven years. The few *Duty* boys who survived were compelled to become tenants of Governor George Yeardley.[21]

Other servants were women. Some were vagabonds and prostitutes who had been "lagged," or kidnapped in London. Others were girls of humble rank who had been seduced by one means or another—the "trepanned maidens" of song and myth. More than a few were young women of "good family" who came willingly in search of a husband. In 1621 a subscription was taken up to send "younge, handsome, and honestly educated Maides" to Virginia, and fifty-seven were dispatched to Jamestown. Most came from London or had friends and relatives in the metropolis. At least eight were daughters of the gentry; most were from families of husbandmen and artisans. Many were orphans or widows or came from broken homes. A few emerge from the records. Alice Burges, the orphaned daughter of a Cambridgeshire husbandman, was twenty-eight years old and "skillful in anie countrie worke. she can brue, bake, and make malte, &c." Ann Harmer, twenty-one years old, came from Hertfordshire, was expert with a needle, and "doe[s] all manner of workes, golde and silke." Mistress Cecily Bray was twenty-five years old, the daughter of Gloucestershire gentlefolk "of good esteeme" and kin to Sir Edwin Sandys, a leader of the Virginia Company.

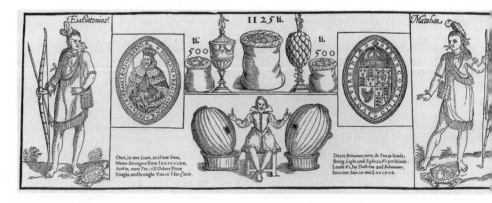

13. The Virginia Company raised part of its capital by public lottery. The loss of lottery rights in 1622 contributed to the bankruptcy of the colony. This image is from a lottery broadside.

Cecily Bray was killed by the Indians in March 1622. Ann Harmer and Alice Burges disappeared, probably into early graves.[22]

Finally, after years of mismanagement and corruption, the English authorities had had enough. In 1622 the company lost its right to raise money by lottery and was driven into bankruptcy. The troubled settlement passed into the hands of the Privy Council, and in 1624 Virginia became a royal colony.

Crosscurrents, 1625–42

After 1624 the new royal colony of Virginia at last began to grow—slowly at first, but with increasing momentum: 1,000 in 1628, 2,000 in the peak year 1634–35. Rates of mortality were still very high. New strains of malaria and tropical fevers took a heavy toll. The population remained small, but at last it was expanding, partly by natural increase: 1,200 in 1625; 4,900 in 1634; 8,000 in 1642. In this period from 1625 to 1642, the colony passed the point at which its survival was in question. It also entered a new era that was critical in the classical sense—a moment when the character of the colony was in the balance.

Major economic problems developed. Virginia's tobacco crop began to glut the European market; prices that had surged to three shillings a pound in the 1620s fell sharply to a few pence in the 1630s. In 1634 a wooden palisade was constructed between tributaries of the James and the York rivers to keep livestock in and Indians out, but fields were beginning to wear out.

The direction of social development was also in doubt. Some areas of the colony became increasingly dominated by small freehold farmers, others by great estates. Large tracts in Berkeley Hundred, Southampton Hundred, and Martin's Hundred were sold to absentee owners. The colony's "public estates" continued to be farmed by "public tenants" on half shares.[23] It was not clear which of these systems would dominate.

Religious trends were in flux. Puritans were beginning to settle in the colony, especially in Norfolk and Nansemond counties and on the Eastern Shore.

Political tendencies were also very mixed. An assembly had been founded in 1619 and became annual in this period—not at the request of the inhabitants but on orders from London. The governor, Council, and men from four boroughs met together as one body and jointly exercised the power of taxation. The authority and autonomy of the House of Burgesses was unsettled. A new system of county government was created in 1634, but county courts and county commissions were controlled by the old company elites who functioned almost as independent warlords, using their servants as private armies.[24]

The first royal governors struggled against these men with small success. Sir Francis Wyatt, after a frustrating time, retreated home "to look after his estates." Governor John Harvey tried to break the old elite by brute force. He arbitrarily imprisoned one councillor and knocked out the teeth of another with a cudgel. The old elite joined together, made a prisoner of Harvey, and sent him to England in 1635. He came back in 1637 and was removed again in 1639. Sir Francis Wyatt was persuaded to return in 1639 for another term that was as troubled and ineffectual as his first.[25]

These disorders arose from tensions that ran deep in the colony. In 1641 Virginia was growing, but in its economic condition, social structure, religious life, and political strife, it was at war with itself.

Sir William Berkeley and the Peopling of Virginia

In the winter of 1641–42 an English gentleman boarded an emigrant ship for Virginia. He was no ordinary passenger. In his baggage he carried the king's commission as royal governor of Virginia, an office that he was destined to hold off and on for more than thirty-five years. Sir William Berkeley was born in 1605 into a powerful West Country family. It had been seated at Berkeley Castle in Gloucestershire since the eleventh century. He belonged to a cadet branch of the family that kept two houses: one in London and the other high on a hill above the ancient wool town of Bruton in Somerset. He lived his youth in a broad belt of territory between London and Berkeley Castle—the English region that was to become the cradle of Virginia's culture.[26]

As a young man Berkeley matriculated at Queen's College in Oxford, took his degree at St. Edmund Hall, and became a fellow of Merton College. After graduating, he was introduced at court and made such an impression that the king appointed him Gentleman of the Privy Chamber Extraordinary. Berkeley also became a literary figure of some consequence and published a "tragy-comedy" called *The Lost Lady* in 1638. In 1639 he was knighted in the

Sir WILLIAM BERKELEY *Brother*
to IOHN *the first Lord* BERKELEY *of*
STRATTON

14. In this portrait by Sir Peter Lely, Sir William Berkeley imitates a favorite pose of Charles I, which appears in Van Dyck's *Roi à la chasse,* now in the Louvre.

field at Berwick-upon-Tweed during the Scottish Covenanters' revolt. Two years later he became royal governor of Virginia.

In many ways Berkeley was not an admirable character. He bullied men beneath him and fawned on those above. He openly enriched himself from his offices and set a sad example for peculation that long persisted in Virginia. In 1667, for example, he wrote to his superior, Lord Arlington, "Though Ambition comonly leaves sober old age, co[v]etousness does not[.] I shal therefore desire of your Lordship [t]o procure of his Ma[jes]tie the customes of two hundred Hogsheads [o]f tobb[acco]."[27]

These were the vices of his age, and Berkeley had them in high degree. He also had its virtues of candor, courage, fidelity to family, and loyalty to a cause. His social values were as highly developed as those of the Puritans — but in a very different direction. And he cared deeply for Virginia. For thirty-five years Berkeley devoted himself to the welfare of his colony with energy, intelligence, and great effect.

When Sir William Berkeley reached Virginia in February 1642, it was a sickly settlement of barely 8,000 souls. The colony had earned the reputation "that none but those of the meanest quality and corruptest lives went there."[28] Its leaders were rough, violent, hard-drinking men. The colony was in a state of chronic disorder. Its rulers were unable to govern, its institutions were ill defined, its economy was undeveloped, its politics were unstable, and its cultural identity was indistinct.

In the thirty-five years of Berkeley's intermittent tenure, Virginia's population increased from 8,000 to 40,000 inhabitants. It developed a coherent social and economic system and its own folkways. Most important, it acquired a governing elite that Berkeley described as "men of as good Families as any Subjects in *England*."[29]

This social system did not spring spontaneously from the soil of the New World. It was the conscious creation of human will and purpose. In that process Berkeley played the leading role, laboring through his long years in office to build an ideal society that was the expression of his own values. More than any other individual, he framed Virginia's political system — becoming, in Thomas Ludwell's words, "ye sole author of the most substantial parts of it either for Lawes, or other Inferiour institutions."[30] When the laws of Virginia were first published, the volume was dedicated to Sir William Berkeley, who was identified as "the author of the best of them."[31]

Berkeley governed the colony through a pliant "long assembly" that he kept in session for fourteen years; he refused to call an election from 1662 to 1676. This assembly's laws expressed the wishes of the governor; many were drafted by his own hand.

Important as his role as a lawgiver may have been, Berkeley had his greatest influence on Virginia in another way. More than any other person, he shaped the process of immigration to the colony during a critical period in its history. That process in turn defined Virginia's culture and largely determined the main lines of development for generations to come.[32]

Virginia's "Distressed Cavaliers"

Of Sir William Berkeley's many projects as governor, the most important was his recruitment of a royalist elite for Virginia. The earl of Clarendon, who knew him well, wrote that Berkeley "invited many gentlemen and others thither" and that "many persons of condition and good officers of war, had transported themselves with all the estate they had been able to preserve."[33] When they arrived, Berkeley promoted them to high office, granted them large estates, and created an oligarchy that ran the colony for many generations.

This migration of cavaliers continued throughout Berkeley's tenure as governor (1642–52, 1660–77). Much of it occurred during the decade of the 1650s, when the Puritans gained the upper hand in England and royalists became refugees from persecution. Many had fought for Charles I in England's Civil War, and some continued to serve him until he was executed in 1649. Others rallied to the future Charles II and fought for him in 1651. Many were younger sons of royalist families who had small hopes in a Puritan commonwealth. So shattered was the royalist cause that William Sancroft wrote, "When we meet, it is but to consult to what foreign plantation we shall fly." Another noted that "Virginia [was] the only city of refuge left in His Majesty's Dominions, in those times, for distressed cavaliers."[34]

These "distressed cavaliers" were actively recruited by Sir William Berkeley himself, who was in England in 1644–45 supporting the Stuart cause. Some had been his kinsmen and friends before they came to America. Many shared his royalist politics, his Anglican faith, and his vision for the colony. Colonel Henry Norwood wrote, "The honour I had of being nearly related

15. Sir Henry Chicheley typifies the many "distressed cavaliers" recruited by Sir William Berkeley. Locked in the Tower of London by Roundheads in 1648, Chicheley came to Virginia in 1650, the year after the beheading of Charles I.

to Sir *William Barkeley* the governor, was no small incitation to encourage me with a little stock to this adventure."[35]

These cavalier immigrants founded the dynasties that would later be called the First Families of Virginia, but they were not chronologically the first in the colony. Most arrived within a decade of the year 1655. The founder of the Carter family came in 1649, as did the first Culpeper, Hammond, Honywood, and Moryson. The first Digges arrived in 1650, together with the first Broadhurst, Chicheley, Custis, Page, Harrison, Isham, Skipwith, and Landon. The first Randolph emigrated from Northamptonshire about 1651, the first Mason in 1652. The first Madison was granted land in 1653, the first Corbin in 1654. The first Washington, a younger son of an Oxford-trained clergyman who had lost his living to the Puritans, crossed the ocean in 1657, as did Colonel William Ball, the ancestor of George Washington's mother, and the first Fairfax in 1659. Of seventy-two founders of Virginia's First Families whose dates of migration are known, two-thirds arrived between 1640 and 1669.

After the Restoration of Charles II in 1660, Sir William Berkeley continued his recruiting. In 1663 he published a pamphlet addressed to the younger sons of England's great families. The governor assured them that "a small summe of money will enable a younger Brother to erect a flourishing Family in a new World; and adde more Strength, Wealth, and Honour, to his Native Country, then thousands did before, that dyed forgotten and unrewarded in an unjust War."[36]

Berkeley himself had been a younger son with no hope of inheriting an estate in England. That "younger son syndrome," as one historian has called it, became a factor of high importance in the culture of Virginia. Many members of its cavalier elite were men of good families and small fortunes, whose pedigrees became their passports to Berkeley's favor.

With very few exceptions, these immigrants were staunch royalists. Of those whose opinions are known, 98 percent came from families who had supported the king in the Civil War. They were Anglican in their religion, and their faith was as important to them as it had been to the Puritans.

These immigrants to Virginia came from every part of England, but two-thirds had lived within a triangle of territory in the south of the country, stretching from the Weald of Kent west to Devon and north to Warwickshire—about 21 percent of the land area of England. If immigrants from London are added to this regional group, its proportion rises from two-thirds

16. Above their front door at Cobbs Hall, Northumberland County, Virginia, the Lees hung this wooden carving of the arms of Richard Lee (d. 1664), founder of the family in Virginia. Worked into the design is a crescent, the heraldic mark of a second son, which appeared on other escutcheons in Virginia.

to nearly three-quarters. Few came from the north of England (8 percent), fewer from East Anglia (7 percent), and only a scattering from Cornwall, Wales, Scotland, Ireland, or foreign countries.

Most had lived within a day's journey of London or Bristol. These cities had been an important part of their world. Many younger sons of landed families had moved to the metropolis and taken up commercial occupations. Their sons in turn moved to Virginia, often after having become merchants and tradesmen, without losing their identity as gentlemen. In houses as ancient as the Berkeleys, younger sons and daughters married London merchants. In families as honorable as the Filmers, country cousins did their city business with traders and lawyers who were their kin. At the same time London merchants intermarried with the gentry of Essex and Kent: an example was the Byrd family, prosperous goldsmiths who were descended from landed gentry and proudly possessed their own arms.

After 1650 these families continued to intermarry on both sides of the Atlantic and moved freely back and forth across the ocean. The result was a tightly integrated colonial elite that literally became a single cousinage by the beginning of the eighteenth century. William Cabell Bruce compared the genealogies of these Virginia families to "a tangle of fishhooks, so closely interlocked that it is impossible to pick up one without drawing three or four after it."[37]

One genealogical example was the Filmer-Horsmanden-Byrd-Beverley-Culpeper-Carter connection. The ancient Kentish family of Sir Edward Filmer produced several sons in the early seventeenth century. Among them was Sir Robert Filmer, author of the royalist treatise *Patriarcha,* which became a favorite target for John Locke and Algernon Sydney. Sir Robert had a son named Samuel Filmer, who married his cousin Mary Horsmanden and moved to Virginia, where he died in the dreaded "seasoning." The young widow married the prosperous planter William Byrd. She became the mother of William Byrd II, the mother-in-law of Robert Beverley and James Duke, and the grandmother of Thomas Chamberlayne, Charles Carter, Landon Carter, and John Page. Within three generations, most of Virginia's First Families were related to Mary Horsmanden Filmer Byrd, whose genealogy might be titled *Matriarcha.*

Another important connection was a Northampton cousinage that formed around the Isham family and included the Randolphs, Washingtons, and Spencers of Althorp. From this connection came William Randolph of

17. Colonel Richard Lee migrated to Virginia in 1640 and became Sir William
Berkeley's chief lieutenant. For his services he received vast land grants that established the fortune of the Lee family. In 1655 agents of the Puritan Commonwealth
seized his baggage and found "200 ounces of silver plate, all marked with his coat
of arms."

18. Anna Constable Lee, wife of Richard Lee, was "a lady of quality" who came to America in the household of Sir Francis Wyatt. In her features the unknown artist represents the cultural values that formed the feminine ideal among Virginia's elite.

Turkey Island and his wife, Mary Isham Randolph. So many FFVs are descended from them that they were called the Adam and Eve of Virginia. These Northamptonshire families were linked to the Filmer connection in Kent. Close ties were cemented by cousin marriages, carefully planned to create a web of kinship as dense as that of the Roman patriciate.

A case in point was the composition of Virginia's powerful Royal Council. Virginia's cavalier elite gained control of this body during the mid–seventeenth century and held it until the American Revolution. As early as 1660 every councillor was related to another member by blood or marriage. As late as 1775 every member was descended from a councillor who had served in 1660.[38] A seat on the Council was not an empty honor. This small body functioned simultaneously as the governor's cabinet, the upper house of the legislature, and the colony's supreme court. It also controlled the distribution of land, and the lion's share went to a group of twenty-five families who monopolized two-thirds of the Council seats from 1680 to 1775.[39]

In company with a larger group of lesser gentry, this small elite kept a firm hand on the economic life of the colony. An imperial official wrote in 1703: "In every river of this province there are men in number from ten to thirty, who by trade and industry have gotten very competent estates. Those gentlemen take care to supply the poorer sort with goods and necessaries, and are sure to keep them always in their debt, and consequently dependent on them. Out of this number are chosen His Majesty's Council, the Assembly, the Justices, and Officers of Government."[40]

Unlike the colony of Maryland, which maintained a large rural middling class through the seventeenth century, the distribution of wealth in Virginia became extremely unequal at an early date. By 1670 in Surry County, 60 percent of the workforce possessed no real estate; 8 percent owned most of the land in the county. Even so, Surry was one of the more egalitarian counties.[41]

So strong was the hegemony of Virginia's First Families through the first century of the colony's history that one well-born immigrant named George Fisher was warned not to displease them. He recalled, "John Randolph, in speaking of the disposition of the Virginians very freely cautioned us against disobliging or offending any person of note in the Colony . . . ; for says he, either by blood or marriage, we are almost all related, and so connected in our interests, that whoever of a Stranger presumes to offend any one of us will infallibly find an enemy of the whole, nor, right nor wrong, do we ever forsake him, till by one means or other his ruin is accomplished."[42]

This small elite was destined to play a large role in the cultural history of Virginia and its westward movement. The formation of southern folkways owed much to their example, which was widely emulated. An English immigrant who came in 1717 observed, "At the Capitol, at publick times, may be seen a great number of handsom, well-dressed, compleat gentlemen." He thought that they made "as fine an appearance as I have seen anywhere." In 1773 a clear-sighted northern visitor to Virginia, Philip Fithian, observed that "the People of fortune . . . are the pattern of all behaviour here."[43] This Virginia elite was firmly established during the governorship of Sir William Berkeley. It remained dominant for more than a century.[44]

Virginia's Great Migration

The era of Sir William Berkeley was the time of Virginia's great migration that supplied the nucleus of its English population. From 1645 to 1665 the population of the colony multiplied more than threefold. Given the high mortality rates in the Chesapeake colonies and the low birthrates during the first generation, the number of immigrants was probably in the range of 40,000 to 50,000 during the period from 1645 to 1670.[45]

Virginia's great migration differed from the Puritan exodus to Massachusetts in many ways—in its English regional origins, in its American destination, and especially in its social composition. New England had drawn its population mostly from the middle of English society. Virginians came in greater numbers from both higher and lower ranks. In quantitative terms Berkeley's "distressed cavaliers" were only a small part of English migration to the Chesapeake colonies. The great mass of Virginia's immigrants were humble people of low rank. More than 75 percent came as indentured servants.[46]

One surviving English register contains the names of approximately 10,000 servants who sailed from Bristol to America between 1654 and 1678. Roughly half went to Virginia. The rest found their way to the West Indies. Scarcely any chose to make New England their home.[47] Virginia's servants were recruited mainly from the lower strata of English society, but not from the very lowest. They came from "the bottom of the middle ranks," one historian has written, "below their older and wealthier contemporaries, but above the poor laborers, vagrants and the destitute." Unlike most immigrants to New England, their passage was paid by others.[48] Two-thirds of Virginia's colonists were unskilled laborers, or farmers in the English sense—agrarian tenants who worked the land of others. Only about 30 percent were artisans (compared with nearly 60 percent in New England). Most were unable to read or write; rates of illiteracy in the Chesapeake Bay were much higher than in Massachusetts Bay.[49]

Patterns of gender in Virginia were also very different from New England's great migration. Altogether, female immigrants to the Old Dominion were outnumbered by males by more than four to one—in some periods, six to one.[50] Few women boarded ships for Virginia with a full understanding of what they were getting into. Some were "trepanned" or "snared" and sent against their will, as an old folk ballad called "The Trappan'd Maiden" tells us:

Give ear unto a Maid, that lately was betray'd,
And sent into Virginny, O:
In brief I shall declare, what I have suffer'd there,
When that I was weary, weary, weary, weary, O. . . .

Five years served I, under Master Guy,
In the land of Virginny, O,
Which made me for to know sorrow, grief and woe,
When that I was weary, weary, weary, weary, O. . . .

I have play'd my part both at Plow and Cart,
In the Land of Virginny, O;
Billets from the Wood upon my back they load,
When that I am weary, weary, weary, weary, O. . . .

Then let Maids beware, all by my ill-fare,
In the Land of Virginny, O;
Be sure to stay at home, for if you do here come,
You all will be weary, weary, weary, weary, O. . . .[51]

In 1643 a woman named Elizabeth Hamlin was sent to Newgate for trepanning girls in this manner. Another ballad tells the tale of an "honest man[,] a Weaver," who sold his wife to Virginia. This practice, bizarre as it may seem, also actually occurred. Wife selling was a common practice in seventeenth-century England.[52]

Most of Virginia's servant-immigrants were half-grown boys and young men. Three out of four were between the ages of fifteen and twenty-four. Only 3 percent were under fifteen, and less than 1 percent were over thirty-five—a sharp contrast with Massachusetts. More than a few of these young-sters were "spirited," or kidnapped, to Virginia. Parliament in 1645 heard evidence of gangs who "in a most barbarous and wicked Manner steal away many little children" for service in the Chesapeake colonies.[53] Others were "lagged," or transported, after being arrested for petty crime or vagrancy. Another ballad tells the story of a London apprentice who was "lagg'd" by a "hard-hearted judge" and "sold for a slave in Virginia":

19. Most indentured servants were young men such as Richard Lowther of Bedford-shire, England, who agreed by this indenture to be the servant of Edward Lyurd, an ironmonger in Virginia.

Come all you young fellows wherever you be,
Come listen awhile and I will tell thee,
Concerning the hardships that we undergo,
When we get lagg'd to Virginia. . . .

When I was apprentice in fair London town,
Many hours I served duly and truly,
Till buxom young lasses they led me astray,
My work I neglected more and more every day,
By that I got lagg'd to Virginia. . . .

But now in Virginia I lay like a hog,
Our pillow at night is a brick or a log,
We dress and undress like some other sea hog,
How hard is my fate in Virginia.[54]

The character of Virginia's great migration thus differed in many ways from the Puritan exodus to Massachusetts. From the start immigrants to the Chesapeake were more highly stratified, more male, less highly skilled, and less literate. Many came from the south and west of England; few came from East Anglia or the north. These patterns did not develop merely by chance. Virginia's great migration was the product of policy and social planning. Its royalist elite succeeded in shaping the social history of an American region partly by regulating the process of migration.

"The Refuge of Our Renagadoes": Emigration from Berkeley's Virginia

Sir William Berkeley and his cavalier elite did not merely recruit immigrants to support their model colony. They also tried to drive out people who did not fit in. Chief among these unwelcome colonists were Puritans and Quakers. Much early movement from Virginia was caused by the departure of religious dissenters—a direct result of policies pursued by the colony's governing elite.

An example was William Stone, a nonconformist Anglican who led a group from Virginia's Eastern Shore to Maryland, where they received 5,000 acres and a promise of religious toleration. Stone later became governor of Maryland and a strong supporter of the Toleration Act in 1649. He also encouraged a larger group of Puritans to emigrate from Virginia farther up the bay, where they founded the town of Providence in what is now Anne Arundel County, Maryland.

After 1660 the Virginia legislature forbade nonconformist preaching, required baptism in an Anglican church, and prohibited Quaker meetings. As a consequence the Quakers began to leave in large numbers—some moving north to Maryland's Eastern Shore and settling in Somerset County.

Sir William Berkeley himself took a leading part in this persecution. When Quaker missionary William Edmundson visited the colony in 1672, he met with the governor and tried to reason with him in the Quaker way but wrote afterward that Berkeley was "very peevish and brittle, and I could fasten Nothing upon him with all the soft Arguments I could use." Later the missionary met with Puritan leader Richard Bennett, who also had run afoul of Sir William. The Quaker wrote that Bennett "asked me, *If the Governor called me Dog, Rogue,* &c.? I said, *No, he did not call me so.* Then said he, *You took him in his best Humour, they being the usual Terms when he is angry, for he is an* Enemy to every Appearance of Good."[55]

At the same time Virginia's cavalier elite also drove out others in a different way. The leaders of the colony arrogated to themselves much of the best land. Young servants found brighter opportunities in Maryland and the southern counties of Delaware. A large part of the lower Eastern Shore was settled in this way. As a result Maryland became a more diverse society, with more room for people of middling estate. Virginia in the late seventeenth century became more closed and homogeneous.

Other servants and debtors fled south beyond the borders of Virginia. Governor Thomas Culpeper, who followed Berkeley, wrote in 1681, "Carolina (I meane the North part of it) always was and is the sinke of America, the Refuge of our Renagadoes." In the critical period emigration as well as immigration in Sir William Berkeley's Virginia contributed to the forming of a hegemonic culture that dominated other groups in the colony.[56]

The Migration of English Culture to Virginia

Berkeley's elite and its indentured servants came from very different strata of England's social order. In other ways, however, their origins were similar. Most shared the same Anglican faith. Nearly all were of the same generation. The great majority came from the same area in the south of England—the territory between Bristol and London, from the Channel to the south Midlands.

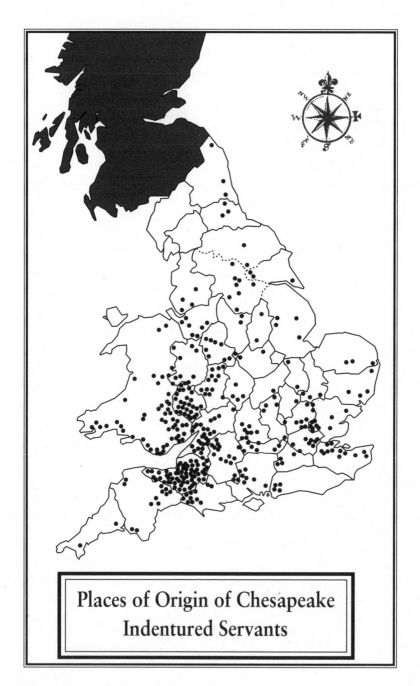

Places of Origin of Chesapeake
Indentured Servants

20

In the seventeenth century that region was an open, wooded, sparsely settled country. In 1600 Dorchester, Dorset's largest town, had 1,500 inhabitants. Hampshire had only two towns (Southampton and Winchester) as large as 3,000 and only six above 1,000. The economy of this region rested mainly on staple agriculture—grain and wool. Virginia's culture was the product of this region. This area's social structure had long differed from that in other parts of Britain. Unlike East Anglia, which had a large number of freemen, the old kingdoms of Wessex and Mercia had held a high proportion of serfs and slaves in the early Middle Ages. Before the Norman conquest slavery had been stronger there than elsewhere in England. By the seventeenth century slavery was long gone, but other forms of social obligation remained powerful. The political character of this region was also distinctive. The old boundaries of Wessex and Mercia coincided almost exactly with that part of England that had been loyal to King John in 1215 and to Richard II in 1381. In the English Civil War, it generally supported the Stuarts. Pockets of Puritanism were to be found in Wiltshire and Hampshire, but most of this territory was royalist. The English emigrants who came to America, both "distressed cavaliers" and indentured servants, created a culture that reflected their British regional origins, their social rank, their Anglican faith, and their period of emigration.

The Virginia accent, for example, developed from a cluster of rural dialects in the south and west of England. Sir William Cope wrote, "The . . . dialect of the counties which formed the kingdom of Wessex has in many respects a great similarity. And of these the people of West Sussex, Hampshire and Wiltshire have many words in common." Most of the distinctive components of a tidewater southern accent have been found in the speech ways of southern England during the seventeenth century. The Virginia patterns were not a matter of linguistic replication. Local variations disappeared, such as the strong *z* sounds of Somerset and the dropped *h* of Sussex speech, but common elements survived. The southern accent began by mixing and merging these ingredients. The elite added more of cultivated London speech, and layers of Indian and African speech were grafted on, but the root of the Virginia accent (which later spread through much of the South) was a set of English regional dialects in the mid–seventeenth century.[57]

A similar pattern appeared in the architecture of Virginia, a broad vocabulary of vernacular forms that derived from English customs. The conventional hall-and-parlor "Virginia house" was a south-of-England building modified to suit American conditions. So also was the great house, of which the prototype was Sir William Berkeley's Green Spring. Likewise, the earliest extant pieces of Virginia-made furniture, though crafted of North American woods such as yellow pine, demonstrate the almost pure importation of Jacobean aesthetics to the New World.

The idea of the family in Virginia was not the covenanted nuclear model that took root in Puritan Massachusetts but another form, more organic, extended, hierarchical, and patriarchal, that had existed throughout the south of England. *Patriarch* was a word that came often to Virginia lips, and *family* referred to everyone under his protection. Demographic conditions reinforced the importance of the extended family by the disruption of nuclear units. Many indicators show that extended relations were stronger in Virginia—this strength appeared in patterns of naming, inheritance, burial, household structure, and language.

Marriage in Virginia was not a contract as in Puritan New England but a quasi-sacrament—a sacred knot that mortal hands could not untie. Gender roles were marked by an exceptionally strong sense of differentiation and inequality. Something of this pattern survives in southern attitudes toward gender even today.

21. Green Spring, the home of Sir William Berkeley, was Virginia's first great house, begun in 1646. This watercolor by Benjamin Latrobe was done in 1796 shortly before the house was pulled down

The naming and raising of children also differed from New England. Less than half of Virginians received biblical names. Males were named after warriors and kings—William, Robert, George, Edward. The eldest sons and daughters were named for grandparents, not parents as in New England.

In place of Puritan will breaking, Virginians actively tried to strengthen the wills of very young children but then subjected them in later childhood to complex rituals of social conformity that did not exist in New England. Dance, for example, was a serious instrument of socialization. Children were taught to cultivate a stoic idea of right conduct, very different from Puritan ethics.

22. The proportions and floral decoration of this cupboard follow English fashions of the early seventeenth century, but it was made in Virginia, c. 1660, of local oak and yellow pine. Its maker used New World materials to preserve Old World traditions that had passed out of fashion in the mother country.

Rituals of worship in Virginia from 1650 to the mid–eighteenth century ran to a liturgical style, rather than the meeting and lecture style of New England. The Anglican establishment was much stronger before 1740 than many historians have believed, and dissent was largely suppressed. Religious institutions in Virginia were not the same as in the mother country. The lay members of the vestry had more power, and ecclesiastical hierarchies much less. More adult Virginians attended Anglican services and took communion than in England.

23. Institutions, as well as individuals, migrated to America. This communion set is the oldest church silver continuously used in the United States. Its chalice and patens were made in London, 1618–19, and given anonymously to the church at Smith's Hundred, Virginia.

As for learning and literacy, Virginia's elite showed strong support for higher learning, but not for common schooling. Berkeley's famous prayer, "But I thank God, *there are no free schools* nor *printing* [in Virginia]," was not an isolated eccentricity but an attitude often repeated by men of his culture on both sides of the ocean.[58] Education and literacy in Virginia were marked by great differences in status—gentlemen were 100 percent literate; servants, 70 percent illiterate.

Foodways ran to a regime of roasting, grilling, frying, and stewing, as in southern England, where "Dorset cooked" means fried. A model dish was the fricassee. The Chesapeake elites created the only haute cuisine in British America and lingered over their dinners. Virginians dined; New Englanders merely ate. In the distribution in probate estates of tablecloths and silver, one finds that something of this difference reached even into the poorest Chesapeake cottages. New foodstuffs emerged from American conditions, but old English foodways were revised rather than replaced.

Sport in Virginia meant blood sports. As in the south of England, the male population was arrayed according to the size of its victims in a great chain of slaughter that embraced the governor's stag, the gentleman's foxes, the yeomanry's coursing after rabbits, the laborers' cockshailing, and apprentices' songbirds, while small boys prepared themselves by maiming toads and butterflies. From Berkeley to Jefferson, Virginians expressed high contempt for games played with the ball and urged young gentlemen to shoot for the sake of the mind. Puritans were appalled.

The work ways of this culture may be seen in a paradox. Sir John Oglander wrote, "I scorn base getting and unworthy penurious saving, yet my desire is to lay up somewhat for my poor children."[59] The result was a set of complex compromises—but always an ideal of independence from manual work, as opposed to the Puritan ethic of work itself.

There were also different ideas about getting and spending. Debt was a common condition not merely of tobacco planters but also of gentlemen throughout the south of England. There were cultural as well as economic imperatives here. In place of the Puritan idea of improving the time, William Byrd II wrote of "kill[ing] the time." In fact, cruel temporal tyrannies controlled Virginia lives—the tyranny of crop time over a tobacco plantation had no equal in New England.[60]

Land in Virginia was distributed by the Council to individual planters in grants that were more than five times larger than in New England. The land

ways of Virginia were less communal, less instrumental, less preservation-
ist. The distribution of wealth from the late seventeenth century was much
less egalitarian than in the Puritan or Quaker colonies. It closely resembled
the prevailing patterns in southern England.

The ways of power and order in Virginia were the familiar English system
of shires (introduced in 1634), parishes, and militia. County courts and
vestries combined an oligarchy of local families with an electoral component.
Voter turnout was heavy among those eligible to vote, heavier than in New
England. Voting was a privilege or liberty. Liberties were not inalienable
rights but were possessed in proportion to one's rank. Those at the bottom
of the social scale were thought to have no liberty, so slavery could thrive in
this culture. Although inegalitarian, ideas of freedom were not wholly authoritarian in Virginia. They were capable of being enlarged.

The Virginia Company of London had failed in its purpose "to plant an
English nation in America," but after its demise a stable, distinctive culture
was developed in Sir William Berkeley's Virginia by cavaliers and indentured
servants. As geographer Donald Meinig observes, "It was, of course, a special kind of 'English nation,' . . . [a] very distinct Virginia variant of an 'English Nation' that had developed over these first fifty years."[61] It was not a
replication of English customs. Important changes were introduced in response to American conditions, but elements of cultural persistence were exceptionally strong in this new environment.[62]

Immigrants in Chains: Convicts and Prisoners

Many immigrants who helped to found a voluntary society in North America did not arrive as volunteers. Some of them came in chains. For them all
the Turnerian clichés ran in reverse. Their America was a place of bondage
rather than freedom, oppression rather than equality, and tyranny rather than
the rule of law.

Many of these involuntary immigrants arrived from Britain as transported
convicts. This traffic began within a few years of the founding of Jamestown.
In 1618 the friends of a highwayman named Henry Reade sought his release
from Newgate Prison on condition that he be transported to Virginia. The
case went all the way to the Privy Council, which refused to agree on the
grounds that the crime had been too heinous.

In the same year, however, a kinswoman of John Throckmorton, who had stolen a hat worth six shillings, offered to pay his way to Virginia. Other convicts were actively recruited by the Virginia Company. A carpenter named Samuel Rogers was saved from hanging for manslaughter because skilled craftsmen were needed in Virginia. In 1619 the king himself ordered that 100 "dissolute persons" be sent to the colony. Through the mid–seventeenth century a small, unsteady flow continued from many parts of Britain. The corporation of Berwick-upon-Tweed flogged seven "very dangerous rogues" in 1665 and sent them to Virginia. During the same year the ship *Recovery* asked permission to sail quickly to Virginia from another part of England before its forty unwilling passengers could escape.[63]

Virginians were of two minds about the convict trade. In 1671 Hugh Nevitt brought over ten criminals and found a ready market among planters

24. *The Fortunate Transport. Rob Theif: or the Lady of ye Gold Watch Polly Haycock,* who, according to the text, is "bound for Virginia." By an unknown artist and engraver, c. 1760–80.

who were desperate for labor. The General Court intervened and made Nevitt carry away all the "Newgate birds" that had arrived in the colony.[64] The previous year the General Court had passed a law forbidding outright the immigration of "any *jaile birds* or such others, who for notorious offenses have deserved to dye in England." The order was allowed to stand by the Crown and appears to have been enforced.[65] Historian Robert Beverly wrote in 1705 that "as for Malefactors condemn'd to Transportation, [the Virginians] have always receiv'd very few, and for many years last past, their Laws have been severe against them."[66]

In 1717 Parliament passed a law for the "more effectual transportation of felons." After that date criminals began to arrive in large numbers. Historians have been revising upward the size of the British convict trade at the same time that estimates of African migration have been falling. Recent studies have reckoned the convict traffic to North America in the eighteenth century at about 50,000 from Britain and Ireland.[67]

Of all British and Irish convicts who were transported to America, as many as half came to Maryland and Virginia. In some years the proportion that came to the Chesapeake was as high as 90 percent. Transportation was a brutal business. Mortality on convict ships was roughly the same as in the African slave trade—between 10 to 15 percent, and sometimes more, died in passage.[68]

The convicts themselves were diverse. Most had been convicted of petty crimes, usually theft. Some were prisoners of war or captives from the many insurrections. In 1717 the ship *Ann and Elizabeth* carried 127 prisoners who had been taken after the Jacobite rising two years before. Once in Virginia they petitioned for freedom under the Habeas Corpus Act, without success.

An occasional prisoner came from the upper reaches of English society. Henry Justice, a barrister of Middle Temple, was transported for having stolen rare books from the library of Trinity College, Cambridge. Most, however, were so poor that they lived on the edge of subsistence and stole to eat. Others were hardened criminals and desperate characters.[69]

About one-fifth were women, of whom 15 percent were in their teens, more than 50 percent in their twenties, and at least 5 percent were over the age of fifty, an unusually large proportion for Virginia. Some had been sold by their own neighbors. The village of Alton in 1730 joined together and arranged to have a neighbor many of them feared transported to America.

The Poor Unhappy

Tranſported Felon's

Sorrowful Account.

O F

His fourteen Years Tranf-

portation at *Virginia* in *America.*

In S I X P A R T S.

By James Revel, the unhapp Sufferer.

S H E W I N G,

How his Father having only this one Son, made
him his Darling, and when he was old enough
put him Apprentice to a Tin-man, near Moor-
fields, where he got into bad Company. How
he ran away from his Mafter, and went a rob-
bing with a Gang of Thieves. How his Mafter
got him back again, but he would not be kept
from his wicked Companions, but went thiev-
ing with them again. How he was tranfported
for Fourteen Years. With an account of the
way the Tranfports work, and the Punifhment
they receive for committing any Fault.

Concluding with a word of Advice to all young Men,

London, Printed and Sold in Stonecutter-
Street, Fleet-Market,

25. James Revel was one among many thousands of felons transported to Virginia.
He arrived between 1657 and 1671 and was bound to a former felon, "a man but
of ill fame, who first of all a transport thither came." Revel's "sorrowful account"
of his "unhappy" experiences went through numerous eighteenth-century editions
in the form of chapbooks, an equivalent to today's comic books.

The convict trade was deeply resented in America. The *Virginia Gazette* on May 24, 1751, reprinted an angry attack that circulated widely in the colonies. The author asked, "Can Britain show a more Sovereign contempt for us than by emptying their jails into our Settlements; unless they would likewise empty their Jakes on our tables!"[70]

As we begin to understand the magnitude of the convict trade to the Chesapeake, we must ask what influence it had on the culture of the region. No doubt it increased violence and disorder. The *Pennsylvania Gazette* of April 11, 1751, published a list of crimes committed by transported felons in Virginia. Some of these convicts escaped to the frontier. In 1748 the inhabitants of Albemarle County asked help to suppress an entire settlement of horse thieves who had "established themselves into a confederacy" on Virginia's frontier.[71]

Americans think of their western frontier as routinely a place of violence, crime, and disorder. So it was in some places, but not everywhere. By any comparative test the frontier of the Delaware Quakers and New England Puritans was much less disorderly than the southern frontier. Patterns of migration and cultural hegemony help to explain the difference.

The African Migration

In 1756 an Ibo child named Olaudah Equiano was kidnapped from his Nigerian village and made a slave. He was bought and sold many times in Iboland, moving farther and farther from home, until he was purchased by a slave merchant for 172 cowrie shells and carried by canoe to the sea, where he saw a great ship riding at anchor. The sight of the ship filled him with surprise, then with terror. Later he remembered, "When I was carried on board . . . I was now persuaded that I had got into a world of bad spirits, and that they were going to kill me." Olaudah saw a multitude of Africans in chains near a boiling copper kettle as big as a man. He wondered if "we were not to be eaten by those white men with horrible looks, red faces, and long hair."

The voyage was long and terrible, "a scene of horror almost inconceivable." Many slaves died miserably in chains. Several hurled themselves into the sea. Olaudah, barely eleven years old, thought that death was his only friend. He refused to eat, and his captors whipped him severely until he took some food.

THE

INTERESTING NARRATIVE

OF

THE LIFE

OF

OLAUDAH EQUIANO,

OR

GUSTAVUS VASSA,

THE AFRICAN.

WRITTEN BY HIMSELF.

VOL I.

Behold, God is my salvation; I will trust and not be afraid; for the Lord Jehovah is my strength and my song; he also is become my salvation.
And in that day shall ye say, Praise the Lord, call upon his name, declare his doings among the people. Isaiah xii. 2, 4.

LONDON:

Printed for and sold by the AUTHOR, No. 10, Union-Street, Middlesex Hospital;

Sold also by Mr. Johnson, St. Paul's Church-Yard; Mr. Murray, Fleet-Street; Messrs. Robson and Clark, Bond-Street; Mr. Davis, opposite Gray's Inn, Holborn; Messrs. Shepperson and Reynolds, and Mr. Jackson, Oxford-Street; Mr. Lackington, Chiswell-Street; Mr. Mathews, Strand; Mr. Murray, Prince's-Street, Soho; Mess. Taylor and Co. South Arch, Royal Exchange; Mr. Button, Newington-Causeway; Mr. Parsons, Paternoster-Row; and may be had of all the Booksellers in Town and Country.

[Entered at Stationer's Hall.]

26. This is the only published account of a Virginia slave brought from Africa.

At last he landed on the island of Barbados and was taken to a slave trader's yard. Olaudah was put up for auction, but nobody would buy him, and he was put on board a small sloop for North America. His treatment grew a little better. The food improved, and he was given plenty of rice and fat pork. The voyage ended in a green and fertile country "up a river a good way from the sea," but the young child was in no mood to admire the countryside. "We saw few or none of our native Africans, and not one soul who could talk to me," Olaudah recalled. "In this state I was constantly grieving and pining, and wishing for death rather than anything else." At the age of eleven, friendless and alone, this small Nigerian child had come to a land called Virginia.[72]

In many ways the story of Olaudah Equiano was typical of the Chesapeake slave trade in the eighteenth century. Virginia's slaves were mixed in their African origins. They came from every part of West and Central Africa, and a few even from Madagascar and Mozambique in East Africa. But not all African regions were equally represented. One area was exceptionally important—the Bight of Biafra. In the great slave marts of this region, especially the towns of Old and New Calabar, the great majority of captives were Ibo or Ibibio.[73] Orlando Patterson calculated that three-quarters of all slaves coming from the Niger and Cross deltas "belonged to the Ibo tribe." The rest were Chambas, Okrika, Andoni, Edoes, and especially Ibibios.[74]

These slaves had been kidnapped from their small villages and farms by other Africans and sent on board slave ships in ports such as Calabar and Bonny on the African coast of Biafra. Often, like Olaudah Equiano, they were carried first to slave markets in other American colonies, where nobody would buy them because they were Ibos.

Slave owners in the eighteenth century early recognized that Ibos were different from other Africans. They were not much wanted in the Caribbean colonies. Jamaican planters thought them "the lowest and most wretched of all the nations of Africa."[75] Another West Indian planter observed more perceptively that Ibos were "turbulent, stubborn and much addicted to suicide; yet they are hardy and susceptible to labour, the women in particular, who are superior to any other, and very little inferior to men. If well treated during their seasoning, and not urged with undue rigour, they frequently turn out to be good slaves."[76]

Christopher Codrington, governor of the Leeward Islands, was of the same opinion. "Eboes or mocoes" when punished were often suicidal, he

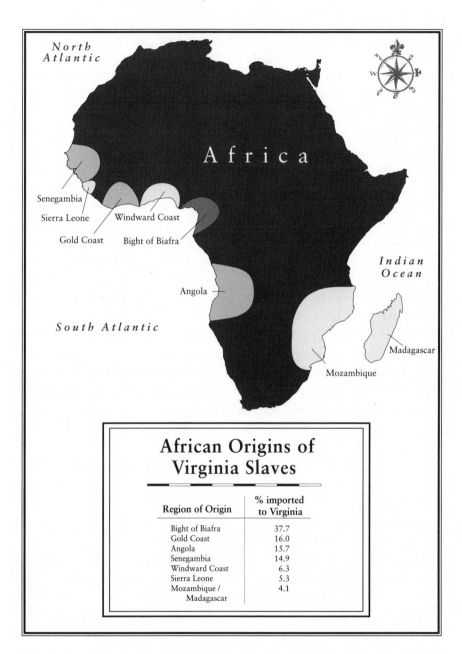

North
Atlantic

Africa

Senegambia

Sierra Leone   Windward Coast

Gold Coast   Bight of Biafra

Indian
Ocean

Angola

South Atlantic

Madagascar

Mozambique

African Origins of
Virginia Slaves

Region of Origin	% imported to Virginia
Bight of Biafra	37.7
Gold Coast	16.0
Angola	15.7
Senegambia	14.9
Windward Coast	6.3
Sierra Leone	5.3
Mozambique / Madagascar	4.1

27

wrote in 1701. "They require therefore the gentlest and mildest treatment to reconcile them to their situation; but if their confidence be once obtained they manifest as great fidelity, affection and gratitude as can reasonably be expected from men in a state of slavery."[77] South Carolinians did not want Ibos. Slave trader Henry Laurens told his suppliers not to send "Callabar slaves" (from the ports of Calabar and New Calabar in the Niger Delta, the prime shipping point for Ibos) because in Charleston "Callabar slaves won't go down when others can be had in plenty."[78] But Virginians were willing to accept Ibos. These Africans were taken to the Chesapeake, where planters knew little about African culture and cared less. A buyer in Northampton County wrote, "If they are likely young negroes, it's not a farthing matter where they come from." The Chesapeake Bay was the end of the line in the African slave trade—a place where slaves were sent who were unsalable in more discriminating markets.[79]

The concentration of Ibos was especially large in the critical period of Virginia's slave trade. It was also highest in the vital center of Virginia's tidewater culture, the estuaries of the York and the James rivers, where Virginia's system of slavery was defined during the eighteenth century. In the period from 1718 to 1726, 60 percent of slaves arriving at York, Virginia, came from Biafra, and perhaps 90 percent of these Biafran captives were Ibo. They brought to Virginia many distinctive traditions, such as using underground cellars—sometimes wood-lined—along the walls or in the corners of a house for storage or hiding places for valuables. A number of these places have been uncovered by archaeologists.[80] Later the origins of Virginia slaves grew more diverse. In the late eighteenth century, an increasing proportion came from Angola, and others from West Africa. But always, by every measure, Ibo slaves remained the largest single group of Africans in Virginia—a pattern that appeared in no other mainland colony.[81] These African origins made a difference in the culture that developed in the New World. The uniqueness of the Ibo people has often been noted. In the twentieth century they came to be called the "Jews of Africa," a people who adapted themselves to Western culture and modern technology with high success. Their individual achievements were a cause of the Biafran war, which arose from deep differences between the Ibo and other major cultures of the Niger basin. In earlier periods the Ibo had a different reputation. They were thought backward and primitive by the standards of other African cultures. Their social system was perceived to be fragmented, atomistic, and individuated. Their polities were more open and less authoritarian. The role of women was different in Ibo society—their status perhaps higher, their cultural role stronger. The high proportion of Ibos may have had an important effect on Chesapeake slavery—in its scale, its social structure, and its cultural values, which differed very much from slavery in other parts of the New World.[82]

Slavery came late to Virginia and grew very slowly in the seventeenth century. In 1625 only 1.9 percent of the population was African American. As late as 1640 a larger number of Africans lived in New England and New Netherland than in Maryland and Virginia. Most servile workers in the Chesapeake Bay were indentured servants until the late seventeenth century. Only after the supply of English servants began to decline did planters turn increasingly to African slaves.

The largest flow of immigration was in the period from 1700 to 1760, when about 59,000 Africans arrived. To be of African descent in Virginia was to be descended from an immigrant who arrived within a generation of the year

28. *The Old Plantation,* watercolor on paper, by an unknown artist, c. 1790

1730. Before 1680 most of Virginia's slaves came from the West Indies. After 1720 nearly all arrived directly from Africa. Mortality was high in the Middle Passage and even higher in the dreaded "seasoning" process in America. A new diet and new diseases, especially European respiratory diseases, took a heavy toll. So also did the cruelty of treatment. African slavery in early America was harsh and very brutal. "A new negro must be broke," wrote Edward Kimber on the Eastern Shore. This task was done with extreme violence.[83]

The slave ships bound to Virginia carried two men for every woman, a more nearly equal ratio than among British servants or convicts. "New negroes" were at first placed in sex-segregated barracks, but at an early date seasoned slaves began to live in conjugal families with children. When families were formed, the black population began to grow rapidly.

If rates of African immigration were small in Virginia, rates of natural increase were large by comparison with other colonies. Most slave populations, from the ancient world to our own time, were unable to reproduce their numbers except by immigration. African-American slavery in Virginia and other North American colonies was different. It expanded by natural increase so rapidly that Virginia's African population grew from fewer than 20,000 in 1710 to nearly 300,000 in 1790.

Like Olaudah Equiano, these African immigrants found themselves in a country occupied mostly by Europeans. They could communicate with their masters and even other slaves only by learning English, which rapidly became the language of the quarters. But this was English with an African accent, a distinctive dialect that became a vehicle of a unique culture.

Most Virginia slaves lived in small "negro quarters" away from their master's house. Black Virginians improvised new marriage ceremonies and rituals. Broom marriages, for example, drew upon both European and African folkways. Caroline Johnson Harris recollected that "when we step 'cross de broomstick, we was married. Was bad luck to tech de broomstick. Fo'ks always stepped high 'cause dey didn't want no spell cast on 'em—Ant Sue used to say whichever one teched de stick was gonna die furst." Tom Epps, however, a Prince George County slave, said, "I hear tell of jumpin' de broomstick, but we never did nothin' like dat on our place." He observed, however, that "all de courtin' an' marryin' was done at night" (so as not to disrupt the work schedule in the day) and that "Marsa would hol' a light, read a lil' bit, an' den tell 'em dey was married." In time the lamps used in these nocturnal ceremonies became part of the wedding ritual, and the custom of lamp

29. Sir Hans Sloane, whose collection became the foundation of the British Museum in 1753, acquired this drum "from Virginia by Mr. Cleark." Sloane thought that it was an Indian drum. Rather, it probably was the product of the Ashanti people of West Africa and was brought to Virginia by ship, either with Africans or Europeans.

marriages spread wherever Virginia slaves migrated, especially to Kentucky and the rest of the Upper South.[84]

African Americans developed new ideas about family in which extended families became more important and nuclear units relatively less so than in European societies. Children were less frequently named for their parents and more often for other kin than was the custom among European Americans. Slaves also followed African taboos against marrying first cousins, a different attitude from that of Anglo-Virginians.

Distinctive attitudes toward work developed in African-American culture that derived from the communal work ethic of Africa rather than the individuated ethic of northern Europe.

Because slaves' bodies were not free, they enlarged the meaning of freedom by seeking it in the soul, spirit, and senses. This expanded sense of freedom often found expression in dance and music. As early as 1698 it was reported that slaves were traveling as far as thirty or forty miles on weekends to gathering places such as the falls of the Potomac River, where they met and mixed. The result was the rapid growth of a distinctive culture.

Music was an aspect of life in which slaves had much autonomy. Accordingly, music and dance were important in emerging African-American culture. In 1774 Nicholas Creswell wrote that Virginia slaves "generally meet together and amuse themselves with dancing to the banjo."[85] In *Notes on the State of Virginia* Thomas Jefferson acknowledged that the "banjar" had come from Africa.[86] Its African precursor seems to have been the *xalam*. The technique used to play it—downstroking—is the one generally used in banjo playing in Virginia and Kentucky today. A study of runaway slave advertisements and other published references indicates that Virginia and Maryland were the cradle of banjo playing in the American colonies. Moreover, the first recorded white banjo player, Joel Walker Sweeney (b. 1810), a native of Appomattox, was taught to play the banjo by his father's slaves. He led a minstrel show that was the principal vehicle for transmitting the African banjo into white culture. Significantly, this first troupe was called the Virginia Minstrels. By the mid–nineteenth century the banjo was a mainstay of American music.[87]

In contrast to the banjo, the fiddle was European—an Italian instrument. African Americans adapted it very early and used it in fashioning a distinctive musical idiom that profoundly shaped the music of European Americans as well.

30. Although a large number of Africans were forcibly brought to Virginia before 1806, this is one of few surviving artifacts that specifically depict the African experience. The four-footed animal that decorates the pipe bowl seems to be an African gazelle.

Virginian foodways were deeply influenced by African and Afro-Caribbean traditions. Slave women added gumbo, eggplant, black-eyed peas, sesame, yams, sorghum, watermelon, bananas, rice, and possibly tomatoes to the Virginian cuisine. Also, from the late seventeenth century onward, many of Virginia's cooks were African American, even in white households, and their contributions have not been fully appreciated. Food historian Karen Hess writes, "In addition to the actual borrowings, there is the thumb print that each cook leaves on a recipe. . . . It's a question of the temperature of the cooking fats, of generosity in measuring, of 'nose,' not to mention palate, of timing, of patience . . . all of which are formed by years of working with food. And so it was that even when thoroughly English dishes were cooked by hands that had known other products, other cuisines, the result would never be quite English."[88]

Altogether, African-American folkways in Virginia constituted a unique syncretic culture. There were many strong elements of persistence from Africa to the New World, but what mainly defined this culture was its extraordinary capacity for combining many different elements.

The Indians of Virginia

One important factor that distinguished colonial Virginia from seventeenth-century England was the presence of an aboriginal population whom the Europeans called Indians. The ancestors of these early inhabitants were themselves immigrants who had moved into Virginia by at least 9,500 B.C. after a west-to-east migration that carried them even farther than Europeans or Africans would travel.[89] By the time of the European encounter, the tribes of the coastal plains of North America had adopted a relatively fixed lifestyle, centered in permanent villages and supported by horticulture and short-range foraging and hunting.

In 1607 many different tribes of American Indians inhabited Virginia. Some west of the fall line were Siouan-speaking people. Three tribes south and southwest of the James River spoke Iroquoian. Along the lower James River basin were Algonquian-speaking groups with whom the Europeans first came into contact. Virginia may have been the New World to English migrants, but to these people it had been their home (according to tribal traditions) for about three hundred years.

The first Europeans with whom the Indians came into contact were not English but Spaniards. In 1570 Jesuits established a mission on the York River. The Indians destroyed it, and the Spanish wreaked vengeance. The need for protection against Europeans facilitated formation of Powhatan's empire, which by 1607 comprised thirty-two subchiefdoms and about 150 villages.[90]

Powhatan was ambivalent about the English. As a result of the Spanish experience, he was wary of these strangers but hoped that the English might be

31. This "American from Virginia, age 23" recently has been identified by George F. Hamell and Christian F. Feest as a Munsee Delaware man called Jacques, who was taken in 1644 from New Amsterdam to Amsterdam, where he was drawn by Czech artist Wenceslaus Hollar. The etching was published in Antwerp in 1645. The term *Virginia* had become sufficiently generic at that period for it to be used to refer even to Dutch New Amsterdam.

useful allies in consolidating his hegemony and in defending his empire against Siouan and Iroquoian tribes to the north and west.

Likewise, the English were of two minds about Virginia's Indians. On the one hand, the native population was seen as part of the natural world along with other animals (a prejudice that is manifest even today, when Indian remains and relics often repose in natural history museums). On the other hand, the Indians were viewed as noble savages or, more precisely, as innocent remnants of man in his natural state before the fall of Adam into sin. This view was encouraged by the literal belief of many Elizabethans in a terrestrial paradise, popularized by works such as Sir John Mandeville's *Travels* in 1496. By offering education and religious instruction, the Europeans tacitly acknowledged the humanity of the Indians. When material gain was at stake, however, it was morally convenient to see them as subhuman obstacles to progress, justifiably removed or even exterminated.[91]

The Powhatans embraced the concept of communal property. To them, open land was a source of food and materials to be shared by all. Sky, land, and water could not be bought or sold. The idea of individual land ownership in fee simple was completely foreign to them. To the English, however, unoccupied land meant that it was not in use and therefore was available for settlement. This misunderstanding was a precondition for conflict. However, it was the insatiable demand for land by the English for growing tobacco that made a clash of cultures inevitable.[92]

Virginia's rivers were fingers of the sea, and it was along them that the English expanded. Alarmed, Opechancanough, brother of Powhatan (who had died in 1618), attacked the English settlements in 1622, killing 347 colonists. In 1644 the aged warrior attacked again (carried to the battle in a litter) and killed more than 500, but the rising was suppressed by Governor Berkeley. The Indians agreed to withdraw north of the York River and to pay a tribute of beaver skins to the English.[93] "Thus," writes geographer Donald Meinig, "the English created a Virginia 'pale,' a clear demarcation as in Ireland, between (in their terms) 'civilization' and 'savagery.'"[94]

In this contest the English had two advantages. One was superior weaponry. The other was a secret weapon, unknown even to the Europeans. Englishmen perished in great numbers in Virginia because of dysentery and fevers, but the "Jamestown Exchange" of diseases was not an even trade. The Indians got the worst of it. Many microbes did not survive the cold of the

Arctic region through which they had to pass when the ancestors of Virginia's Indian peoples made their way across the Bering land bridge from Asia. This "cold screen" (as anthropologists call it) meant that the Indians' descendants, who reached Virginia generations later, came without many of the infectious diseases that plagued other continents. Virginia's aborigines were exposed to these illnesses all at once by their contact with Europeans and Africans after 1607.[95] The English and Africans who died from disease could be, and were, replaced by others from abroad. The Indians of Virginia, however, entered into an inexorable decline. By 1669 only about 1,800 were left, compared to more than 20,000 when the English arrived.[96]

Diseases were not all that the Europeans and Indians exchanged. There were material and cultural transfers as well. The Indians quickly adopted and became dependent on European tools and implements such as kettles, needles, fishhooks, knives, and guns, as well as woolen cloth and even pottery. The English introduced swine to Virginia, but "using the Indian method of cooking bear or venison, barbecued pork became typical of Virginia's cuisine," and even the Indians soon came to rely on it.[97] Colonists learned new methods of shellfishing with nets. They cultivated new crops such as tobacco, maize, squash, wild rice, and beans. Indian words entered the English vocabulary: tobacco, hominy, sachem, succotash, and powwow. Captain John Smith observed that the Indians called a hatchet a tomahawk. Not only words were adopted; there were also such cultural borrowings as the canoe, buckskins, moccasins, and pemmican (a concentrated food for long journeys) that influenced how Europeans dressed, moved, ate, and made a living.

After 1650 men such as Abraham Wood and William Byrd sent agents to the hinterlands to trade with the Indians, and they became important transmitters of English culture. But many of them adopted Indian ways, and in later years there was in the backcountry a group of people whose ethnicity and lifestyles were mixed. For example, Moravian missionaries found "a kind of white people, who live like savages. Hunting is their chief occupation." The Moravians observed that these people lived in bark-covered wigwams and "the clothes of the people consist of deerskins."[98] L. Daniel Mouer contends that a creole culture emerged in the Virginia backcountry in the second half of the seventeenth century.[99] That some genetic and cultural blending took place is undisputed; how widespread this culture was is debatable. In any event, it was overtaken by the hegemonic culture of the Scotch-Irish and English and Scottish borderers in the eighteenth century. Until then the population of the backcountry was very small, and these creoles no more determined the general lines of development than did any of the small groups cited by Wilbur Zelinsky in his "doctrine of first effective settlement."

Not only were aspects of Indian culture integrated into the larger culture of Virginia, but Indian culture itself also persisted. Though greatly reduced in numbers, Indians never vanished from eastern Virginia. Some functioning tribal units, such as the Pamunkey, survive to this day.

The Cultural Emergence of Colonial Virginia

By the end of the seventeenth century, the culture of colonial Virginia had crystallized in its classic form. Its gestation had been slow and painful, with many false starts and major setbacks: disaster at Roanoke, defeats at Jamestown, the failure of Captain John Smith's plans for the colony, the collapse of corporate institutions under the Virginia Company, and difficulties under the first royal governors.

With the arrival of Sir William Berkeley and the formation of his cavalier elite, a cultural order began to emerge in Virginia. It was strong enough to survive mortal challenges in the English Civil War and Bacon's Rebellion. By the late seventeenth century a strong set of cultural institutions had emerged.

The dynamics of change and continuity in Virginia in its first century offer little support for the Turner thesis. There was no process of democratization at work on this frontier and no emergence of modern individualism or capitalism. The colony that Charles II dubbed his "Old Dominion" was not in any meaningful sense an open society. Its institutions were in many ways more closed than those in England. Its labor system was more coercive than those of Europe. Its laws allowed less latitude to freedom of expression than did those of the mother country.

At the same time the history of seventeenth-century Virginia does not conform to the *Altlandschaft* model, one version of the germ theory that Turner was arguing against. The first settlers of Jamestown did not determine the direction of Virginia's development. Neither did Captain John Smith, or the leaders of the Virginia Company of London, or the first royal governors of Virginia. The major break came in the period from 1640 to 1690, and the central actors were Sir William Berkeley and his small elite of younger sons, who shared a vision of a cavalier utopia and worked systematically to impose that idea on their colony.

They did not have everything their own way. A cavalier utopia required a servile underclass, which was not easy to recruit by voluntary means. The failure of Berkeley's elite to build a social hierarchy with English servants led to other expedients—convict laborers in large numbers and African-American slaves. These involuntary immigrants made a difference, along with the continuing presence of the Indians.

The result was a colonial society that was a new-modeled American version of an old European ideal—hierarchical, conservative, constraining, but increasingly restless, dynamic, and diverse.

2

Migration in Virginia

For most Virginians the Atlantic crossing was only the beginning of their American migrations. Once landed in the New World, they commonly moved again. This general trend occurred everywhere in British America, but in Virginia a distinctive pattern of internal migration developed, different from that in other colonial regions.

Immigrants to Massachusetts tended to move once or twice after reaching America and then settled down after the mid–seventeenth century. Virginians kept on moving; their rates of internal migration remained high throughout the seventeenth and eighteenth centuries. Further, New Englanders did most of their moving when they were young, then found a place and stayed there. Virginians were more restless all their lives. As a consequence, it was not uncommon for 20 percent of the population in a Virginia county to disappear within a single year and for 50 percent to vanish in a decade. These tendencies persisted for many generations.

Other distinctive patterns also appeared. In New England rates of migration were comparatively egalitarian. A study of Hingham, Massachusetts, found that people of different ranks moved at about the same rate. In Virginia frequency of migration differed greatly by social rank. By and large the poor moved more than the rich. This was so partly because former servants were rarely able to find land in the counties where they had worked—less than 10 percent gained land in Lancaster (1662–78), and 9 percent in Northampton (1663–97), and 17 percent in Accomack (1663–97). There was a continuous migration of people who were looking for land and work. This pattern of population movement in Virginia was similar in some ways to that in England, except that distances were greater and removals more frequent.[1]

Virginia's ruling elites were not happy with this incessant movement, even though their policies had caused it. They specially feared a floating population of landless former servants and the poor. In Accomack County on the Eastern Shore there were complaints that "Loose & vagrant persons, That have not any Settled Residence, do too comonly enter themselves singly, and not in any house Keepers' List of Tithables, . . . and when the time comes that the Sheriff goes about to collect the publique dues, they abscond, and remove from place to place, on purpose to defraud the County of their Levies, being sensible they have no visible Estate." When the authorities cracked down, these "removers" left the colony altogether.[2]

Most migration, however, remained within the colony. In the mid–seventeenth century this movement assumed a pattern that persisted for many years. Former servants gravitated to areas of inferior land that had been left behind by the great gentry. In New Kent County the population that collected on poor land between the Chickahominy and Pamunkey rivers was called "rabble" by social superiors in the 1670s. Others moved toward the far fringe of settlement, preferring to take their chances with the Indians rather than challenge Sir William Berkeley's cavalier elite.

At the same time the elite itself moved toward the best lands, the most navigable streams, and (not least important) the fairest prospects. Hugh Jones wrote in 1724, "Gentlemen and planters love to build near the water, though it be not so healthy as the uplands and barrens."[3]

Virginians, rich and poor alike, seemed happiest when putting a large space between themselves and their neighbors. In 1754 planter Peter Fontaine wrote to his brothers, "I look upon a small estate, which will . . . set [me] above the necessity of submitting to the humors and vices of others, the most happy state this life affords. One thousand acres of land will keep troublesome neighbors at a distance."[4]

This attitude became a powerful stimulus to migration. It also created an open pattern of settlement and weakened the strength of social bonds. Another important consequence was a process of population sorting which created the cultural regions of Virginia.

Migration and Regions within Virginia: The Central Tidewater

The cultural hearth of colonial Virginia was the central tidewater, between the James and the Rappahannock rivers. This region reached inland from the Chesapeake Bay to the line of falls that marked the head of navigation. Its area was defined mainly by access to the sea. The Chesapeake Bay was fed by hundreds of streams and forty-eight navigable rivers, some of immense size. The James River was larger than London's Thames; the Potomac was longer than the Seine.[5]

This "watery maze" of rivers and streams created vast tracts of rich alluvial soil, a "low moist and fat mould" of exceptional fertility. Captain John Smith accurately described the tidewater as a succession of "pleasant plaine hils and fertle valleyes, one prettily crossing an other, and watered so conveniently with their sweete brookes and christall springs, as if art it selfe had devised them." When cleared and cultivated, the western shore took on a quiet, pastoral beauty that reminded homesick English gentlemen of southern and western England.[6]

The best land was appropriated by Governor Berkeley's royalist elite for their large plantations. When William Hugh Grove sailed into the York River in 1732, he observed that it was "Thick seated with gentry on its Banks. . . . the prospect of the River render them very pleasant [and] equall to the Thames from London to Richmond, supposing the Towns omitted."[7]

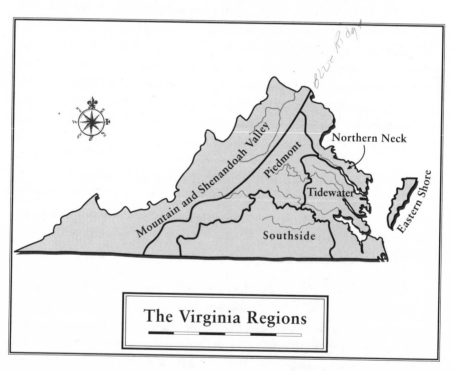

The Virginia Regions

There was also another reason for living near the water's edge. Virginia planter Robert Beverley wrote that oceangoing ships could anchor directly "before that Gentleman's Door where they find the best Reception, or where 'tis most suitable to their Business."[8]

Between the navigable rivers were "necks" or ridges that tended to be thin and barren land. Here former servants and poor whites pitched their small houses and scratched out a miserable living from the earth. Upland soil sold for as little as 5 s. an acre in the eighteenth century. The price of rich bottomland was £5 an acre—twenty times greater.[9]

To its first English colonists, the Chesapeake country appeared another Eden, demiparadise. John Smith thought that "heaven and earth never agreed better to frame a place for mans habitation."[10]

The area would have been ideal, were it not for one terrible defect. To colonists from northern Europe, the Chesapeake proved to be desperately unhealthy. The best lands on the water's edge became death traps in the summer and fall. For Europeans who insisted on living near the water's edge, the tidewater always had been very dangerous. With time it became in some ways even more lethal. The seasoning process, by which a minority of the European population became hardened to the dangers, was overbalanced by new diseases that were introduced by the immigrants themselves. Microbes, as well as people, were migrants to the New World. European respiratory diseases took a toll on Africans in America. Even more deadly to Europeans was Africa's revenge, the tropical diseases that were imported with the slave trade.[11]

In the tidewater it was discovered that African immigrants survived in larger numbers than Europeans. This inexorable fact transformed the culture of the region. Of the many thousands of English servants and convicts who landed in the tidewater, few survived. Some moved away as soon they were free to do so, but most experienced what Lorena S. Walsh has called "vertical mobility into the grave."[12]

In their place an African-American population began to grow at a rapid rate. This was one of the few slave populations in history to multiply abundantly by natural increase. As late as 1680 Africans had been a very small minority. By 1755 they were a majority of the inhabitants between the James and the Rappahannock rivers, two-thirds of all the people living in the old heartland of James City County and Warwick County, and an even larger proportion of the population on bottomlands along the rivers. By the mid–eighteenth century the old Virginia tidewater was predominantly an African country, with a small white minority who owned and ran it.[13]

The tidewater points up another important aspect of our problem, one that was entirely neglected by early historians of the westward movement, including Turner himself. Every American region was not only an economic entity, defined by its material resources. It was also a biological environment, changing through time. The causal relations were complex. Biological conditions fixed the limits of life itself and shaped the process of settlement. In turn, migration and settlement changed the biology of a region in fundamental ways. Nowhere was this more clearly the case than in tidewater Virginia.

Sir William Berkeley's Fall-Line Frontier: The Cavalier Turned Forester

In the early years of Sir William Berkeley's governorship, the frontier was near the head of navigation on Virginia's rivers. As the population began to grow more rapidly, the zone of European settlement advanced west, north, south, and even east across the Chesapeake Bay.

The power of the Indians was still very great. Many continued to live close to the English plantations. When their great leader Opechancanough heard of the outbreak of civil war in England, he reportedly resolved that "now was his time or never, to root out all the English" before they could be reinforced from "their own country."[14]

On Holy Thursday, April 18, 1644, the Indians attacked with all their strength. More than 500 colonists were killed, a toll greater even than the attack on Good Friday of 1622. This time, however, the outcome was different. Governor Berkeley began a major war against the Indians. Under his leadership and that of acting Governor Richard Kemp, fighting continued until October 1646, when finally the Indian leaders sued for peace.

The Indians were expelled from the European settlements. An English pale was erected on the perimeter of the colony, and the Indians were forbidden to cross it unless they were wearing passport badges. Even Indian messengers could not enter the English pale unless dressed in special striped coats. Another war followed in 1676. It broke the power of the eastern Indians and forced them to accept tributary status under English sovereignty.

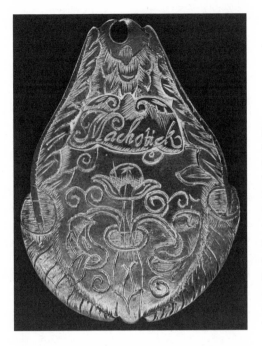

33. This silver badge was presented c. 1661–77 to the king of the Machotick Indians as both a decoration and a passport. Indians were forbidden to enter English territory without wearing such a badge, which was made of silver for chiefs and copper for anyone else. Two similar badges survive that were given to the Patomeck and Pamunkey chiefs. They were emblems of English hegemony during the era of Sir William Berkeley.

Thereafter resistance to Anglo-American expansion came only on the western frontier.

The edge of this English settlement was the fall line on the several rivers, where Governor Berkeley encouraged the construction of a chain of forts. The most important was Fort Henry, built in 1645–46 at the falls of the Appomattox River (now the city of Petersburg). The commander was Colonel Abraham Wood, a rough-cut, self-made immigrant who arrived as an indentured servant in the ship *Margaret and John* and became one of the few of that humble origin to rise into the upper ranks of Sir William Berkeley's elite. With the governor's blessing Wood organized a trading network with Indians beyond the fall line. Each year a party of 100 horses left Fort Henry and returned laden with furs and deerskins.

Wood's agents also ranged far into the interior on missions of exploration. Among them was James Needham, the younger son of a Hertfordshire gentry family, who had moved to Virginia as one of Berkeley's cavalier elite. In 1673 Needham was sent from Fort Henry into the Tennessee Valley and made contact with the Cherokees. Later he made a second trip and was killed by his Indian guide.

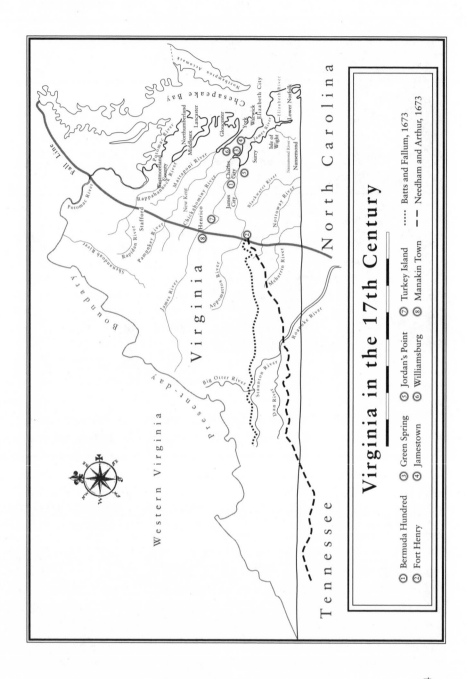

Virginia in the 17th Century

① Bermuda Hundred ③ Green Spring ⑤ Jordan's Point ⑦ Turkey Island ⋯⋯ Batts and Fallum, 1673
② Fort Henry ④ Jamestown ⑥ Williamsburg ⑧ Manakin Town − − Needham and Arthur, 1673

In 1670 John Lederer searched in vain for a pass through the Appalachians, but on September 1, 1671, Thomas Batts and Robert Fallam left Fort Henry with a commission "for the finding out the ebbing and flowing of the waters on the other side of the Mountaines in order to the discovery of the South Sea." They followed the New River, which penetrates the mountain chain, and reached what is now Giles County near the West Virginia border. They marked a tree with Governor Berkeley's initials and claimed the region for Charles II. Yet another of Wood's men was reputed to have reached the Mississippi.[15]

The commanders of Berkeley's forts were favored with land grants so large that they were measured not by the acre but the mile. William Byrd I inherited three square miles near the fort at the falls of the James. He moved

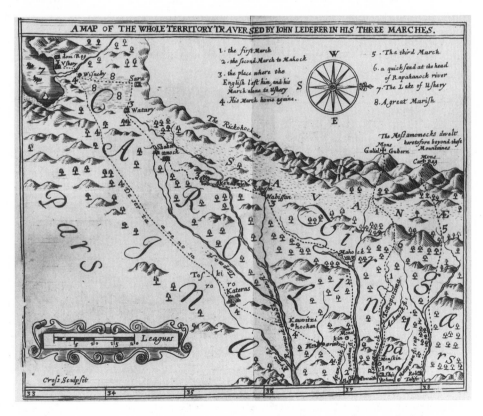

35. In 1669–70 John Lederer was the first European who is known to have reached the crest of the Blue Ridge and look beyond it. He was appalled to find more mountains farther to the west, higher than those he had crossed.

there, took command of the fort, and agreed to recruit 250 settlers. For his trouble Byrd was given eleven square miles.

Another fort was owned by Major Lawrence Smith on the Rappahannock. A third on the Potomac River was commanded by Henry Fleet (1600–1661), the son of a Kentish gentleman and a kinsman of the Filmers and of Sir Francis Wyatt. Fleet was captured by the Indians and held a prisoner for five years. He learned the languages and the ways of the woods. When he returned to freedom, his new skills and connections brought him large holdings of land.

These English cavaliers adapted quickly to American conditions. They did not know themselves as "pioneers" or "frontiersmen"—anachronistic terms that did not come into common use until many years later. The first William Byrd preferred to call himself a "forester," a word that might remind us of his temporal distance from later western leaders.

Sir William Berkeley's cavaliers-turned-foresters maintained their manners as gentlemen. They were as much at home in a London salon as in the American wilderness. Henry Fleet traveled back and forth across the Atlantic and maintained his connections with the great families of England, as also did the Byrds.

At the same time that Berkeley promoted exploration and trade by his cavalier-foresters, he also tended to restrain distant settlement beyond the fall line. At the end of his long tenure, Berkeley found himself increasingly at odds with Virginians who were moving rapidly beyond the fall line into the piedmont as hunters, traders, and even settlers. By 1675 the frontier had reached Stafford County, 100 miles northwest of Jamestown.

The Indians resisted, especially the Susquehannocks to the northwest, who were themselves on the move, having been pushed south to the valley of the Potomac by wars with the Iroquois. They in turn drove other tribes before them. Two cultures, Indian and European, both in motion, collided violently. The flash point was reached in Stafford County on a summer Sunday in 1675, when a party of Virginians on their way to church found settler Robert Hen lying on his threshold, dying from tomahawk wounds.

Stafford County's militia was commanded by Colonel George Mason, still another of Berkeley's cavalier-foresters, who had fought for the king and emigrated from the English Staffordshire in 1651. Mason mustered his men, chased the Indians twenty-four miles, and killed ten in their village. The

Indians retaliated by slaying thirty-six Virginians on the upper Rappahannock, and a bloody war began.

Sir William Berkeley and a group of tidewater leaders called the Green Spring faction (who took their name from the governor's mansion) sought to deal with the problem by reinforcing their forts and trading posts. Small settlers and large landowners with eyes on the West desired a more forward policy. They made common cause against Sir William Berkeley and rallied to Nathaniel Bacon, a former protégé of the governor. "How miserable that man is," Berkeley wrote, "that Governes a People wher six parts of seaven at least are Poore Endebted Discontented and Armed."[16]

Nathaniel Bacon led an armed rebellion against the governor. The rising spread rapidly through the colony. It ended only when the climate killed Bacon and crippled Berkeley. In the aftermath the governor punished the rebels with such extreme violence that he fell from royal favor. Charles II was reported to have said, "That old fool has hang'd more men in that naked Country, than [I have] done for the Murther of [my] Father." Sir William Berkeley's long tenure ended in disgrace. He died in England in 1677.[17]

Historians have interpreted Bacon's Rebellion in various ways. Some have seen it as a protodemocratic movement and a precursor of the American Revolution. Others have viewed it as an insurrection led by aggressive planters who owned large tracts of western lands and hungered for more. One scholar has argued that the gentry's distrust of the lower classes led to greater reliance on African labor.

However that may be, historians agree that Bacon's Rebellion began with an argument over frontier policy. It ended in the termination of Sir William Berkeley's governorship, a heavy defeat for the Indians, and the movement of Virginia's frontier farther to the west.[18]

The Northern Neck: Regional Culture in the Fairfax Domain

As the area of settlement expanded in the seventeenth century, other distinctive regions began to develop in Virginia. One of them, called the Northern Neck, was the land between the Potomac and the Rappahannock rivers. This vast domain of nearly five million acres stretched from the Chesapeake Bay to the Shenandoah Valley. In 1649, when Charles II was a young king without a country, he awarded this great tract to his royalist supporters—

John Culpeper, baron of Thoresway; Henry Jermyn, baron of St. Edmundsbury; Ralph Hopton, Baron of Stratton; Sir William Morton, Sir Dudley Wyatt, Thomas Culpeper, Esq., and Sir John Berkeley (brother of Sir William Berkeley).

The first land grants in the Northern Neck of Virginia were made in the 1650s. Much of the land in this territory went to a small elite. Some were "distressed cavaliers" such as Sir Thomas Lunsford, who had been lord of the Tower of London in 1641, and Sir Henry Chicheley, a royalist who had been locked in the Tower by Roundheads in 1648. Others were men in Berkeley's

36. Thomas, sixth Lord Fairfax. His claim to 5,282,000 acres in Virginia was upheld by the Privy Council in 1745.

circle such as Richard Lee, the founder of a Virginia dynasty. Many were young men of gentle families in mercantile careers: Raleigh Travers, William Ball, Thomas Powell. In 1674, 5,000 acres were granted to exiled royalist John Washington, great-grandfather of the future president, on condition that he "seat and plant" the tract within three years and pay in perpetuity a rent to the proprietor.

These men gave a distinctive tone to the Northern Neck by the end of the Berkeley era. Historian Edmund Morgan writes, "Lancaster [County] in the seventeenth century was a rich man's county, . . . not a land of opportunity for its newly freed servants." Of 247 servants who gained their freedom in Lancaster from 1662 to 1678, only twenty-four appeared as householders in 1679. Similar patterns appeared even more strongly in Northumberland and especially in Westmoreland County.[19]

The king's proprietary grant of the Northern Neck passed from his consortium of supporters to one family alone—the Culpepers. Through them, it was inherited by the Fairfax family. The Fairfaxes were an interesting English dynasty who combined cavalier manners with parliamentary principles. The third Baron Fairfax had commanded the army of Parliament against Charles I. The sixth Baron Fairfax also had the same strong sense of English law and liberty, which he linked to the conduct and character of a highborn English gentleman.

Lord Fairfax employed as his colonial agent Robert Carter who, by granting lands on the Northern Neck to his sons and friends, founded the wealth and power of the Carter family and won for himself the nickname of "King" Carter. When he died in 1732, his 300,000 acres and 1,000 slaves made him the richest man in Virginia.[20]

Virginia maintained that the western boundary of Fairfax's domain was "the first falls" of the Potomac River, but he claimed the headwaters of that river, which at that time was unexplored. In the disputed region beyond the first falls, both the Virginia Council and Fairfax made grants, and Lord Fairfax ultimately came to Virginia to defend his interests. In April 1736 a group of horsemen headed by the proprietor himself arrived in a new settlement called Frederick (now Winchester) and informed the inhabitants that they were on his land. Fairfax was reasonable; he merely required that they pay their rents to him instead of to Virginia.[21]

Other Virginia grandees were not happy about the size of Fairfax's holdings. William Byrd II, acting for the colony, protested that Fairfax's claim to 5,282,000 acres "is about as much Land as at present pays Quit rents to his Majesty in all the rest of Virginia."[22]

The Privy Council in London had directed that surveys be made of the disputed territory. The result has been remembered as the battle of the maps. Fairfax and the Virginia commissioners each hired a different man to make a survey. Virginia employed William Mayo, a native of Wiltshire, England, who came to Virginia in 1723 and "formed a very elegant map of the whole Northern Neck by joining all the particular surveys together." Fairfax hired John Warner, another "noted surveyor" who made an even more elegant map. With its aid Lord Fairfax won the case in 1745. Revised editions of the map were issued, showing the western boundary as now confirmed by the Crown. Thus defined, the proprietary consisted of 5,282,000 acres.[23]

The Northern Neck rapidly developed into a distinctive region of Virginia with a character that was largely defined by Lord Fairfax himself and his friends and agents, who included the Washington, Lee, and Marshall families.

Fairfax liked the country so well that he returned as an immigrant in 1747 and made his permanent home in Virginia. He built himself a long, rambling hunting lodge called Greenway Court and a small stone land office high in the Shenandoah country at the western end of his domain. At the same time he became justice of the peace of all the counties in the Northern Neck, county lieutenant, and commandant of the militia. Lord Fairfax acquiesced in the American Revolution and was treated always with honor both by the people of the Northern Neck and the Virginia General Assembly. He died at Greenway Court in 1781 at the age of eighty-eight.[24]

In the course of his long life, a circle formed around him. Lord Fairfax's drawing room became a school of manners for young gentlemen of the Northern Neck—among them, many Washingtons, Lees, Marshalls, and others who shared a distinctive set of values and beliefs.

The Northern Neck was very much a part of the culture of Virginia, but it gave that culture a special meaning. On this frontier there was little of democracy and nothing of equality, but a strong tradition of service, character, right conduct, and the rule of law.

We have been trained by the materialism of American social science to think of regional culture as a reflex of economic interests and environmental conditions. So it is sometimes, but the culture of the Northern Neck was shaped when it was a frontier, in large degree by the interplay of culture,

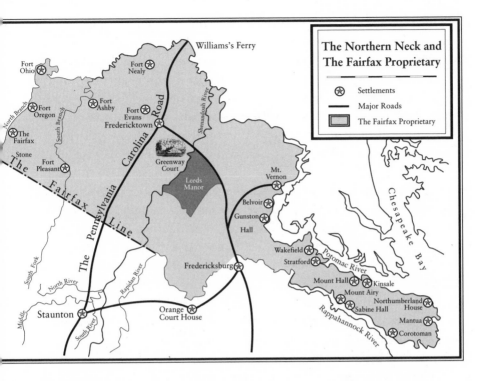

The Northern Neck and
The Fairfax Proprietary

⊛ Settlements

— Major Roads

▭ The Fairfax Proprietary

37

environment, and the purposes of a single individual. A cultural tradition
was planted by Lord Fairfax at Greenway Court. It took root in the fertile
soil of the Northern Neck and flowered in the careers of George Washington in the Revolution, Robert E. Lee in the Civil War, and George C. Marshall in World War II.[25]

The values of this tradition were in many ways different from the liberal
ideas on which the American republic was founded. Yet this tradition supplied that nation with many leaders who served it in a distinctive way. The
Northern Neck was the cradle of their culture, and Lord Fairfax was its
founding father.

The Southside: Virginia's Pocket Frontier

Another distinctive region of Virginia was the Southside, a broad crescent of
territory below the Appomattox River (some would say below the James) and
extending from the tidewater to the mountains.[26]

This region was slow to develop, because of its remoteness. Its soil was rich, and its growing season was the longest in Virginia, but its rivers (the Meherrin, Nottoway, Roanoke, and Dan) were not navigable and flowed south, away from the Chesapeake Bay. More than a century after the founding of Jamestown, Southside Virginia was scarcely occupied at all by Europeans. Its oldest counties bear eighteenth-century English names that tell us the time of their adoption: Prince George (1702), Brunswick (1720), Amelia (1734), Lunenburg (1745), Dinwiddie (1752), Halifax (1752), and Prince Edward (1753).

The first European settlers in this region were desperately poor squatters. William Byrd II, on a mission to survey the southern boundary of Virginia, met one of them named Cornelius Keith, near the Roanoke River. Byrd wrote that Keith "lived rather in a pen than a house with his wife and six children. I never beheld such a scene of poverty in this happy part of the world. The hovel they lay in had no roof . . . for want of nails it remained uncovered. . . . The man can read and write very well and by way of a trade can make and set up quernstones [grindstones for hand mills], and yet is poorer than any Highland Scot or bogtrotting Irishman."[27]

Byrd called the region Lubberland and described the inhabitants as a race of "indolent wretches," but he was not an impartial judge. These people had initiative enough to pick up and move away from the tenant farms on which they were exploited by men such as Byrd himself. They deserved better than they received from that arrogant grandee.[28]

In the eighteenth century the great gentry of Virginia gained large tracts of the Southside lands. Chief among these speculators was Byrd himself, who built a hunting lodge called Bluestone Castle. Although he acquired 105,000 acres along the Dan and Roanoke rivers, he never found many buyers. He sought Swiss immigrants, whom he thought ideal, but was forced reluctantly to solicit offers from north British borderers and Scotch-Irish, whom he likened to "the Goths and Vandals of old." These people were not sufficiently deferential to suit him, but he thought that they were more industrious than the English squatters who preceded them.[29]

A sharply focused stream of migration began to flow into the Southside during the early and mid–eighteenth century. Most settlers (55 percent, according to one study) came from the counties of Henrico, Goochland, and Hanover in central Virginia near the falls of the James. Few arrived from Isle

38. In Virginia the gentry spearheaded and organized the settlement of the frontier. William Byrd II, shown here in a c. 1724 painting by Hans Hysing, was quite successful in developing the piedmont, founding Richmond and Petersburg, but he was less fortunate with his Southside lands.

of Wight County, and none from Nansemond or Norfolk, which had their own hinterlands.

Here again, as throughout Virginia's westward movement, migration fields and streams were as sharply defined as in Europe, with a few dominant seed counties as points of origin. The turnover of population was great. Many moved on to the Carolinas, and there were backflows in both directions.[30]

A few Virginia grandees settled in the Southside. Chief among them were the descendants of Sir Grey Skipwith, a British baronet who fled to America after the English Civil War, became part of Governor Berkeley's cavalier elite, and settled near Petersburg. Grey Skipwith's grandson was Sir William Skipwith, who inherited the English title but remained in America and moved deeper into the wilderness.[31]

Sir William's son, and Sir Grey Skipwith's great-grandson, was Sir Peyton Skipwith, born in 1740. He was accused of toryism during the American Revolution, but no charges were brought against him. In 1789 he began construction of a great stone house that was called Prestwould after the family's

39. Prestwould (1789) was the home of Sir Peyton Skipwith, progenitor of a gentry family in Southside.

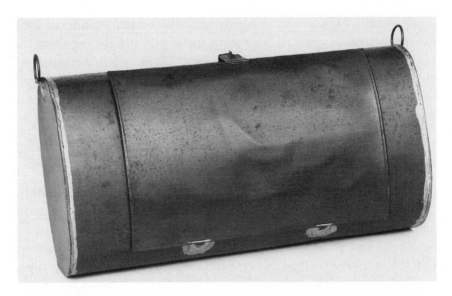

40. Jean, Lady Skipwith, was the second wife of Sir Peyton Skipwith (her sister had been his first wife). She laid out an English garden but planted it with American wildflowers which she collected in this very rare eighteenth-century vasculum.

ancestral estate in England. It was situated on a high hill where the Dan and Staunton rivers meet to form the Roanoke.

The house was surrounded by a deer park and formal gardens laid out in the classical English taste at the direction of Jean, Lady Skipwith, daughter of Hugh Miller of Scotland and Virginia. She took great pleasure in planting her English garden with American wildflowers. She reconstructed the culture of the Old World from the materials in the New World—a paradigm example of the social process that created the colony of Virginia.

The Skipwith family carefully maintained its English connections. Sir Peyton Skipwith relinquished the title to his eldest son, Sir Grey, who moved back to Britain and sat in Parliament for Warwickshire 1831–34. Other children remained in America and multiplied at a rapid rate. Today many thousands of Americans proudly trace their descent from this extraordinary Southside dynasty.[32]

For many years the development of the Southside lagged behind other regions of Virginia. The area remained largely a subsistence economy, so remote from markets that squatter Cornelius Keith had been unable to buy even a few nails to fasten a roof on his house. That condition continued until the late eighteenth and early nineteenth centuries, when the improvement of overland communications made the Southside more accessible to commerce. Then the region developed rapidly along familiar lines. Slaves began to arrive in such large numbers that by 1810 two-thirds of the population was African American.

The Southside's institutions were very Virginian, but with a distinctive regional character that arose from its history. One regional peculiarity was the distribution of wealth. An inventory of estates shows that the distribution of wealth, by Virginia standards, was more egalitarian than in other areas. Towns were small, schools were weak, and in the mid–eighteenth century 50 percent of adult males were unable to sign their names. Communities in the Southside centered on crossroad churches, which have continued to dominate the cultural landscape from the eighteenth century to our own time. In the rhythm of its history and the structure of its institutions, the Southside is a classic example of a recurrent phenomenon in the westward movement — a pocket frontier that the first wave of settlement passed by and that later developed with great rapidity.[33]

Virginia's Eastern Shore: An Alternative Frontier

In the complex geography of colonial Virginia, other regions also developed distinctive customs, which were created by the interplay of culture and environment. Everywhere, the course of growth was shaped in large part by the folkways of their founders and by the pivotal choices that people made throughout their long history.

To the east, across the broad waters of the Chesapeake Bay, lay the Eastern Shore of Virginia. In the seventeenth century it was as much a frontier as any other region, with its own forts and Indian wars and patterns of settlement.

This region expanded north into a large area of Maryland's Eastern Shore below the Choptank River. It also spread into Sussex and Kent counties in Delaware. From the perspective of Baltimore, H. L. Mencken contemptuously called it Trans-Choptankia, but he understood it very little. As this region grew it developed a vibrant culture different from other regions of Virginia — distinctive in patterns of landholding, religion, politics, and community.

Two trends were specially important in that respect. First, after an initial period in which the officers of the Virginia Company gave large grants to themselves on the Eastern Shore, land began to pass to individual freeholders in small parcels of 100 acres. Second, the Eastern Shore also became a seat of religious dissent—Puritan and Quaker in the seventeenth century, Methodist in the eighteenth and nineteenth.

At an early date its inhabitants formed close-knit comities, in organic rural communities of unusual density. In the eighteenth and early nineteenth centuries, when other parts of Virginia were Whig, the Eastern Shore was often Tory in its sympathies. When most of Virginia became Jeffersonian Republican, the lower Eastern Shore voted Federalist.

These cultural patterns began to appear in the seventeenth century. In that process the settlement of the Eastern Shore of Virginia made a classic study in the comparative history of frontiers.[34]

Norfolk and the Chesapeake Islands:
Virginia's Maritime Frontier

Yet another regional culture developed in the neighborhood of what are now the cities of Norfolk and Newport News, on the western shore near the mouth of the Chesapeake Bay.

This area was the seat of Puritan and Quaker settlements until Sir William Berkeley and the cavalier elite drove out their leaders and suppressed their meetings. In the eighteenth century the seaport towns began to develop and attracted their own pattern of immigration by Scottish merchants, captains, maritime artisans, and seamen from throughout the empire.

The frontier of this area stretched southward to the Dismal Swamp and the coastal counties of North Carolina and Albemarle Sound. In the 1730s William Byrd II wrote that the frontier began a few miles south of Norfolk, and he made light of its inhabitants. The cavalier gentry did not think highly of these folk. Byrd himself called them Dismalites. Yet they developed the resources of the swamp itself into a naval stores industry that supported their maritime activities.

In a larger sense the sea itself became their frontier. They explored and exploited it with the same enterprise that other Virginians brought to the opening lands of the West. The water's edge, like Turner's terrestrial frontier, was also the "edge of the unused." It presented another "field of opportunity" and a different "zone of interaction." These hardy maritime frontiersmen made the most of these possibilities. They lived by their wits and survived by the speed of their sharp-built Chesapeake schooners. Those beautiful craft were American artifacts as distinctive as the Conestoga wagon. They became fitting symbols of yet another regional culture that developed in the Old Dominion.

The Chesapeake Islands: The People of the Bay

One of Virginia's smallest but most distinctive and persistent regional cultures took root in the Chesapeake Bay itself, especially on Smith and Tangier islands. They became home to communities of watermen who made the bay their frontier and fished it for three centuries.

This way of life was shaped by an austere environment and also by the culture that was carried to it. Like other communities of Anglo-American watermen, from the lobster gangs of Maine to the conch culture of the Florida Keys, the people of Smith and Tangier islands came disproportionately from the west coast of England—not the region between the Vale of Gloucester and the uplands of Kent that produced so large a part of Virginia's servant migration and cavalier elite. Its cradle was a different part of England—the fishing ports of Devon and Cornwall.

Even to this day the dialect of Smith and Tangier islands (*zink* for sink, *noyce* for nice) derives from the southern seaports of seventeenth-century England. The speech of these islands brings out with exceptional clarity the phenomenon that linguists call "cultural lag," that is, a tendency toward the conservation of culture that happened everywhere on the American frontier, if not always in the same degree.[35]

The Piedmont Frontier

Beyond the fall line lay one of the largest regions in the Old Dominion—the piedmont of Virginia, extending from the Chesapeake tidewater to the Blue Ridge Mountains. The area's many valleys reached like outstretched fingers toward fresh lands in the interior.

The piedmont was attractive to settlement in many ways. Its deep red clays were highly fertile. Its wooded, rolling countryside was very beautiful. Most important, its climate was healthy. A French visitor in tidewater Gloucester

County had been appalled by the sallow faces of English settlers, who "looked so sickly that I judged the country to be unhealthy." On higher ground in Rappahannock and Stafford counties, he remarked that complexions were "clear & lively."[36]

During the late seventeenth century a scattering of former servants moved into the piedmont and settled as squatters on the land. They were quickly pushed aside by the grandees of the tidewater, who acquired title to the best soil through their access to power. The men who sat in the Council and controlled the granting of lands in the colony awarded a large part of the piedmont to their own families.

Chief among them was William Byrd I (1652–1704), who came to Virginia before 1670, inherited 1,800 acres at the falls of the James, and settled there. As part of Governor Berkeley's program for protecting the frontiers against the Indians, he was granted 7,251 additional acres on condition of settling 250 tithables. He took over Fort Charles, one of Berkeley's frontier posts, and made it a major trading post with the Indians. The Indian trade, like westward expansion, fell to those who had capital and influence in the Virginia government. In 1737 Byrd's son founded Richmond, mainly to defend his own commercial interests. The area around the falls was becoming heavily farmed. Had Byrd not acted quickly, others would have gained control of tobacco shipped from the area.

Opening the Piedmont: The Valley of the James

A circular relationship developed between family and land in this region. Extended family connections regulated access to the land, and land in turn reinforced family connections. Beyond the falls of the James River, the leaders of exploration and settlement were the vast Randolph clan. The highborn English immigrants William and Mary Isham Randolph settled on Turkey Island Creek near the confluence of the Appomattox and James rivers. Three of their sons established large plantations along the river. Richard Randolph settled Curles Neck near Turkey Island. Thomas Randolph moved inland and built Tuckahoe plantation, the first large estate above the falls of the James. Isham Randolph went farther west and founded Dungeness plantation.

Other gentry families moved up the James River and intermarried with the Randolphs. Thomas Jefferson, great-grandfather of the third president,

41. William Randolph (c. 1650–1711), younger son of a Warwickshire royalist who suffered during the English Civil War, typified the cavalier gentry recruited by Governor Berkeley.

42. Mary Isham, who married William Randolph, was born in Virginia and descended from a leading Northamptonshire family. So large was their progeny that they have been called the Adam and Eve of Virginia.

settled at Osborne's, now in Goochland County. His grandson, land surveyor Peter Jefferson, married Jane Randolph, daughter of Isham Randolph. From their union the future president was born. Bollings, Carters, Pages, Flemings, Walkers, Meriwethers, and Lewises all acquired large tracts and intermarried with Randolphs and one another. They moved up the James to the Rivanna and settled a large area that was organized as Albemarle County. "Thus," writes historian Thomas Perkins Abernethy, "we find family connections playing quite as important a part in the Piedmont section as in the older Tidewater."[37]

The Valley of the Rappahannock

The upper Rappahannock Valley was opened in a different way. In this area the central role was played not by a family but by a single individual. He was a character of high importance in Virginia's westward movement, yet very far removed from the stereotypical image of the pioneer.

Alexander Spotswood was born to an ancient north British family that had fallen on hard times. His father was an army surgeon (no job for a gentleman in the seventeenth century), who helped to gain the young man a commission in the army. Spotswood sought his fortune on the battlefield in the duke of Marlborough's European campaigns. The motto on the family's coat of arms was *Patior ut potiar,* "I endure that I may secure," which became the story of young Spotswood's career. To his cousin he wrote, "If the war lasts and I live, some lucky hits may happen towards the making one's fortune."[38]

By desperate courage Spotswood won the patronage of Marlborough and was rewarded with an appointment as lieutenant governor of Virginia. The governor through most of Spotswood's tenure was an old army friend, George Hamilton, earl of Orkney, who never visited the colony in a tenure of twenty-seven years. Spotswood was given the disagreeable but highly lucrative task of actually running the colony.[39] This gallant young officer arrived in 1710 with his mistress Katherine Russell, who charmed the gentlemen of Virginia. He was still too poor to marry.

Spotswood was appalled to discover that access to the colony's land was firmly controlled by a small clique of great planters. After trying unsuccessfully to curb their power, he decided to join them. Quickly he recognized

43. Governor Alexander Spotswood was instrumental in opening up the Rappa-
hannock and Shenandoah valleys. During his 1716 jaunt he dubbed the Shenandoah
River the Euphrates, which, had it stuck, would have precluded a wonderful
American ballad.

that the pathway to prosperity in the colony ran through the river valleys to the west. The valley of the James was closed to his ambition and so firmly in the grasp of the Randolph clan that not even the acting governor could break in. Spotswood turned his attention instead to the Rappahannock. In 1712 iron deposits were found near the falls of that river. In 1714 and 1719 Spotswood granted a tract of ten square miles on the upper Rappahannock to several of his clerks, who promptly reconveyed it back to Spotswood. He recruited a group of miners and settled them with their families at a fortified post called Germanna, thirty miles beyond the nearest settlement, where they developed mines on the governor's property.[40]

In time Spotswood managed to acquire some 83,000 acres (about 130 square miles) in the western piedmont and the Shenandoah Valley. This land was organized in 1720 as Spotsylvania County, now the area west of Fredericksburg. Spotswood threw his energy into its development and became the owner of fifty-seven plantations, with many mills, mines, and ironworks.[41]

Spotswood and the grandees of Virginia created a distinctive culture in the piedmont. They did not favor speculators or absentee landlords, and in 1713 they passed a law requiring property holders to cultivate three acres out of every fifty in their possession, on pain of forfeiture. This statute fostered rapid development, discouraged absentee owners, and forbade speculators to hold large tracts of undeveloped land for long periods. Settlers in new counties of the piedmont were also exempted from taxes for ten years, another spur to swift occupation. By 1727 the line of settlement had nearly reached the Blue Ridge.

At the same time, except for Spotswood's own vast holdings, many of the best lands went to well-connected gentry families in grants of 1,000 to 15,000 acres.

This expansion was not merely a replication of tidewater culture. The healthier climate of the piedmont made for stronger families and tighter kinship nets. It allowed a new spirit of domesticity to develop in plantation houses.

Slaves were introduced from the start, some from Africa directly, most from the tidewater. Among Virginia-born piedmont slaves, the sex ratio was more nearly equal, and population grew even more rapidly than in the tidewater. Large numbers of young children lived on piedmont plantations. Naming patterns showed stronger family ties and extended kin networks in the slave quarters, as well as in the big house.

The proportion of slaves to the general population was smaller in the pied-mont than in tidewater—rising rapidly to 40 and 45 percent but remaining in that range for many years. As a consequence, African slaves assimilated more of European ways—creating a syncretistic Afro-European culture in America.[42]

By the mid–eighteenth century the piedmont had become the dominant region of Virginia—larger, more dynamic, more prosperous, and more healthy than the tidewater. It generated a large surplus population of both blacks and whites, many of whom emigrated farther west. In that process the piedmont replaced the tidewater as the leading hearth of Virginia's hege-monic culture. It became a great seed region that spread its folkways widely through the American South.

"To Encourage Gentlemen to Venture Backwards": Alexander Spotswood and the Valley of Virginia

At the same time that Alexander Spotswood promoted the settlement of the piedmont and enriched himself in the process, he also made another con-tribution to Virginia's westward movement by encouraging exploration and settlement of the mountains and valleys that lay beyond.

Through the late seventeenth century, Virginians who were beginning to be called rangers explored the rising country to the west. On June 12, 1716, Spotswood informed the Board of Trade that these men had found a way through the "great mountains to the westward."[43]

Two months later Spotswood himself led a major expedition to explore the country. It was an event of high importance, not merely for what it did but also for how it was remembered. On August 20, 1716, Spotswood left Williamsburg with sixty-two men, mostly gentlemen and their servants, led by fourteen hardened Virginia rangers and four Indian guides. The acting governor traveled in his chaise, and the gentlemen rode on horseback, with a raucous pack of hunting dogs and large supplies of food and drink. Their route took them north across the York River, then west through the valleys of the Rappahannock and Rapidan, over the Blue Ridge, and to the Shenan-doah River (which they named the Euphrates).

They had a merry time. One of their number, John Fontaine, remembered that at the end of each day their servants built handsome camps where they gathered round a huge bonfire and feasted on bear and venison. One of the company described an evening's entertainment in detail: "We drank the King's health in Champagne, and fired a volley — the Princess's health in Burgundy, and fired a volley, and all the rest of the Royal Family in claret, and a volley. We drank the Governor's health and fired another volley." Lesser toasts were drunk in Virginia red and white wine, brandy, shrub, two rums, canary, cherry punch, and cider. The next morning they were off again. They took possession of the country by marking it with papers sealed in the many wine bottles that they had emptied the night before.[44]

When they returned to Williamsburg, Lieutenant Governor Spotswood decided to commemorate the event by presenting a decoration to each gentleman who had accompanied him. Hugh Jones reported, "For this expedition they were obliged to provide a great quantity of horse-shoes; (things seldom used in the lower parts of the country, where there are few stones:) . . . the Governor upon their return presented each of his companions with a golden horse-shoe, (some of which I have seen studded with valuable stones resembling the heads of nails) with this inscription on the one side: *Sic juvat transcendere montes:* and on the other is written the tramontane order."[45]

Thus was born the legend of Alexander Spotswood's Knights of the Golden Horseshoe, created to "encourage gentlemen to venture backwards" — that is, to the backcountry. From this event a myth arose. It became in itself an important part of southern culture and a factor in its westward expansion.

The Knights of the Golden Horseshoe entered deep into the folklore of Virginia. They were given new life in the nineteenth century by William Alexander Caruthers, an expatriate physician who signed himself a Virginian even when he was living in Georgia. Caruthers published romantic fiction about the land of his birth and in 1845 brought out a popular novel called *The Knights of the Horse-Shoe.* "Few more bold, daring and chivalrous adventures have been undertaken," he wrote, "even in this land of wild adventure."[46]

Thus in southern folklore the romance of the frontier was joined to the legend of gauntlet and glove. Here was another image of the westward movement, led not by pioneers in coonskin caps but by acting Governor Alexander Spotswood in his chaise, with a panoply of gentlemen on horseback.

This myth was grounded in one reality and gave rise to yet another. During the turbulent decade of the 1850s, it inspired the formation of another southern group who called themselves Knights of the Golden Circle and sought the expansion of slavery. These nineteenth-century knights-errant dreamed of joining all the lands bordering the Gulf of Mexico and the Caribbean in one enormous slaveocracy, to the limit of a "golden circle" with a radius extending 1,200 miles from Havana. The myth of Alexander Spotswood's expedition gave an aura to the expansion of southern culture that was far removed from the stereotype of the American pioneers.

The Opening of Virginia

At the same time that Virginians were moving west to the piedmont and Shenandoah Valley, the social institutions of the Old Dominion became more open. These processes were connected, but not in a Turnerian way.

In the Berkeley era Virginia had been a closed society. Freedom of speech, press, and religion were narrowly constrained. The repressive spirit of its government was captured in Sir William's immortal diatribe: "I thank God, *there are no free schools* nor *printing,* and I hope we shall not have these hundred years; for *learning* has brought disobedience, and heresy, and sects into the world, and *printing* has divulged them, and libels against the best government. God keep us from both!"[47]

Berkeley's outburst was not a private prejudice. It became an official policy in the colony, actively shared by other governors and enforced for many years. In 1682, for example, Berkeley's successor, Thomas Culpeper, second baron of Thoresway, and his Council severely chastised a printer named John Buckner, who had appeared in the colony and published the colony's laws. Buckner was forbidden to print anything at all. Not for another fifty years would the laws of the colony appear in print. The next governor, Lord Howard of Effingham, was given instructions that bound him to allow no person to use a printing press "on any occasion whatsoever."[48]

The growth of a closed society in an open environment was not unique to Virginia. In most colonies American conditions caused European leaders to become more repressive, not less so. The first effect of the American environment was actually the opposite of what the frontier thesis suggested. The Puritans, for example, became cruelly intolerant on the New England frontier, while Puritans in Old England were moving in the opposite direction. Dutch rulers such as Peter Stuyvesant in New Netherland grew increasingly hostile to nonconformists and dissenters, while toleration was taking root in the Low Countries. The Spanish Inquisition became even more horrifying in Mexico and South America than it had been at home. The rulers of Quebec outdid the authorities of France in tyranny and oppression.[49]

So it was in Virginia, where royalist officials punished dissent and nonconformity more rigorously than did the king in England. That story was much the same in most colonies. The dangers, anxieties, uncertainties, and fears that were part of life in the New World drove Europeans in America to repression.

In Virginia this system of repression began to break down during the early decades of the eighteenth century, but not in the way that the Turner thesis suggested. A spirit of toleration began to grow, but not at first on the frontier, and not from an American root. It was imported from abroad.

In England the Glorious Revolution of 1688 was followed by a Declaration of Rights, a Bill of Rights that greatly expanded the rights of British subjects, and a Toleration Act that allowed dissenting Protestants the right to worship while excluding them from public affairs.

The challenge to Virginia's repressive system arose within this new regime. Its leader lived not in the new western settlements but in an old-settled area on the Eastern Shore. Francis Makemie (1658–1703) came to America as an impoverished Irish Presbyterian missionary about the year 1682 and roamed the American colonies as an itinerant evangelist. He was much disliked by authorities in several colonies. New York's Governor Edward Hyde, Viscount Cornbury, called him a "Jack of all Trades; he is a Preacher, a Doctor of Physick, a Merchant, an Attorney, or Counsellor at Law, and, which is worse of all, a Disturber of Governments."[50]

During the 1690s Makemie married Virginia heiress Naomi Anderson and settled down in Accomack County on the Eastern Shore. There he became a prosperous merchant and landowner. In 1699 he obtained a certificate under the English Toleration Act and demanded that the government of Virginia give him license to preach freely in Accomack County. The license was granted, and the Anglican monopoly was officially broken.

Once the old system of intolerance was breached, a flood followed. Other permissions were granted by the Governor and Council in 1700 to French Huguenots in King William County who were "left at their own liberty to agree with and pay their minister." By 1702 toleration was extended to at least three English Quaker meetings and three north British Presbyterian churches. By 1714 a Baptist fellowship was recognized in the Southside, and by 1730 a German Lutheran church was allowed at Germanna.[51]

All this happened under English law. In America local gentry and Anglican clergy were not happy about the new regime. Persecution continued in many rural neighborhoods, and juries convicted dissenters without regard to English law. When Virginia courts did not clearly recognize a right to worship freely, Presbyterian minister Samuel Davies of Hanover County appealed directly to the attorney general in London and obtained an opinion that the Toleration Act was in force throughout British America.

This libertarian system was at first very limited. It extended only to religious toleration, not to a more broadly defined idea of religious freedom. Even so, the new toleration had to be forced on Virginia from abroad, as it was upon other American colonies. Freedom of speech and worship did not rise spontaneously from the early American frontier. If anything, the environment of the New World had the opposite effect.

Once Virginia began to move in the direction of toleration, however, something interesting began to happen. The new spirit from Europe opened the colony to increasing diversity, and the abundance of land gave it room to grow. In the eighteenth century this openness brought a flow of many different people to Virginia. A new naturalization act allowed Protestants from other European states to be admitted to rights of citizenship after seven years. Many of these immigrants settled on the frontier. Germans of varying sects and denominations began to arrive. North British borderers and Scotch-Irish from the north of Ireland settled in large numbers. French Huguenots founded their own settlements. The Quakers returned in large numbers.

The process was encouraged by some landowners, who discovered in the new libertarian regime a union of principle and interest. Lawrence Washington wrote to Lieutenant Governor Robert Dinwiddie, "It has been my opinion, and I hope ever will be, that restraints on conscience are cruel in regard to those on whom they are imposed, and injurious to the country imposing them." Those words were written as part of a campaign to attract German settlers to his lands.[52]

The population of Virginia grew more diverse, especially in the upper piedmont and the Shenandoah Valley. As it did so, multiple religious establishments began to take root along the frontier. This diversity led in turn to the need for a new framework within which these competing groups might

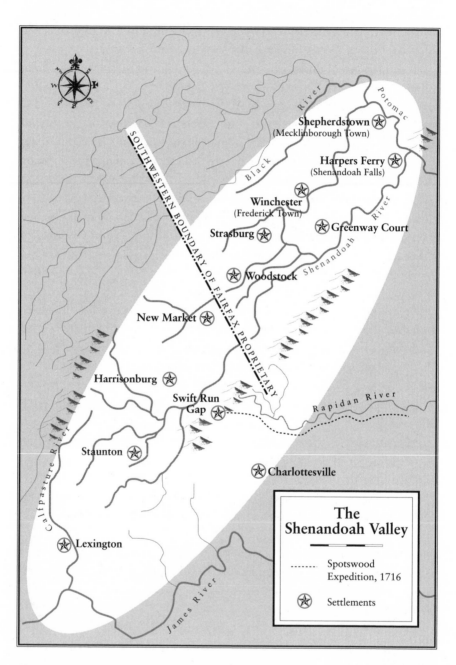

The Shenandoah Valley

------- Spotswood Expedition, 1716

⊛ Settlements

Shepherdstown ⊛
(Mecklinborough Town)

Harpers Ferry ⊛
(Shenandoah Falls)

Winchester ⊛
(Frederick Town)

⊛ Greenway Court

Strasburg ⊛

⊛ Woodstock

New Market ⊛

Harrisonburg ⊛

Swift Run Gap ⊛

Staunton ⊛

⊛ Charlottesville

⊛ Lexington

SOUTHWESTERN BOUNDARY OF FAIRFAX PROPRIETARY

Potomac

Black River

Shenandoah River

Rapidan River

Calfpasture River

James River

44

coexist. That frame was developed in eighteenth-century Virginia by the great libertarian leaders of the Revolutionary era—Thomas Jefferson, James Madison, and many others. These men created a set of ideas that replaced old ideas of toleration with new and more spacious conceptions of freedom.

In Virginia the cradle of this new thinking was in the piedmont, where the population was rapidly growing mixed in its origins and ethnicity. In that way the frontier became a factor of great power—though not a first cause—in extending an opening process that was already under way.

The relationship between freedom and the frontier was highly complex. It cannot be understood either by a simple Turnerian model or by its various antitheses. The history of Virginia can help us to find a deeper and more accurate meaning for the significance of the frontier in American history. Western conditions were not the first cause of an expansion of freedom in the Old Dominion. In the beginning freedom was an alien seed in America. It came to Virginia as an extension of the English Toleration Act, through the strivings of the immigrant evangelist Francis Makemie. Once that seed was planted in Virginia, however, it was nourished by the soil of the New World. In a new environment ideas of freedom grew far beyond the possibilities of an old world. English toleration expanded rapidly into an idea of American freedom.

Turner was right in asserting a close relationship between freedom and the frontier in American history. He was wrong in his understanding of its nature, direction, and cause. In the history of Virginia, the linkage was clear. In the early eighteenth century, a new toleration, imposed from abroad, opened Virginia to new diversity. The frontier and the process of voluntary migration created conditions in which that idea of toleration grew into a broader, more expansive concept of freedom needed to cope with and codify the multicultural society that Virginia had become. All of this development happened in Virginia in the early and middle decades of the eighteenth century.

Virginia's Huguenot Settlers

One of the first groups to gain from the new toleration were Huguenots. Their numbers were small, but many became prominent in the life of the colony.

In 1700 Daniel Coxe, an English speculator, proposed to plant a colony of Huguenots on Virginia lands near the Carolina border. The grandees of the Virginia Council had their own ideas and required that the Huguenots settle in another place, in what now is Powhatan County. The result was Manakintown, a French community that grew in the heart of old Virginia. Its aristocratic Huguenot founders, the marquis de La Muce and Charles de Sailly, recruited 207 settlers, including many women and children, who hoped to produce fine French wines for planters' tables. They were allowed to bring their own ministers and were given their own separate parish of King William.

The Huguenots rapidly assimilated the culture that surrounded them. French vineyards yielded quickly to Virginia grain and tobacco. Slaves were acquired in large numbers. French ministers became part of the Anglican establishment. The Manakintown Huguenots also joined the incessant migration of Virginians. Many moved away and were replaced by English settlers. By the eighteenth century the Huguenots of Manakintown had become part of the society around them.

Other Huguenots also settled in Virginia. In the Valley of Virginia, the son of a Frenchman settled at what became New Market, married a British wife, and became part of the English-speaking culture around him. His son, John Sevier, was raised in the north British culture of the backcountry and became a prominent leader of westward expansion from Virginia to Tennessee.

Yet another Huguenot, John Fontaine, was raised as a gentleman in Ireland. He gained a commission in the British army, came out to Virginia, and became a friend of Spotswood, one of his Knights of the Golden Horseshoe. Fontaine founded a family, moved freely throughout the British empire, and became part of the imperial elite.

The careers of these Virginia Huguenots have something important to teach us about assimilation in the westward movement. Turner's thesis hypothesized that the frontier was a zone of assimilation that created a composite nationality. The history of the French Huguenots tells a different story. Assimilation was not a reflex of material conditions but a cultural and a historical variable. Some ethnic groups assimilated rapidly and virtually disappeared as distinct groups. Others assimilated slowly and retained their own culture for many generations. The contrast between the French Huguenots and German Mennonites is a classic example. Religion and related constellations of cultural value made all the difference—more so than nationality, class, or material conditions, which were comparatively weak in this setting, though stronger in others.

Further, the Huguenots of Virginia assimilated different American cultures, even within the same colony. The French vintners of Manakin became piedmont planters. John Fontaine joined the imperial elite. John Sevier became part of the north British backcountry culture in the Valley of Virginia. In these patterns of assimilation, we can see the strength of hegemonic cultures that created another dimension of diversity, more powerful than national origin itself. This pattern is an important clue to a cultural meaning for the westward movement, very different from material models that center on class relations and the environment of the frontier.[53]

The Return of the Quakers

Early in the eighteenth century, the new spirit of toleration in Virginia was officially extended to Quakers. The House of Burgesses in 1705 allowed the Society of Friends "the same liberty of giving their evidence, by way of solemn affirmation and declaration, as is prescribed by an Act of Parliament." In 1738 Quakers were exempted from military service if they supplied a substitute.[54]

As a consequence Quakers began to return to Virginia in large numbers. The epicenter of this migration was the Delaware Valley, where a growing scarcity of land, increasing tenancy, and rising real estate prices caused many Quakers to move west and south. By 1725 they had begun to settle in western Maryland. In 1732 they had crossed the Potomac, and a group headed by Alexander Ross obtained a charter for 100,000 acres in Frederick County, Virginia. By 1776 perhaps 5,000 Quakers had moved into the colony and founded at least fifteen monthly meetings—mostly in the piedmont, the Valley, and the west.[55]

This movement had its own distinctive character. The typical Quaker migrants of the eighteenth century were married couples with a family. They were propertied people who traveled "with horse and wagon and cattle." Of those who joined a meeting in Virginia, the median age was twenty-seven, much older than other groups. They were not movers but resettlers. The average number of removals in a lifetime was one or two.[56] An observer described the Quakers as "honest industreous people" who moved long distances, often "4, 5, 6 and 7 hundred miles by land."[57]

The Friends were looking for land in places where they could build rural communities and raise their children among neighbors of the same faith. In 1774 the price of real estate in Frederick County, Virginia, was half the price in Pennsylvania. Another factor was the disappearance of game in eastern Pennsylvania. Quaker leader John Churchman wrote of the Shenandoah Valley in 1741, "I believe that the delight in hunting, and a roving idle life, drew most of them under our name to there." The search for game was a major and often overlooked factor in the westward movement, even among Quakers.[58]

Primary areas of settlement were in the north, in what is now Frederick, Loudoun, and Fairfax counties, and also in Hardy, Hampshire, Berkeley, and Jefferson counties of what is now West Virginia. Smaller Quaker communities settled in the piedmont, around Louisa County, farther east in Henrico County, and in Bedford and Campbell counties. Native communities formed in the southeastern counties and persisted on the Eastern Shore.[59]

Tensions developed between the Quakers and their southern neighbors. They did not get on well with the Scotch-Irish and British borderers. Stephen B. Weeks has observed that the movement of Quakers "is parallel to that of the Scotch Irish. These two waves passed over the same ground at the same time but the two did not intermingle, for the gentle and peaceloving Friend, who decried all war . . . had little in common with the restless, aggressive, fighting, ruling Scotch-Irish, or with the democratic but stern tenets of Calvinism."[60]

Increasingly, the Quakers were hostile to slavery, and many had difficulties with southern land offices. A contemporary observed that many "like Israll of old begin to wish themselves back in Pennsylvania."[61] There was much reverse migration in all of these flows, back to Pennsylvania and even to the north Midlands of England, where the Society of Friends had originated. One Quaker immigrant, Joseph Elam, moved about 1750 from Brighouse in Yorkshire to the Henrico Monthly Meeting in Virginia. He went back to Brighouse in 1755, returned to Henrico by 1758, was back in Brighouse by 1764, and remained there for twenty-four years during the period of the Revolution. By 1786 he was back in Henrico and stayed until 1788, when he moved to Philadelphia and disappeared from the records.[62]

By these close ties with Friends in other places and by keeping their distance, Quakers remained, in Stephen Weeks's description, an "imperium in imperio." They did not assimilate with other groups in Virginia but preserved their distinctive ways.

Pluralism in the Piedmont and Valley: The Virginia Germans

Among the leading beneficiaries of the new toleration were German immigrants. The first settlers that Alexander Spotswood recruited for his iron mines in the Rappahannock Valley were not English but German-speaking. He did so mainly to save money. English servants were in short supply, of doubtful quality, and increasingly costly. For a bargain price—£150 for the lot—Spotswood was able to buy a group of forty Swiss German redemptioners.

By 1715 they built for him a five-sided wooden fort and a little town called Germanna. Traveler John Fontaine visited the place on November 12, 1715, and found a tightly integrated community that was very different from English settlements in Virginia. From the start Germanna was a close-built family community. Fontaine observed, "There are but nine families, and they have nine houses, built all in a line; and before every house, about twenty feet distant from it, they have small sheds built for their hogs and hens, so that the hog-sties and houses make a street."[63]

The Germans were deeply religious. They brought a minister with them, and Ensign Fontaine reported that "they go to prayers constantly once a day, and have two sermons on Sunday. We went to hear them perform their service, which was done in their own language, which we did not understand; but they seemed to be very devout, and sang the psalms very well."[64]

The redemptioners were hardworking but did not put their wealth into consumption. Fontaine was appalled to find that they "live very miserably" and could offer him nothing better than straw to sleep on and "a bit of smoked beef and cabbage, which was very ordinary and dirtily dressed." He moved thankfully to the home of an English gentleman whose housekeeper "entertained us well" with "a good turkey for supper and beds to lie on."[65]

The Swiss Germans were as displeased with their British employer as Fontaine had been with them. When their term of service ended in 1721, twelve families left Germanna and established Germantown in the foothills of the Blue Ridge Mountains, the most westerly settlement in Virginia. They were replaced by seventy Germans from the Palatinate, and a new European culture began to multiply in Virginia.

This was a small part of the great *Auswanderung* of perhaps as many as a million German-speaking emigrants from central Europe in the century after 1683. They were fleeing war, conscription, taxes, confiscation, oppression, persecution, and tyranny in a European world that was a system of organized bullying, where Thomas Jefferson observed that every man was either a wolf or a sheep, a hammer or an anvil.

These German emigrants came from many parts of *Gross Deutschland* but mainly from an area in southwestern Germany. From that heartland they fled in many directions. Many traveled east to Siberia and southeast to Hungary and the Balkans. Roman Catholics among them went to France and Spain. About 100,000 Protestants came to British America in a series of waves that began with William Penn's recruitment of German-speaking Pietists in 1683 and continued until the American Revolution. Half may have come in one great wave from 1748 to 1754.

One may observe two classic types of European emigration through the full span of American history. One was a flight from persecution that was mainly a movement of families. The other was a movement mostly of unattached young men, toward economic opportunity.

The German emigration was very much a movement of families. Of 3,200 migrants to America from Rheinpfalz and the Saarland from 1683 to 1776, three-quarters traveled in family groups. A large proportion of single males came after 1760, but always families predominated.[66]

The Germans came not only in families but also in entire neighborhoods and in congregations of many different denominations. Most who came from the Palatinate, Württemberg, and other parts of southwest Germany were Lutherans. Others were Quakers and Pietists from the lower Rhine; Calvinists (called German Reformed) from Alsace; the Brethren (called Dunkers or Tunkers after the German word *tunken,* to dip) from Hesse; Amish from the Swiss canton of Berne; Mennonites from Zurich, Basel, and much of the Rhineland; Schwenckfelders from Silesia in eastern Germany; and Moravians from Bohemia, Moravia, and Saxony.

Many were helped on their way by authorities who wished to be rid of them. The Swiss officials of Berne were deporting Anabaptists to America as early as 1709. Mostly, however, this migration was voluntary. Marianne

Wokeck writes: "Within this overall international context, the migration to British North America stands out because it was not the result of a concerted government effort. These people made their own way to the New World. They were helped by private entrepreneurs who made a business of transporting immigrants, often cruelly exploiting them in the process."[67]

Their travel route was different from earlier migrations to Virginia. Many sailed to the Delaware Valley, then found their way west into the countryside in search of land. They followed the fertile valleys southwest through Pennsylvania and Maryland and after 1730 began to settle in the northern end of Virginia's Shenandoah Valley. The first land grants in the Valley were made to Virginians—Larkin Chew's 10,000 acres along Happy Creek, soon followed by grants to Benjamin Borden and William Beverley, one of the Knights of the Golden Horseshoe. The first German grantee was Adam Miller in 1727.

A major leader of the movement was Jost Hite, an imposing Alsatian who was called the "old German Baron." He settled in the Shenandoah Valley with three sons-in-law, Jacob Chrisman, George Bowman, and Paul Froman. In 1734 Hite was granted 100,000 acres of land, which he resold to other Germans, mostly in family farms of 100 to 500 acres. The court records of Frederick and Orange counties contain "innumerable records of land sales by Jost Hite."[68]

There were many other promoters of settlement, not always of good character. Jacob Stover was an unscrupulous Swiss entrepreneur who got a large land grant by "giv[ing] human names to every horse, cow, hog and dog he owned." He then sold the land for £3 for a hundred acres and "went off with the money."[69]

Another early promoter was Peter Stover, who founded the town of Strasburg, Virginia, which he named after his place of birth in Lorraine. Other Germans moved up the Potomac Valley and founded the town of New Mecklenburg (now Shepherdstown), West Virginia.

A group of Lutherans and Calvinists settled in the Hebron Valley; communities of Dunkers and Mennonites settled in other areas. The heaviest concentration of Virginia Germans was in the northern Shenandoah Valley, between the towns of Winchester and Staunton. Their distribution appeared in a survey of place-names by John Walter Wayland. He found a total of eighty-five German names in the Shenandoah Valley: twenty-seven were in modern Rockingham County, twenty-two in Shenandoah County, eleven in Augusta, eight in Frederick, seven in Page, six in Jefferson, only three in Berkeley, and one in Warren.[70]

Substantial German populations also settled the piedmont counties of Loudoun, Culpeper, Madison, and Floyd. They soon found their way to the Roanoke Valley, especially Botetourt County, and into the Southwest Virginia counties of Smyth, Bland, Washington, and Wythe. By 1790 a majority of inhabitants in Wythe County were Germans or Swiss. Overall, 28 percent of white Virginians in 1790 were of German ancestry.[71]

In the heart of this area German culture and language established itself. Palatine dialects dominated the Shenandoah Valley. Virginia German was spoken with a Swabian accent in the Hebron Valley.

Massive stone-built German houses and barns rose throughout this region. Their interiors were heated not with English fireplaces but German stoves. Patterns of dress were highly distinctive. The cut of a German bonnet revealed the religious sect and the regional origin of the woman who wore it.

German foodways were different from those of English settlers. An abundance of *Kraut, Pfannhass* (scrapple), and raisin pies appeared on the tables. Thrifty German cooks made use of organ meats; one delicacy was pig's stomach stuffed with sausage and potatoes, which English-speaking neighbors unkindly called Dutch goose. Sauerkraut was a ceremonial dish, always served on Christmas and holidays, a custom that spread to English-speaking households throughout Maryland and the Valley of Virginia. Food was served on German stoneware with bright glazes.

Besides their distinctive language and publications, Germans also brought to Virginia a distinctive decorative arts tradition of lavishly applied decoration on furniture. Important family events were recorded on fraktur documents with cheerful folk designs. Houses and barns were painted with hex signs and distelfinks in red, green, and yellow.[72]

Equally distinctive were attitudes toward family, gender, wealth, and power. Gender roles were sharply defined, but in a manner different from English-speaking cultures. Both sexes labored at different tasks in the home and the field, and daughters inherited land along with sons. In general the German settlers were uncomfortable with slavery, preferring to do their own labor.

They also developed distinctive ideas of freedom. German concepts of freedom tended to be more personal and social, less political than the attitudes of their English neighbors. They had a stronger sense of personal and

45. Fort Stover, Page County, Virginia, is a sturdy stone-built house with a traditional three-room German floor plan.

46. The German inscription on this stove plate translates "Each one shall live without fear under his own vine and fig tree." It expressed the principal motives that brought Germans to America and their idea of freedom, which had less to do with politics than with privacy.

48. A *Taufschein,* or baptismal certificate, became an artifact of the migration process, carried west as proof of church membership. This one was taken to Ohio.

47. (opposite page) Virginia Germans brought strong folk traditions in decorative arts. This chest from the northern Shenandoah Valley was painted and probably made by Johannes Spitler (1774–1837), who moved on to Ohio—one of many who carried their German heritage from Virginia to the Midwest.

familial responsibility but a weaker sense of public responsibility. Historian A. G. Roeber has characterized this culture as "self-reliant, thrifty, religious, and withdrawn. . . . The sense of public responsibility for liberties, never strongly rooted in the German past, apparently remained fragile." There was an intense hostility to taxes, which in the long experience of German-speaking people had paid for governments that had oppressed them. Liberty meant for them an autonomy for their churches, communities, and families—an attitude at variance with their highly political English neighbors.[73]

German culture persisted with remarkable tenacity in the Shenandoah Valley of Virginia. The churches were important in maintaining Old World tradition; German-language schools were maintained for many years throughout the region. There were continuing linkages to the fatherland (Britons, of course, spoke of the mother country). Many of these immigrants came from propertied families, and professional agents moved among them to secure inheritances and land titles to German estates. German-language publications circulated from Philadelphia, Lancaster, and Baltimore. Books and newspapers were printed in German within Virginia as well, although not until the early 1800s. Even non-Germans such as Quaker Isaac Zane produced cast-iron products with German inscriptions.[74]

The history of this culture can be traced in the career of German printers in Virginia. Among them was Jacob D. Dietrich, whose migration experience followed a familiar pattern for German Americans. Dietrich moved in stages from his native Philadelphia to central Pennsylvania and then to western Maryland. By 1804 he was in the Shenandoah Valley of Virginia, first at Winchester, then in Staunton where he published English and German editions of a Republican newspaper, the *Staunton Eagle,* to counter a Federalist gazette already established there. Mounting debt persuaded Dietrich to move farther west. He accepted a job as a printer in Lancaster, Ohio, serving a community founded by Shenandoah Valley Germans. There in 1811 he published the *Ohio Eagle* in both English and German editions.

Another family of German printers were the Henkels of New Market, Virginia. They came from the Philadelphia area and began to operate their press in 1806. It continued to be a source of German-language publications for fifty years, until 1854. By then the market for such publications had greatly diminished, partly because many Germans like Dietrich had moved on the Midwest, partly because new immigration from Germany to the Shenandoah Valley ceased.

More important, however, was the relentless tide of Anglicization. A recent study concludes that "as early as 1833 the writer Samuel Kercheval could reminisce fondly about the heyday of German culture in the region."[75] German settlers were quick to assimilate much of the official English-speaking culture. At the same time they preserved other ancestral folkways, long after they ceased to speak the language of their fatherland.

Today the Virginia Germans are "chiefly made up of the descendants of early immigrants . . . descended almost entirely from the immigrants of the early eighteenth century." The language has been lost, but cultural attitudes and customs have persisted even to our own time.[76]

The Swarming of the
Scotch-Irish and British Borderers

Another folk migration populated the southern end of the Shenandoah Valley. In a period of sixty years (1715–75), more than a quarter of a million people moved from the borderlands of north Britain and northern Ireland to the American backcountry.

Many think of this migration in ethnic terms and call it Scotch-Irish or Celtic. These labels fit some emigrants but not all or even most of them. Many came not from Ireland or Scotland but from the north of England. Most did not speak Celtic languages but English. They were very mixed in their ethnicity, religion, and place of residence. In many ways, however, they shared a common culture, the product of a distinctive region that might be called the borderlands of north Britain.

The culture of the borders derived from one decisive fact. For 700 years the kings of England and Scotland could not agree who owned this region and fought constantly for its possession. Incessant violence created a warrior ethic of great intensity, a family life in which the clan became an important unit of protection, a polity defined mainly by personal loyalty, a system of age relations that resembled the rule of tanistry (a system of life tenure conferred by election upon the strongest), a structure of gender inequality common to warrior cultures, an economy that rested on herding and extensive agriculture, a comity that combined high rates of internal migration with strong kin bonding, a strident prejudice against strangers, a style of impermanent cabin architecture for ordinary folk, a habit of religion in mobile field meetings, a special type of nescient fatalism common to people who live

48th

Saturday 28th May 1774

Nothing remarcable this day, in the evening ÿ Colonel
and his Lady returned from their visits. —

Sunday 29th

There is no Church nearer Belvidera than
Frederichsburgh, and for want of a sadle I was
obliedged to stay at home all day and when I was alone
in the school I the thought on ÿ following verses.

1st

In Virginia now I am, at Belvidera settled
but may they ever mercÿ find, who hade the cause
that I am from my dearest wife, seperated
And obliedged to leave my Infant Children, Fatherlefs

2d

As a schoolmaster, I am here;
and must for four years, remain so;
May I indeavour the Lord to fear,
and always his commands do.

3d

For in Gods strength I do rely,
that he at his appointed time;
will bring me back to my familly,
if I his precepts do but mind.

4th

O May my God provide for them,
who unto me are near and dear;
tho they afar off me are from.
O Jesus keeps them in thy fear.

do—

49. This poem was written by John Harrower, who had to leave his family in the
Shetland Islands to go to Virginia as an indentured servant for passage and "Bed,
Board, washing and five pounds during the whole time."

120

constantly at risk of violent death, an idea of order dominated by the rule of *lex talionis,* and a concept of liberty as "natural freedom."

In the sixteenth, seventeenth, and eighteenth centuries, a new system of order was imposed on this region by a process as violent as the world it destroyed. Many people were set in motion by these events—some to northern Ireland, others to America. Most of the borderers were extremely poor, but they emigrated in family groups with strong networks of support. They were not welcomed in eastern settlements and were hurried on their western way. In the southern highlands from Pennsylvania to Georgia, they quickly established a cultural hegemony. Through the southern backcountry as a whole, 60 percent of the European population was from northern Ireland, Scotland, and northern England. North Britons were 73 to 80 percent of the population in Virginia's Augusta, Fayette, and Lincoln counties, 75 percent in Pennsylvania's Washington County, 90 percent in some counties of Tennessee and Kentucky, and nearly 100 percent in the Hillsboro district of North Carolina and parts of the South Carolina upcountry.[77] These areas became the seed settlements of the southern highlands.

Among these emigrants was a small elite who had been called the "ascendancy" in northern Ireland. These leaders included the family of Patrick Henry, who was a cousin of the great Cumbrian Whig Lord Brougham, and the ancestors of Sam Houston, who were a family of border baronets. The forebears of Zachary Taylor were of the border ascendancy in the north of England.

North British borderers rapidly established a cultural hegemony in the backcountry, partly by weight of numbers, partly by the integration of elites, and partly by the nature of border culture itself, which proved to be exceptionally well suited to backcountry conditions. Much of what Americans think of as frontier culture was adapted from the borderlands of north Britain and northern Ireland in the eighteenth century.

In speech patterns, for example, strong continuities ran from north British speech and the "Scotch-Irish dialect" in the eighteenth century to the family of American regional dialects called southern highland speech. The latter is spoken today in variant forms from the Appalachians to the Ozarks, Texas and Oklahoma, and westward to southern California. It is familiar today as the speech of country and western singers, cinematic cowboys, and backcountry politicians.

In vernacular architecture one also finds similar patterns of persistence and change. The log cabin, icon of the backcountry and frontier, is a good example. The development of the log cabin is a study in cultural continuity and change. Turnerian scholars believed that the log cabin was a spontaneous invention on the American frontier. This was not the case. English settlers—those from the south of England particularly—did not build log cabins in seventeenth-century America. Their rude structures tended to be adaptations of English architecture.

Two other European models were combined to create the American log cabin. One of them was a tradition of building in logs that had flourished in Germany and Scandinavia. A study by two geographers, Terry G. Jordan and Matti Kaups, has traced one particular type of log architecture from a region of Finland to the Delaware Valley.[78]

These Scandinavian structures were log buildings, but they were not log cabins. The architecture of the cabin, like the name itself, came from buildings in north Britain and northern Ireland. These were small, impermanent structures with a few small windows, an open fireplace, and dirt floors. In the borderlands they were mostly made of stone or turf and were well adapted to a hostile environment in which more imposing structures invited destruction. North British cabins tended to be a standard size, commonly one pole, perch, rod, or lug in width, which normally was five and a half yards.

In the American backcountry border immigrants built cabins of the sort that they had known at home, with only a single alteration. The building material changed from stone to wood. Otherwise, the plan, dimensions, design, and name of the structure remained the same. Border settlers borrowed methods of log building from Scandinavian and German settlers, but they used that technology to create a log cabin. Thus a distinctive American building type was created, mainly by north British borderers in the American backcountry.

Similar patterns appeared in the furnishings of log cabins. In a recent study of inventories of material culture in northern Ireland and in the Valley of Virginia, Warren R. Hofstra concludes that "the most remarkable feature is the high degree to which the inventories agree. To the extent that material possessions sketch the outline of a way of life, men and women at Ballyhagen [in Ireland] and Opequon [in Virginia] lived quite similarly. . . . In other

The Flight
from
Northern Britain

■ Highland Counties
□ Other Counties

Orkney

Caithness

Sunderland

Ross and
Cromarty

Nairn

Moray

Banff

Aberdeen

Inverness

Scotland

Kincardine

Skye

Angus

Kinross

Cluckmannan

Fife

Argyll

Stirling

Edinburgh

W. Lothian

Midlothian

E. Lothian

Renfrew

Lanark

Peeb

Berwick

Ayr

Sel

Bute

Ayr

Dumfries

Roxburgh

Kirk-
cudbright

North-
umberland

Newcastle -on- Tyne

North
Atlantic
Ocean

North
Channel

Outer Hebrides

Inner Hebrides

Coleraine

Portrush

Donegal

Londonderry

Derry

Larne

Antrim

Tyrone

Belfast

Sligo

Fermanagh

Down

Sligo

Leitrim

Monaghan

Armagh

Newry

Roscommon

Cavan

Long-
ford

Dundalk

Louth

Wigtown

Wigtown

Kirkcud-
bright

Cumberland

West-
moreland

Durham

Whitby

Mayport

Whitehaven

Scarborough

ISLE OF MAN

England

Yorkshire

Bridlington

Morecambe

Lancashire

Hull

Liverpool

Irish Sea

W. Meath

Meath

King's

Dublin

Kildare

Dublin

Anglesey

Merseyside

Flint

Cheshire

Derby

Notting-
ham

Lincolnshire

Ireland

Caernarvon

Denbigh

Norfolk

Queen's

Wicklow

Carlow

Merioneth

Mont-
gomery

Shropshire

Stafford

Leicestershire

Kilkenny

Radnor

Warwick

North-
ants

Hunts

Cambs

Suffolk

Tipperary

Wexford

Cardigan

Here-
ford

Worcester

Beds

Waterford

Carmarthan

Breck-
nock

Herts

Essex

Pembroke

Mon-
mouth

Gloucester

Oxon

Bucks

Glamorgan

Berkshire

MDX

London

North Sea

Bristol

Wiltshire

Surrey

Kent

St. George's Channel

Hampshire

Somerset

Sussex

Dorset

Strait of Dover

Devon

Isle of Wight

Cornwall

English Channel

50

words, cultural persistence as much as change shaped the emigration and assimilation process."[79]

Other folkways showed the same linkages between the north British borderlands and the American backcountry. Family ways were marked by the importance of the clan, by a large number of mutually supportive nuclear households sharing a common name, and by the memory of a common origin. A process of chain migration brought many of these clans to the backcountry. Marriages were celebrated by ritual reenactments of ancient customs of bridal abduction. Gender ways were those of a warrior society, with sharply drawn differences in gender roles for male warriors and female workers. Attitudes toward sex were distinctive in the open celebration of sensuality. Dress displayed extreme differences in gender. Male clothing was cut broadly across chest and shoulders with horizontal seams to display masculinity; women wore open bodices, tight waists, and high hems that emphasized femininity. Sports of the borderers stressed the martial arts—contests in wrestling, fighting, running, leaping, weapon throwing, and shooting.

51. The folkways of the British borderers were well matched to conditions in the southern backcountry. They shared a culture of austerity in which a few possessions served multiple purposes. The settle or saddle bed was a bench or fold-out bed that, without the bedding, could be used as an infant playpen.

The rearing of male children was intended to instill a sense of masculine honor and a warrior's courage in the young. Female child rearing was very different. Child naming was distinctive in the frequency with which Andrew, Patrick, and David (the patron saints, respectively, of Scotland, Ireland, and Wales) appeared as forenames. The religion of these people ran in the eighteenth century to the theology of the new light and field meetings that were virtually identical with what would later be called camp meetings in America.

Foodways drew heavily on border customs. Ingredients changed as Indian corn replaced oats and pork substituted for mutton, but methods of cooking stayed much the same. Food preparation was dominated by pot boiling and hearth baking. Staples were boiled grain (oatmeal to grits and hominy), clabber, and whiskey.

The actual distribution of wealth in the backcountry contrasts sharply with Turnerian models of the frontier. Tax lists in nineteen southern Appalachian counties during the eighteenth century showed the highest levels of inequality in early America, with Gini ratios of .7 to .9, higher even than in eastern Virginia.[80]

At the same time land use showed an exceptionally strong sense of impermanence and the highest rates of internal migration in the American

52. British border culture was distinctive in its spartan foodways. Ingredients changed in the southern backcountry, but the diet remained remarkably the same: oatcakes and oatmeal yielded to cornbread and grits, old mutton to salt pork, and Scotch whiskey to bourbon. This harnen (from *hardening*) stand was used to toast grain cakes before an open fire.

colonies. Social order was conceived mainly as a system of *lex talionis,* the rule of retribution. The power ways of the border and the backcountry were dominated by the politics of personal loyalty, more so than in other ethnic groups. Ideas of freedom were highly articulated in the borderlands and the backcountry, but in a distinct way. This ethnic group held an idea of natural freedom in which every man was his own master and, in the backcountry proverb, the sheriff on his own hearth. Freedom meant a man's natural right to be let alone, with plenty of elbowroom and as little government as possible.

This culture was planted in the southern end of the Valley of Virginia, mainly in Augusta County, which at its founding included the entire southern half of the Shenandoah Valley. It spread into the mountains beyond the Valley and was carried throughout the southern highlands.[81]

Leaders of this movement from the British borderlands became a backcountry ascendancy. One of the members of this elite was James Patton, an ancestor of General George S. Patton (who personified this culture in many ways). James Patton became agent in the Shenandoah Valley for William Beverley, one of Spotswood's Knights of the Golden Horseshoe. Later, Patton was a partner in the James and Roanoke River Company. In 1745 he obtained 100,000 acres on the New, Holston, and Clinch rivers in Southwest Virginia. Many of the settlements that emerged there were offshoots from Augusta, one of the great seed counties in American history and the backcountry hearth of this culture.

Anxiety, Nostalgia, and Cultural Conservatism on the Frontier: The Saga of Mary Moore

The persistence of ethnic culture in western Virginia poses an interesting problem about the dynamics of change on the edge of settlement. The germ theory linked cultural determinants to social continuity. The frontier thesis, on the other hand, connected the environmental conditions to social change.

Both models were mistaken. We find repeated evidence that the prevailing mood on the edge of settlement was profoundly conservative. New settlements tended to remain remarkably old-fashioned in their folkways. The cause of this conservatism was complex. One part of it was a sense of distance from "home." Another was the anxiety that many felt on the frontier.

he good of our
y lament the
resignation;
ffection assure
ave given rise
d to you, we
of the people,
e this publick
pect for your
our vigilance
, this united
imony, while
oppofition to
ial meafures
ointed cut and
refolution kd
extenfive po-
atly indebted,
ich the troops
were continu-
the firmnefs,
which formed
nduct towards
pprobation of
il leave upon
il impreffion.
nmediate con-
e continuance
Ve know your
ufes; we have
our abilities,
r views; and
may be to un-
ation, we truft
tice fhall pre-
an honourable

diamond, and had to her a lady's fteel
chain, with a feal of *Virginia* ftone fet in
gold, ornamented with a coat of arms.
Whoever delivers it to the printer fhall be
genteelly rewarded.

LOUISA, *March* 18, 1776.

RUN away from the fubfcriber on the
16th inftant (*March*) a likely negro
fellow named JACOB, who is about 5
feet 5 or 6 inches high, 30 years old,
fquare and well made, is very black, and
has a down look; had on, and took with
him, a coarfe blue cloth great coat, a fine
brown mixt coloured broadcloth body
coat, double-breafted fcarlet cloth waift-
coat, a pair of very good buckfkin
breeches, knit yarn ftockings, very good
hat and fhoes, and alfo feveral fhirts of
white and brown linen, and fome money.
He was born in *Pennfylvania*, bred a farmer, pretends to great fkill in farriery,
fpeaks in the *Scotch-Irifh* dialect, and in
converfation frequently ufes the words
moreover and *likewife*; and as he can read
and write, will probably forge a pafs.
Whoever takes up faid flave, and fecures
him fo that his mafter may get him again,
fhall have 40s. if taken in *Louifa*, *Albemarle*, or *Orange*; if in any other county
in the colony 5l. and if taken out of the
colony 10l. paid by

DAVID HOOPS.

RUN away from the fubfcriber, on
Sunday the 10th inftant, a negro man
named JAMES, who is a fhort thick
fquat fellow, marked with the fmall pox,

53. One of the strongest local hegemonies was the north British and Scotch-Irish
culture of the southern backcountry, which influenced even those there who belonged
to other groups. This advertisement in the *Virginia Gazette* of March 22, 1776, reports
that the runaway slave Jacob "speaks in the Scotch-Irish dialect, and in conversation
frequently uses the words *moreover* and *likewise*."

The force of those feelings may be observed in the sad story of Mary Moore (1776–1824) of Tazewell County, known as "the captive of Abb's Valley." She was taken prisoner as a child by the Shawnees, during the surge of westward movement that followed the end of the American Revolution. Her captors carried her to Ohio, and in the mid-1780s she was sold as a slave in Canada. Five years later, at the age of fifteen, she returned to Virginia and resumed her former life.

Mary Moore seemed at first to readjust well to her former society. She married a clergyman named Brown and had eleven children. As an older woman, however, perhaps because of her captivity experiences, she could only sleep in a special bed, constructed exactly like a baby's cradle but to the size of an adult. It was perhaps not unlike the cradle in which Mary Moore had slept peacefully as a child, before she was taken by the Indians.[82]

Here was an interior dimension of the westward movement that has left few traces in the history textbooks: the sharp stab of fear that came suddenly

54. Captured by Shawnees at the age of ten, Mary Moore (1776–1824) returned to Virginia five years later but as an adult woman could sleep only in this cradle, which perhaps recalled childhood security before her ordeal. It is a rare artifact of an interior dimension of the westward movement—the psychological terror of frontier living, anxiety for the future, and nostalgia for the past.

with the bark of a dog at dawn or the screech of an owl in the dark, the long sleepless nights and weary days, the consuming anxiety for others even more than for oneself, the alternation of dreary tedium and desperate terror, and most of all the uncertainty of life on the frontier. All these feelings took their inexorable toll.

These people were not passive victims. Like Mary Moore, they found the strength to keep on with their lives. To remember the depth of their suffering is to understand something of their courage and resolve.

It is also to comprehend more clearly the complex dynamics of the cultural process that we call the westward movement. The anxiety and pain of life in a new settlement often were accompanied by nostalgia for the half-remembered comfort of the older world that had been left behind.

Just as Mary Moore found peace by returning to something like the cradle of her childhood, so others preserved what they could, with a determination that became all the stronger for the changes and uncertainties that were part of their new lives. Here is a key to the paradox of "cultural persistence" and "colonial lag." Old ways survived in new settlements not merely by a kind of cultural inertia but as an act of will and purpose.

With the growth of toleration, a consequence of cultural persistence was cultural pluralism on the frontier. On the frontier English, Germans, and Scotch-Irish settlers did not form a single hybrid culture. They all tended to cling stubbornly to their own special folkways.

Freedom, the Frontier, and the Flowering of Virginia

During the late eighteenth century, the new toleration encouraged a vast expansion of settlement in Virginia and the growth of a population of increasing diversity. By 1790 the Old Dominion was by far the most populous state in the American confederation, nearly as large as the next two states combined (Massachusetts and Pennsylvania).

Every major part of the state had been settled to some degree. The regions of eastern Virginia had taken on their own unmistakable character. The central tidewater had evolved into a plantation system in which most of the population were African-American slaves, with their own highly distinctive culture. The Southside was growing rapidly as communications improved into a land of modest farms and small plantations, also with a large black population. The Northern Neck was yet another distinctive region, more than ever a "rich man's country" of large plantations and tenant farmers. Maritime Virginia was flourishing, as Norfolk developed into a center of commerce with the West Indies. The most dynamic regions were the piedmont and the Valley of Virginia, where prosperous farms and plantations multiplied at a rapid rate. Grain farming, orchards, and livestock replaced tobacco, and Sir William Berkeley's dream of a more diversified agricultural economy was being realized at last.

The population of Virginia also had become diverse in ethnic terms. Still, the old cavalier elite controlled the Council and had great strength in the House of Burgesses. New elites were growing rapidly, however: Scottish merchants in Norfolk, German farmers in the northern Valley, Scotch-Irish and British borderers farther south in Augusta County, colonies of Quakers, English Methodists, French Huguenots, Swiss Pietists.

At the same time it is important to remember that ethnicity was merely one dimension of cultural diversity. Many other dimensions of pluralism also developed in Virginia. The expansion of settlement not only allowed room for old ethnic and religious differences to coexist in the New World. It also encouraged a new pluralism of regional cultures. This process occurred not only on a broad sectional level where it is familiar to all Americans but also within sections and even states.

A case in point was the cultural history of Virginia's distinctive regions. The tidewater, Northern Neck, Southside, Eastern Shore, piedmont, and Valley each slowly developed its own folkways. The history of speech is an example of this process. Although a general Virginia accent was evident to strangers by the mid–eighteenth century, natives of the Old Dominion were highly conscious of regional variations in pronunciation and vocabulary. Research by Hans Kurath and Phyllis Nixon found, for example, that the crawling creature called an *earthworm* along the lower James became an *angleworm* on the Northern Neck, a *fishing worm* in the piedmont, and a *redworm* west of New River. A *griddlecake* in the tidewater was a *hotcake* on the Eastern Shore and a *flannel cake* west of the Blue Ridge. Flat and fertile alluvial fields were *lowlands* in the Northern Neck and *lowgrounds* in the Southside. The *living room* or *parlor* or *sitting room* of a piedmont house was called *the chamber* in the tidewater and *the front room* in the Southside. Similar patterns of regional differentiation within Virginia appeared in vernacular architecture and other folkways.[83]

This very rich pattern of regional diversity developed within a common frame. Most of Virginia's regions and many of its ethnic groups participated in the colony's social and political system. Regional differences coexisted with a high degree of regional integration in economic and social relations. Furthermore, the diffusion of slavery encouraged backcountry settlers to identify with tidewater and piedmont gentry despite wide disparities of wealth. Richard R. Beeman has shown how the growth of slavery brought Southside Lunenburg County into the mainstream of colonial culture. Turk McCleskey documents a similar phenomenon in Augusta County in the Valley of Virginia.[84] Albert H. Tillson, Jr.'s study of the southern Valley shows how an isolated country populated by borderers nonetheless had many ties to eastern planters and merchants. The area's elite, unlike Beeman's Lunenburg leaders, was partially successful in creating a deferential political culture in some ways similar to the tidewater. Even as these elites came to resemble each other in some respects, they cultivated their differences, which in turn supported a strong sense of cultural diversity.[85]

As Virginia's regional and ethnic elites became more diverse, while at same time having to coexist with one another, new patterns of social thought began to develop—a ferment of ideas that flourished in Virginia perhaps more than anywhere else in America or the Atlantic world. These new ideas were in many ways part of large intellectual movements that were sweeping through the Western world in the eighteenth century. At the same time they developed in ways that were highly specific to the regional and ethnic cultures that had formed in more than a century of the westward movement in Virginia.

These new ideas shared a central theme. They were models of a society that was organized around a principle of freedom—not merely the grudging and expedient toleration of England's settlement in 1688 but a fundamental belief in the right to be free.

One of these ideas of freedom flourished in the tidewater, among such men as George Wythe and the Williamsburg leaders—an idea that stressed the rule of law and the integrity of social institutions. Another developed on the Northern Neck, in the circle of Fairfaxes, Washingtons, Marshalls, Carters, and Lees. This was a conservative idea of a free society led by an elite of character and dedication, organized around a sense of decency, honor, and service.

Another kind of freedom flourished in the Southside, an idea of natural liberty, the freedom to be left alone. Patrick Henry was the great spokesman of this tradition, which horrified Virginians of the tidewater.

In the western piedmont, where a plural society of diverse ethnic groups was developing, the most interesting and original idea of freedom emerged in the thinking of James Madison and Thomas Jefferson. These men were comfortable with diversity. Madison celebrated it as a positive good in *The Federalist* No. 10.

As seen in Jefferson's idea of ward government, they were also happy with a high degree of decentralization and popular participation. This new idea of a free society developed in an area where many different groups lived in proximity to one another, not mixing and merging but preserving their differences.

The development of these ideas was an interesting pattern in which the westward movement had an important role, but in a highly complex way, very different from the simple materialist mechanisms of the old frontier thesis. When tidewater Virginia had been a frontier, a strong but repressive system of government was firmly planted in its soil by Sir William Berkeley and his cavalier elite. At the end of the seventeenth century, a new spirit of toleration was imposed on Virginia from abroad. This new toleration opened the colony to settlements of increasing diversity. That diversity in turn required a framework for its coexistence. In response to that need, ideas of toleration grew into models of freedom. This development happened in many parts of Virginia, but most powerfully in the piedmont, where settlement was most diverse. The result was a new set of libertarian ideas.

This more open social order and the ideas of freedom that developed rapidly in Virginia's Revolutionary generation did not arise from the American environment alone, or from European imperatives by themselves, but from their creative interplay.

New ideas of freedom were further enlarged and reinforced by the incessant movement of Virginia's population. The royal governor Lord Dunmore complained to the earl of Dartmouth: "The established authority of any government in America, and the policy of the Government at home, are both insufficient to restrain the Americans. . . . They acquire no attachment to place: but wandering about seems engrafted in their nature; and it is a weak-

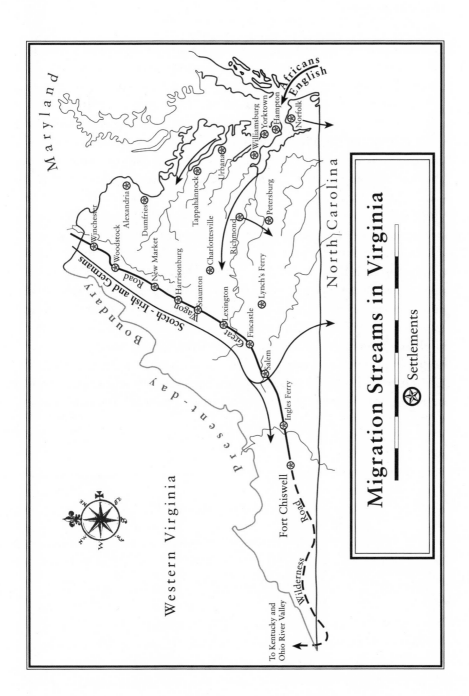

Migration Streams in Virginia

⊛ Settlements

ness incident to it, that they should forever imagine the lands further off, are still better than those upon which they are already settled."[86]

But these libertarian ideas also had their limits. Most ideas of freedom in Virginia coexisted with slavery and did not challenge the peculiar institution's right to exist in an unequivocal way. Virginia's libertarian tradition developed from the hegemonic freedom of the cavaliers, who believed that people of different ranks possessed different liberties and that some had no liberty at all. Despite that limiting source, these ideas of freedom were expansive in their applications to the master class and open to enlargement in the future.

That process of racial enlargement came slowly and painfully. When the Revolution broke out, Lord Dunmore issued a proclamation calling on slaves to abandon their masters and rally to him. Thousands did. Nothing Dunmore did was more appalling to Virginia's leaders. Their ideas of freedom did not yet extend to slaves. In time that limitation too would be overcome. Meanwhile, the words "all men are created equal," though not meant for black ears, stirred black souls and worked powerfully on black minds. Nat Turner, in planning his slave uprising, initially scheduled it for the Fourth of July. The issue of slavery and its westward migration would dominate the new century and ultimately result in yet another "new birth of freedom."

3

Migration beyond Virginia

AFTER THE Revolution the Republic attracted a new class of foreign visitors. They were not casual tourists but serious students of American institutions who hoped to find in the New World a clue to the future of the Old.

Of all the many sights they saw in the United States, none surprised them more than the human flood of migration that flowed westward from seaboard states to the interior of the continent. What most amazed them was not the magnitude of the movement, or the vast distance that it spanned, but the spirit in which it was undertaken.

"The active genius of the Americans is always pushing them forward," Brissot de Warville observed in 1788. "After they have spent some time on any piece of land, they move on to another where they hope to do better." On the road in Maryland, he passed a convoy of wagons heading across the mountains. "These caravans had an appearance of gaiety that surprised me," he wrote. "Apparently for Americans a migration to a place several hundred miles away is no more serious than moving from one house to another and is taken in the spirit of a pleasure party."[1]

English traveler Isaac Weld, Jr., was equally astounded by what he called the "roving disposition" of the Americans. "Nor having once removed, are these people satisfied," he wrote. "Restless and discontented with what they possess, they are for ever changing. It is scarcely possible in any part of the continent to find a man, amongst the middling and lower classes of Americans, who has not changed his farm and his residence many different times."[2]

These attitudes toward migration were thought by foreign visitors to be peculiar to a place. They were also specific to a period. Earlier travelers to the American colonies in the seventeenth and early eighteenth centuries had not, in general, made these remarks. Many things had changed in the era of the American Revolution—not merely in the political institutions of the new nation but in its cultural life as well.

Backcountry to Frontier: Changing Perceptions of the West

An important part of that change was a revolution in American thinking about the westward movement, and even about the West itself. Before 1776 the noun *West* as we use it today scarcely existed in American speech. In Mitford M. Mathews's *Dictionary of Americanisms,* the earliest usage of *the West* to denote that part of the United States that lay beyond earlier settled regions was recorded in 1798.

Before that period the word *frontier* commonly meant a boundary between countries or colonies or a zone of conflict between enemies. As late as July 12, 1832, the Boston *Transcript* referred to the Massachusetts state line as "the Connecticut frontier." American usage of *frontiers* in the seventeenth and eighteenth centuries commonly referred ambiguously to boundary zones between hostile people, such as the Indian frontiers or the Spanish frontier. This meaning was what Roger Williams intended when in 1655 he referred to "our dangers (being a frontier people to the barbarians)."[3]

Frederick Jackson Turner had something different in mind. "The American frontier," he wrote in 1893, "is sharply distinguished from the European frontier—a fortified boundary line running through dense populations. The most significant thing about the American frontier is, that it lies at the hither edge of free land. In the census reports it is treated as the margin of that settlement which has a density of two or more to the square mile." That usage was not his invention. It had been introduced by a census publication in 1874.[4]

Before 1776 the region that Frederick Jackson Turner called the frontier was known as the "back settlements," or the "backcountry," or merely the "back parts." Scarcely anyone thought of it as the "frontier" in Turner's sense during the first two centuries of American history. The fact that colonists thought of it as the "back" rather than "front" of their world tells us which way they were facing.[5]

That usage changed suddenly and very broadly in the early years of the Republic. The earliest recorded use of *frontier settlement* was in 1789; *frontier man,* 1782; *frontiersman,* 1814. Mitford Mathews found that the first recorded use of the word *trail* was in 1790, and *trailblazer* in 1814. *Pioneer* in the western sense first appeared in 1817.

An important part of this change was another new vocabulary of migration. Words such as *mover* (1810), *moving wagons* (1817), *relocate* (1814), even the verb *to move* in its present migratory sense of resettling, date from this period. Before 1790 Americans thought of themselves as *emigrants,* not *immigrants.* The word *immigrant* was an Americanism, probably coined in that year. It entered common usage by 1820.[6]

These semantical changes were superficial indicators of a profound and radical transformation in the way that Americans thought about their place in the world. Before 1776 their thoughts were directed east toward Europe; the back settlements lay behind them. By the early nineteenth century, they were beginning to look west toward the interior of their own continent. They had begun to identify themselves with their destinations rather than their origins. This changing perception gave new meaning to the westward movement. In an intellectual sense it marked the beginning of the American West.

Magnitudes

The westward movement carried about a million people out of Virginia. There are no precise statistics, but in 1847 Henry Ruffner, president of Washington College in Lexington, Virginia, made a study of the subject. He estimated that in the period from 1790 to 1840 the Old Dominion lost more of its inhabitants than did all of the original states above the Mason-Dixon Line combined. Ruffner concluded: "In the ten years from 1830 to 1840, Virginia lost by emigration no fewer than 375,000 of her people, of whom East Virginia lost 304,000 and West Virginia 71,000. At this rate Virginia supplies the West every ten years with a population equal in number to the population of the State of Mississippi in 1840!"[7]

The Federal Census of 1850 found more than 388,000 native Virginians living in other states, compared with Virginia's remaining population of 949,000. This figure did not include a much larger number of emigrant Virginians who were no longer living in 1850. Nor did it embrace their children and grandchildren, who were reckoned in millions by 1850.

Destinations

The direction of this great movement changed through time. During the eighteenth century the first great wave of emigration from Virginia went mainly south, to the Carolinas and Georgia. Something of its scale may be seen in the fact that of South Carolina's six congressmen serving in 1795–97,

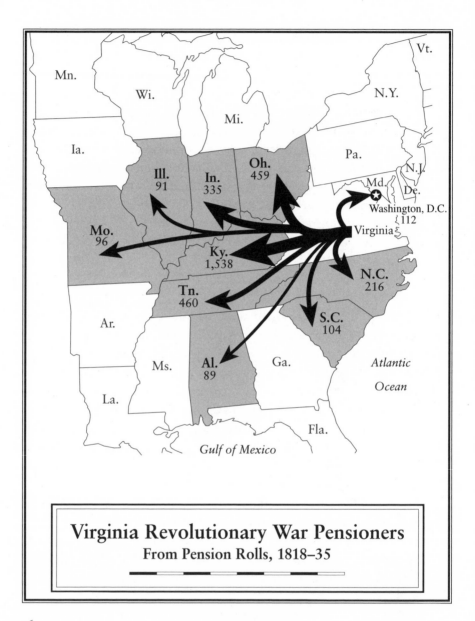

Virginia Revolutionary War Pensioners
From Pension Rolls, 1818–35

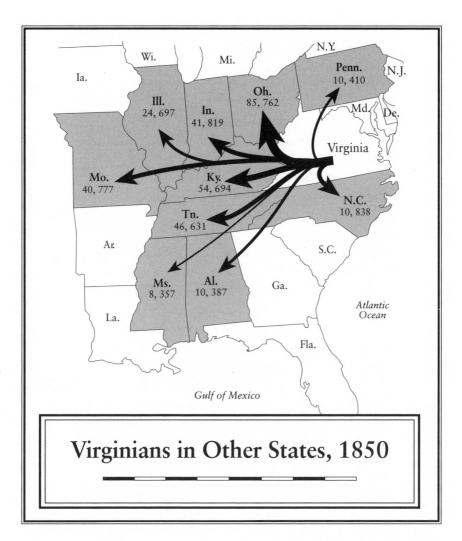

Wi.

Ia.

Mi.

N.Y.

Penn.
10, 410

N.J.

Ill.
24, 697

In.
41, 819

Oh.
85, 762

Md.

De.

Virginia

Mo.
40, 777

Ky.
54, 694

N.C.
10, 838

Tn.
46, 631

Ar

S.C.

Ms.
8, 357

Al.
10, 387

Ga.

*Atlantic
Ocean*

La.

Fla.

Gulf of Mexico

Virginians in Other States, 1850

four were native Virginians, one was a North Carolinian, and only one had been born in South Carolina itself. In Georgia patterns were much the same. During the same two years, four men were senators from Georgia. Two were Virginians, one was an immigrant from Britain, and only one was a native Georgian. The movement south was the largest migration stream from the Old Dominion in the eighteenth century.[8]

During the early Republic a second and larger wave of migration began to move more strongly to the West. A study by Phyllis Hunter of migration patterns as revealed in Revolutionary pension rolls from 1818 to 1835 found that nearly half of all veterans of Virginia units living outside Virginia were in Kentucky (1,538 of 3,599). Tennessee (460) and Ohio (459) were tied for second place.[9]

A little later in the nineteenth century, a third wave of emigration occurred, leaving its traces in the U.S. Census of 1850, the first to record place of birth as well as place of residence for Americans. In this movement the largest number of emigrant Virginians went to Ohio, which in 1850 had 85,762 immigrants from the Old Dominion. Although Virginians moved to all parts of the Buckeye State, they were most numerous on the bounty lands of the Virginia Military District.

The next largest number of emigrant Virginians was in Kentucky— 54,694. Then came Tennessee (46,631), Indiana (41,819), Missouri (40,777), and Illinois (24,697). Other favored destinations were Alabama, Mississippi, and Louisiana, in a period when Dr. James Somerville wrote of "a perfect mania for Chickasaw lands."[10]

The Census of 1860 supplied evidence of a fourth wave of migration, beyond the Mississippi. The leading state for emigrants from Virginia was still Ohio, but now it was followed by Missouri. Other prominent states were Kentucky, Indiana, Tennessee, and Illinois, as before. Strong flows also appeared in Texas, the Pacific slope, and northern cities.[11]

These figures included only the free population—both black and white. They did not count slaves, whose numbers were also large but could not be studied through the census in the same way.

Structures of Voluntary Movement:
Migration Fields and Streams

Altogether, quantitative evidence of movement from Virginia shows a pattern of migration fields and streams that were sharply defined in spatial terms and yet also extraordinarily dynamic. Leading destinations changed through time: the Carolinas and Georgia in the eighteenth century, Kentucky and Tennessee in the early Republic, Ohio a little later, and by 1860 the trans-Mississippi West.

A striking paradox presented itself in this migration. The westward movement was voluntary for most free people. Individual Virginians freely chose when to leave and where to go. Yet the process of this voluntary movement was elaborately structured in many ways.

Some of these structural patterns were spatial and temporal. The great outpouring of people from Virginia tended to flow in distinct streams, not only to particular destinations outside its boundaries but also from specific regions within the state. The first great flow of emigration to the Carolinas came mainly from the Southside and southern parts of the Shenandoah Valley. The second wave left from the Valley of Virginia to the Southwest, from the piedmont to Kentucky, and from the Northern Neck, western Virginia, and the northern Valley to the Ohio country.

These great rivers of movement were supported by a web of smaller tributaries. Every county of the Old Dominion contributed to each major flow. In general, however, Virginia's migration was a classic example of migration streams, with specific origins and destinations.

Virginia's various migration streams also had different social characteristics. Some were more heavily dominated by elites. This was notably the case in Kentucky, where the gentry of Virginia had special advantages that arose from historical circumstances. The movement south to North Carolina had a different texture. In every migration stream leaders can be identified—specific individuals who set the flow in motion, led it to its destination, and organized the society that took root there. In this vast movement individual motives, values, purposes, and cultural beliefs made a difference, just as they had done in the movement of Sir William Berkeley's elite from England to America. The story of migration out of Virginia was in many ways similar to what had preceded it within the Old Dominion itself. We find the same patterns of cultural persistence and increasing cultural pluralism. Different groups of migrants preserved their distinctive ways as they moved into new environments. Let us examine this complex process in some of its individual parts.

The Coastal Stream: Southern Virginia
to the Carolinas and Georgia

The first large movement from Virginia began early in the seventeenth century and flowed not west but south. As early as 1607 men sailed from Jamestown to explore "by sea and land" the coast of what is now North Carolina. Settlers followed close behind. The first to appear in the records was Nathaniel Batts, a Virginian who built a house in what is now Bertie County, North Carolina, sometime before 1657. He was still there in 1672 when George Fox passed through, scouting possible sites for a Quaker colony.[12]

That stretch of coast was called South Virginia on early maps. It became the colony of a colony, called Albemarle, with a governor appointed by Sir William Berkeley. By 1675 the population had increased to an estimated 4,000 settlers, mostly from Virginia, and was expanding rapidly.

From the start the settlement had a distinctive tone, with more small farmers and nothing like Berkeley's cavalier elite. Several of the Albemarle Council were unable even to sign their names. Sir William Berkeley wrote of his own appointee, Governor Samuel Stephens (1629–1670), a native Virginian, that "he had not that fullness of understanding wch men bred in Europe and early accustomed to manage affaires of great Importance usually have."[13]

The Piedmont Stream: The Southern Highlands

The migration from Virginia to coastal Carolina was followed in the eighteenth century by a larger flow from the Southside and the southern Valley of Virginia into the Carolina backcountry. Most of these emigrants merely passed through Virginia on their way south; many were British borderers.

Typical of this migration was Benjamin Cleveland. Like many of the backsettlers who are remembered as Scotch-Irish, his roots were in the border counties of northern England. His family had emigrated from Yorkshire's North Riding to Virginia. Benjamin Cleveland was born near Bull Run in 1738 and grew up in Orange County near the Albemarle line. He disliked the routine of farming and became a hunter, roaming widely through the southern highlands. As a young man he acquired 10,000 acres in North Carolina, built a home called Roundabout in a horseshoe bend of the Yadkin River at the foot of the Blue Ridge Mountains, and joined the backcountry gentry.

The spirit of this elite was very different from that of Virginia's gentry. The rules of order in Surry County's Committee of Safety required that "every person keep their seats . . . only one to speak at a time . . . and that any member behaving disorderly either by getting drunk, swearing, or any other vices, shall be fined." During the Revolution, Cleveland led a band of backcountry riflemen called Cleveland's Devils. They fought at Kings Mountain, hunted Tories across the countryside, and hanged them without the formality of a trial. One day they caught two "tory horse thieves." One was hanged instantly. Cleveland turned to the other, pointed toward the Tory who was twisting at the rope's end, and said, "You have your choice, either take your place beside him or cut your ears off and leave the country forever." The Loyalist asked for a knife, whetted it on a brick, gritted his teeth, amputated his own ears, and "with blood streaming down his cheeks, left the country."

After the Revolution, Cleveland discovered that the title to his own beloved estate of Roundabout was "improper." He was forced to surrender the property and moved on to South Carolina where he lived as a squatter in the Tugaloo Valley until his death in 1806. His offspring moved on to Georgia, as did many other Virginians.[14]

The Georgia Piedmont

Many others followed. A favored destination for Virginians from the piedmont was the piedmont county of Wilkes in Georgia. A study of that county's planters in the 1850s found that many were descended from Virginians who arrived in the 1780s and 1790s. The pioneers of this group arrived during the War for Independence. One of the first was John Williston Talbot (1735–1798), who came to Wilkes before 1782. The heaviest stream, however, consisted of Revolutionary veterans who moved south after the war and reached Wilkes through the Broad River valley.

Of these migrants E. Merton Coulter has written, "The Virginians were a remarkable group, constituting an element whose importance is hard to overestimate."[15] They came from every part of Virginia. John Pope

(1749–1802) and Margaret Hunter Pope (1758–1836) left Westmoreland County on the Northern Neck. George Willis (1754–1827) and his wife, Susanna Baker Willis (1747–1843), came from New Kent and King William counties.

But most settlers who found the Georgia piedmont attractive emigrated from the piedmont counties of Virginia in search of lands similar to those they had known at home. Among these emigrants were Colonel Benjamin Taliaferro (1750–1827) and Martha Meriwether Taliaferro of Amherst County, who came in 1784. John Anderson (1741–1801), a Revolutionary veteran, and Mary Southland Anderson left Hanover County in 1785 and arrived in Wilkes in a party led by her family. John Fanning, who arrived about 1787, came from Sussex County. Richard Fortson (1777–1836) was from Orange and his wife, Lucy Arnold Fortson (1778–1847), from Louisa. William Brooke (1740–1832) and Edith Brooke (1741–1822) from Amelia and Lunenburg counties reached Wilkes about 1791. James Anthony of Henry County came in 1793. Christopher Irvin and Louisa Tucker of Campbell County moved first to Oglethorpe County, then Wilkes, in 1792–94. The children and grandchildren of this elite moved rapidly into positions of eminence in Georgia politics. Robert Toombs (d. 1815) and Catherine Huling Toombs were the parents of Georgia's U.S. congressman and senator Robert Toombs (1810–1885), a secretary of state of the Confederacy and nearly its president.[16]

This piedmont migration continued for many years. As late as the 1850s a region called "Little Virginia" was settled in Cherokee and Cass counties. The leader was David Mahan, who saw possibilities for tobacco growing in Georgia. A historian of Bartow County writes, "These Virginians grew tobacco successfully along the Salacoa creek and erected four factories and packing houses until the revenue tax became so high there was no profit and operations ceased."[17]

The Valley Stream: Virginians in East Tennessee

Other streams of population movement flowed in a different direction, from Virginia to the Southwest. The sweep of settlement through the Valley of Virginia led inexorably into the valley of East Tennessee. In 1769 William Bean of Virginia raised a cabin along the Watauga, a tributary of the Holston, thereby becoming the first white settler in what later became the state of Tennessee. Within three years several hundred settlers followed, including

John Carter and William Tatham, who wrote the Articles of Association adopted by the Watauga settlers in 1772.

These people came believing the region belonged to Virginia, but the Lochaber survey line run in 1770–71 showed that most of the area belonged to North Carolina. Because the settlers were too remote to be served by either colony, they adopted a form of local government "taking (by desire of our constituents) the Virginia laws for our guide, so near as the situation of affairs would admit."[18]

This ad hoc arrangement was called the Watauga Association. It has been remembered as a precursor of the Declaration of Independence, largely because Virginia's last royal governor, Lord Dunmore, misread it. He declared that the settlers had "erected themselves into though an inconsiderable, yet a Separate State; the Consequences of which may prove hereafter detrimen-

58. Captain John Smith was the first Englishman to mention the "tomahack," an Indian artifact quickly adapted by Europeans to their own uses. This silver inlaid example was not for scalping foes or hacking brush. It was the fashionable accessory of gentleman-pioneer Daniel Smith, who studied at the College of William and Mary, became a noted surveyor, moved to Nashville in 1783, and was appointed Tennessee's first secretary of state in 1796. It could also be smoked as a peace pipe.

tal to the peace and Security of the other Colonies; it at least Sets a dangerous example to the people of America, of forming Governments distinct
from and independent of His Majesty's authority."[19]

The purpose was in fact very different. The settlers were not disassociat-
ing themselves from England but associating with Virginia. The Watauga Association specifically reenacted the laws of the Old Dominion on new lands
beyond the Appalachians. It represented the migration not only of Virginians but also of their customs and beliefs.

Backcountry Gentry: John Sevier

A leader of this community was John Sevier. In his family migration was a
way of life. His grandfather was a French Huguenot who moved to London,
married an Englishwoman, and changed his name from Xavier to Sevier. His
father, Valentine Sevier, moved again from England to Maryland and settled
on the frontier in the Shenandoah Valley of Virginia, where he became a
prosperous farmer and Indian trader.

John Sevier was born in what is now Rockingham County, then part of
Augusta County. Even as a child he was often on the go. When the French
and Indian War began, the family moved east to the comparative safety of
Fredericksburg, where he attended the local academy. Two years later the Seviers returned to the Valley to find their farm burned by the Indians. The
family started over and soon was prospering once again.

Responsibility came early to young people in that world. At the age of sixteen, John Sevier married Sarah Hawkins, by whom he fathered ten children.
Later by his second wife, Catherine "Bonnie Kate" Sherrill, he had seven
more children. At nineteen he laid out the Valley town of New Market, sold
lots, and built a tavern there. In his twenties he moved his family to the Holston Valley in what is now Sullivan County, Tennessee. His lands were believed to be part of Virginia until a survey in 1779–80 ascertained definitively
that they belonged to North Carolina instead.[20]

This was only the beginning of Sevier's westward movement. In the words
of Arthur Whitaker, "For the next seventeen years he continued to move
down the valley with the advancing frontier." On the Tennessee frontier John
Sevier made his reputation as a warrior. He survived thirty-five battles against
the British and Indians, innumerable backcountry brawls over land and

power, a feud between the Seviers and Tiptons, an altercation with fiery young Andrew Jackson, an arrest for fighting in North Carolina, and a jail-break organized by his backcountry friends.

John Sevier was the new model of the western leader, very different from Sir William Berkeley's cavalier-foresters or Alexander Spotswood's backward-venturing gentlemen. Sevier was the prototype of what W. J. Cash called the upcountry "hell-of-a-fellow." He had been raised and married within the north British border culture that had adapted so successfully to the American backcountry. So popular did Sevier become among his fellow frontiersmen that he was elected Tennessee's first governor and was returned to office five times. He won his following not by social rank but by courage and charisma.

59. John Sevier (1745–1815), of Huguenot descent, married into the culture of north British borderers and became an archetype of the "hell-of-a-fellow" leader who flourished in the southern backcountry.

Virginians in Middle Tennessee

In 1779–80 settlement skipped over the forbidding Cumberland Plateau to the more inviting lands of the Cumberland Basin (now Middle Tennessee). The leaders of these pioneering expeditions were Virginians. The first map of Tennessee was drawn by Virginian Daniel Smith, who had surveyed the Virginia–North Carolina line in 1779. His work verified that both the Watauga and Cumberland settlements were within North Carolina rather than Virginia.

Settlement was led by men from several regions of the Old Dominion — two men in particular. One was James Robertson, a Brunswick County native of north British border stock, who led the overland party to the French Lick (now Nashville), arriving on Christmas Day 1779.

The other was John Donelson, whose roots were in the tidewater. He was born on the Eastern Shore, married Rachel Stockley of Accomack County,

60. James Robertson (1742–1814), a native of Brunswick County, Virginia, is called "The Father of Tennessee." He was among the first settlers in East Tennessee and in 1780 was cofounder of Nashville and Middle Tennessee with another Virginian, John Donelson.

and moved west in search of land, first to Brunswick County, then to Pittsylvania County, and on to the Tennessee country.

Donelson led a flotilla of flatboats 985 miles down the Holston and Tennessee rivers, north on the Ohio to the Cumberland River, and up the Cumberland to a meeting with Robertson at their rendezvous, which they named Fort Nashborough. This was a migration of families; traveling with Donelson and several other men were 120 women and children. Another child was born onboard a flatboat and later killed by the Indians. Donelson himself commanded the expedition from the flatboat *Adventure,* which carried his wife, eleven children, his slaves, his household silver, and furniture. His Virginia-born daughter Rachel, then thirteen, later became the wife of Andrew

61. When John Donelson (c. 1725–1786), a native of Virginia's Eastern Shore, made his epic voyage to Tennessee in the flatboat *Adventure* (1779), he carried with him this handsome desk, made in Virginia about 1770. Donelson used it on the frontier until 1786, when he was killed by Indians. Five years later his Virginia-born daughter Rachel became the consort of Andrew Jackson.

Jackson. They reached their rendezvous with Robertson on April 24, 1780, four months after they had embarked on the Holston River.[21]

Westward Migration and Upward Mobility: The Life of Thomas Hardeman

The fertility of Middle Tennessee attracted many migrants of middling and even humble circumstances. Typical was Thomas Hardeman of Pittsylvania County, Virginia. The first Thomas Hardeman in Virginia had arrived before 1660. His descendants were coopers who became justices of the peace, militia officers, and members of the House of Burgesses. John Hardeman III migrated from the tidewater to Goochland, then to Albemarle, where his son Thomas was born in 1750. The family moved again, to Pittsylvania County in Southwest Virginia. In 1768 Thomas joined a party of hunters who crossed the mountains into the valleys of the Holston and Powell rivers and went as far as what became Nashville. Then he returned to Virginia, married, rented acreage, and worked as a tenant in the Dan River lowlands. He and his wife shifted annually from one location to another, acquiring a few livestock but chafing under the "restraint and monotony" of tenancy.[22]

Hardeman disliked his subordination to the tidewater planters who held the backcountry in a form of vassalage. He had seen the lands to the west and in 1777 or 1778 moved his family to what became Tennessee. Indian attacks, however, forced them to return to Pittsylvania. Finally they settled at Boone's Creek in the Watauga area.

Hardeman fought at Kings Mountain and after the Revolution, as a reward for his services, received 640 acres on the Little Harpeth River. He and his family, like the Donelsons, traveled from East Tennessee to Nashville by flatboat. With each move westward to an area of cheaper land, Hardeman bettered his holdings, although at the cost of heightened danger to his family and himself. Soon the former tenant was a planter with 7,000 acres.

Hardeman had thirteen children and was resolved that none would be a tenant. He gave sizable parcels to his sons and smaller but significant holdings to his daughters. When the last child was grown, the widower Hardeman, age sixty-one, left Tennessee for Missouri with two or three slaves, a one-horse cart, a saddle horse, and a long rifle.

His son John followed in 1817 and in 1823 married a girl from a Virginia family. Later, John Hardeman moved on to New Mexico. A brother went

62. Ann Neely Hardeman married Nicholas Perkins Hardeman in Tennessee, where he had moved with his father in 1778.

to Texas. Their children pushed on to Oregon and California. Of old Thomas Hardeman and his siblings, three went to Georgia and four to Tennessee. None remained in Virginia.[23]

Alabama

The migration stream that flowed through the western valleys of Virginia and East Tennessee continued farther south. Virginia settlers followed the Tennessee River to the rich alluvial black-soil lands that stretched in a great crescent across the northern part of what is now the state of Alabama.[24]

This movement was led by many of Virginia's greatest planter families — the Tayloes of Mount Airy, the Cockes of Bremo, and the Hooe family of King George County.[25] A large number of Virginia craftsmen followed: housewrights, carvers, cabinetmakers, wagon makers, tailors, and others who catered to Virginia tastes. In the period from 1818 to 1830, the rising town of Huntsville, Alabama, was home to Virginia silversmiths George Stuart, Littleton Figg, and James Cain, who supplied the needs of planters in surrounding Madison County. Their presence was an important part of the transit of culture into the Southwest.

Kentucky Fever: Virginians on the Dark and Bloody Ground

Two stock figures in American folklore are the rough western pioneer and the polished southern gentleman. They are remembered as opposites, but in the expansion of Virginia these two types were one. Nowhere was linkage stronger than in the emigration to Kentucky, which in terms of numbers became a more important destination for Virginians than Tennessee.

This movement began in 1750 with the travels of Dr. Thomas Walker, a classic example of the gentleman pioneer. Like so many of the First Families of Virginia, Walker's ancestors were people of substance who migrated in the mid–seventeenth century from Staffordshire. The second son of Thomas and Susanna Peachy Walker of King and Queen County, Virginia, he studied medicine in Williamsburg and practiced in Fredericksburg. By his marriage to Mildred Thornton in 1741, he acquired an estate of 11,000 acres on the edge of settlement in what became Albemarle County.

For the rest of his life, Walker was caught up in the westward movement. While working as a physician and planter, he was also a storekeeper and developed a trading network from the piedmont to the Valley of Virginia and beyond. In 1748 he also helped to lay off 100,000 acres along the Holston River in Southwest Virginia for Colonel James Patton of Augusta County. The next year Walker, Edmund Pendleton, Peter Jefferson, and Joshua Fry were among the founders of the Loyal Land Company, which received a grant of 800,000 acres beyond the mountains in the West from the governor's Council on the condition that they settle the area.

Walker was chosen to lead an expedition to locate 800,000 fertile acres that would be sold in small allotments to actual settlers. He set out from Louisa County in March 1750 and on April 13 reached an opening through the Appalachian Mountains that he was the first to call Cumberland Gap.

Walker traveled more than 700 miles in all—into the rugged terrain of eastern Kentucky—but never reached the fertile bluegrass country that lay just beyond. He was not the first explorer to pass that way, but his expedition was the earliest to demonstrate that the Cumberland Gap was the best way into Kentucky.

Others followed in his footsteps. Ten years after Walker's discovery, a party of "long hunters" brought back accounts of the rich lands in the bluegrass country. Among these hunters was Daniel Boone. On a trip during the winter of 1772–73 he found that land speculators from Virginia had sent agents to survey tracts along the Ohio River, and some had reached the Kentucky River. Knowing that settlement soon would begin, he was determined that his family should be among the first. The party of forty or fifty emigrants that he led was ambushed at the entrance to the Cumberland Gap and had to retreat to Southwest Virginia.

This was one of several incidents that led to Lord Dunmore's War, a response of the Indians to repeated incursions into the Ohio Valley. Virginia's royal governor, John Murray, Lord Dunmore, himself led the men of Virginia into battle against the formidable Shawnee warriors. Dunmore and Colonel Andrew Lewis of Augusta County each led divisions from old Fort Pitt (renamed Fort Dunmore). Scottish chieftain that he was, the governor marched on foot with his men and carried his own pack.

Lewis's division was surprised at Point Pleasant (now in West Virginia) on October 10, 1774, but managed to defeat the Shawnees under Chief Cornstalk and the Mingos under Chief Logan. Dunmore then marched to the Shawnee towns along the Scioto River (now in Ohio) and dictated a peace that, although denounced by many frontiersmen as too moderate,

63

made more secure settlement of what is now West Virginia and opened up Kentucky.

Thereafter settlement began again, and Boone led a party along the Wilderness Road in 1775, the first of many groups that he escorted into Kentucky. Fighting with the Indians continued for years, however, not only in the parts that today are West Virginia and Kentucky but also in Virginia proper.

Virginia laid claim to the "dark and bloody ground" of Kentucky as part of its own dominion. On December 31, 1776, the new state government of Virginia approved a petition carried by George Rogers Clark and organized the region as Kentucky County—partly to block the rival ambitions of North Carolina land speculator Richard Henderson.

Among the pioneers were two rough-hewn Virginians, Benjamin Logan and Simon Kenton. Both were instrumental in defending the infant settlement against Indians, British, and Carolinians alike. The two came from British border stock and carried that culture into Kentucky.

Benjamin Logan (1743–1802) was typical of the backcountry ascendancy that came to dominate the southern highlands. He had been born in Augusta County, Virginia, of Scotch-Irish stock. Largely self-taught, he was described as a "large, raw-boned man, fully six feet [tall, who] sometimes fought at fisticuffs" and was "somewhat arbitrary and overbearing." Logan was among the first to accept Virginia's offer of 400 acres to anyone who would move to Kentucky, build a cabin, and raise a corn crop. During the Revolution, when Kentucky was nearly abandoned, Logan stood his ground until reinforcements arrived. After the war he became a man of wealth and a popular political leader. In 1796 he won a plurality of votes for governor of Kentucky but was defeated in the electoral college. He held many other high offices in Kentucky.[26]

Simon Kenton is thought to have been born in Fauquier County, Virginia, the son of a Scotch-Irish immigrant father and a Scotch-Welsh mother. Thinking he had killed a rival in love, he fled west to escape a hanging. He changed his name, wandered two years in the wilderness, became a scout in Dunmore's War, saved the life of Daniel Boone, served in the Revolution, was captured by the Indians, made to run the gauntlet eight times, and bound three times to a stake for burning. Handed over to the British, he escaped and made his way home. His adventures made him a famous figure on the frontier, but he never learned to read or write and could barely sign his name. After the war Kenton discovered that the man he thought he had killed was still alive. He resumed his name and brought his father's family to Kentucky, but he himself kept wandering and moved to Ohio, where he died in poverty. Some writers made him into the prototypical pioneer. More accurately he was one type among many others, a footloose fugitive living precariously on the edge of settlement.

On the heels of these men, a human deluge poured down the western rivers and along the Wilderness Road. One observer reported that "one would think . . . that half Virginia Intended to Kentuck." Another Virginian wrote, "People are Running Mad for Kentucky Hereabouts!" The Reverend Lewis Craig, a Baptist preacher in Virginia, said, "Heaven is a Kentucky of a Place," and his entire congregation moved there as a body. By 1783 there were 12,000 white inhabitants — by 1785, 30,000 — half of them from Virginia. They came mainly from two regions of the state — the Valley and the piedmont, particularly the seed counties of Augusta and Albemarle.[27]

This movement westward into Kentucky quickly came to be dominated

64. Benjamin Logan was a self-made backcountry leader who made a fortune in western lands and narrowly failed of election as governor of Kentucky. Lack of formal education was cited as the cause, which may explain the presence of a book in this portrait.

65. Simon Kenton (1755–1836) personified another western type. A footloose fugitive from the law in Virginia, he became a frontier hero in Kentucky and died a pauper in Ohio.

by an elite of gentry families from Virginia. Settlement of the piedmont and Valley regions of Virginia had taken place largely on this group's terms. Squatters were few there. The Royal Proclamation of 1763 deterred settlement beyond the Appalachians by planters, but small farmers who were willing to chance the lack of formal paper titles continued westward, weakening gentry control of the process.[28]

To reassert that control, Kentucky County was created in 1776. Gentry families moved early into Kentucky and often were able to obtain title to good land before they left. Many owed their first contact with Kentucky to government service, fighting Indians in Lord Dunmore's War or campaigning in the War of Independence, or to experience as surveyors of rival land claims. They used their influence with great effect. As early as 1780 a petitioner to Congress complained that "almost the whole of the lands . . . are Engrossed into the hands of a few Interested men, the greater part of which live at ease in the internal parts of Virginia."[29]

These gentry coordinated their migration and settlement with others to whom they were related. One finds in Kentucky during the 1780s and 1790s a Preston-Breckinridge-Brown family group and a Christian-Fleming-Trigg network,[30] just as seventeenth-century Virginia had its Filmer-Byrd-Beverley-Carter-Culpeper-Berkeley cousinage and its Northampton connection.[31]

A case in point is the career of John Breckinridge, attorney, planter, and legislator from Albemarle County. He was well placed to receive accurate information about Kentucky, and his wealth and connections enabled him to act on that knowledge. Just as William Byrd II had used slave gangs to open new areas of Virginia to settlement, Breckinridge sent eighteen of his slaves ahead to Kentucky. In the customary way he made an exploratory journey himself before returning to Virginia to arrange for the actual move in 1793. The West was not only an escape valve for the discontented, as students of Frederick Jackson Turner stressed, but a destination for those who were already well off.[32]

By 1789 the demand of Kentuckians for self-government was irresistible. Kentucky was admitted to the Union as a state in 1792. This event marked the end of Virginia as the West and its claims to the West but was only the beginning of the story of Virginians in the West. By 1800 Kentucky had 220,000 people, most of whom were Virginians or their offspring.

The Portable Planter: David Meade
of Virginia and Kentucky

In 1796, three years after the Breckinridges, fifty-two-year-old David Meade left his Virginia plantation for Kentucky. His grandfather had come to Virginia late in the seventeenth century and acquired an estate at the mouth of the Nansemond River, where David Meade was born in 1744. At the age of seven he was sent to England to be educated. He returned in 1761, married in 1768, and in 1769 served briefly in the House of Burgesses. In 1774 he sold the Nansemond estate he had inherited and bought Maycox, a plantation of 600 acres south of the James River across from Westover. There he lived until 1796.

The estate did not flourish. Except for a few acres along the James, Maycox consisted "of very poor land." Apparently Meade suffered reverses during the Revolution. Thereafter, a French visitor to Maycox observed that Meade "cannot prevail upon himself to make his negroes work. He is even so disgusted with a culture wherein it is necessary to make use of slaves that he is tempted to sell his possessions in Virginia and remove to New England."[33]

Meade was unable to bring himself to take so radical a step and began to look in another direction for a solution to his problems. During the early 1790s he admitted to having an advanced case of "Kentucky fever," and in November 1794 he offered his Virginia lands for sale. In 1795 he sent his son to Kentucky, who bought for his father a 320-acre tract nine miles from Lexington.[34]

Meade moved his entire plantation to Kentucky in a single expedition. He wrote that the "cavalcade consisted of the coachee, my chair, our baggage waggon, two hired waggons with the first teams in Frederick, altogether twenty-one horses and about fifty souls," black and white.[35] Meade led this procession first to his brother's home in Winchester, Frederick County, then through western Maryland into Pennsylvania, and on to Red Stone Fort on the Monongahela River, where they boarded "Kentucky boats," or flatboats, that took them down the Ohio River to Limestone (now Maysville), Kentucky. From there they proceeded overland to Lexington.

Meade warned his nephews that to come out they would need £500 or £1,000 beyond traveling expenses. He did not discourage them, however. He described Kentucky as "the most fertile tract of country in the world." Of the county in which he lived, he wrote, "No part of Virginia is as thickly set-

66. David Meade was a child of privilege. Born in 1744 on a large plantation, he was educated in England where this portrait was painted, c. 1760. In 1796 he moved his entire plantation to Kentucky and became one of the Virginia elite who dominated the first western state.

67. Sarah Waters Meade (d. 1828) moved to Kentucky with her husband and became mistress of a great plantation and arbiter of frontier society. One of her many guests wrote, "She is very mild and lady-like, and . . . plays upon her piano-forte, the first one brought to Kentucky, with the facility and cheerfulness of a young girl."

tled as Fayette." In Meade's view the possessor of £2,000–£3,000 and some slaves could live "as well or better" than in Virginia and with more opportunity "in the way of procuring lands for his children."[36]

To his sister Meade wrote, "How much it would contribute to our happiness if some of our friends were inclined to come out and settle here. . . . how abundantly and handsomely would some of my Virginia friends live in Kentucky upon two or three hundred acres." He asked his sister to circulate his letter. "I would particularly convince my nephew Richard," he wrote, "that He has been too much prejudiced against Kentucky." Richard should "look to it as a refuge from the evils which I have experienced for a few years past to the East." He conceded that his nephew David, who held a lucrative office, should remain in Virginia, but even he should buy "Military lands for the benefit of his Sons."[37]

Meade built a great house in the wilderness, a Virginia mansion made entirely of logs. He quickly made acquaintance "with many genteel people" in Kentucky, mostly Virginians. His nearest neighbors were Colonel Joseph Crockett, captain of the 7th Virginia Regiment of the Continental Line in

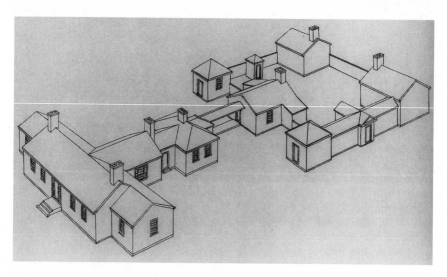

68. Virginia planter David Meade built a house in Kentucky and called it La Chaumière des Prairies (the cottage in the meadows). It was made of logs in the frontier manner but followed the Georgian symmetry of tidewater Virginia and southern England. A visitor wrote, "There were cooks, dining room servants, coachmen, footmen, valets and chambermaids."

the Revolution, and Colonel Gabriel Madison, brother of Bishop James Madison of Virginia. Upon first arriving in Kentucky, Meade had stayed in Lexington for a time to "fix our females for a few weeks in as large a society as possible to divert their thoughts as much as I could from the objects which they had left behind in Virginia. . . . our daughter Salley was indeed very unhappy. . . . The vapor soon exhaled and after a ball or two—many tea parties and much flirtation—her ladyship soon became as zealous Lexingtonian as any in it."[38]

Certainly, Meade did his share to transplant Virginia gentility to the frontier. Once he was established, his house servants wore livery. "The magnificent solid silver plate, which was brought from England, and the costly china and cut glass were on such a lavish scale, that one hundred guests could easily be served at one time."[39]

Horace Holley, who visited the Meades in the 1810s, wrote: "He and his wife dress in the costume of the olden time; he wears the square coat and great cuffs, the long court vest, knee breeches, and white silk stockings at all times: the buttons of his coat and vest are of silver with the Meade crest on them. Mrs. Meade had the long waist, the stays, the ruffles at the elbow and the cap of the last century. She is very mild and lady-like, and though between sixty and seventy, plays upon her piano-forte, the first one brought to Kentucky, with the facility and cheerfulness of a young girl."[40]

Although a traditionalist in dress and manners, David Meade was a thoroughgoing Jeffersonian and carried west an ideology that was at once elitist and libertarian. He was the very embodiment of the intensely practical Virginia gentry who had unsentimentally cast aside the British connection as an encumbrance and took the same attitude toward emigration. He also was a classic example of what Marion Nelson Winship has called the "portable planter," an agrarian elite that identified itself more with a system of production than with a single place or property.

There were many of this type. Another "portable planter" was Thomas Jones, who sold his Essex County plantation and moved to Kentucky with eighteen slaves. Like Meade, he expected to replicate his lifestyle in Kentucky. Indeed, they believed that it could only be maintained by moving their entire plantations out of Virginia.[41]

Though sometimes discontented by reduced circumstances, this elite sought not to escape or change a way of life but to preserve it by expanding and transplanting the culture into which it had been born.

A Lamentation for the Long Hunter: Daniel Boone

And what of the men these Virginia gentry elbowed aside? What of old Daniel Boone? The historical Boone did not flourish in Kentucky as the Virginia planters had done. The romantic view was that he was Rousseau's natural man, who could plant settlements but not abide to live in them. The truth was more prosaic. Boone invested all that he could in land and during the 1780s acquired warrants, certificates, and rights valued at between £7,000 and £10,000. These documents enabled him to file claims for more than 39,000 acres. Each claim, however, had to be defended through a process of survey and grant of patent, and if some other claimants could show prior or better rights, the entry and investment were lost.[42]

Virginia's chaotic metes-and-bounds system of claiming land and the intense speculative fever made Kentucky a crazy quilt of overlapping or "shingled" claims and a fertile field for aspiring attorneys such as John Brown and Henry Clay. Boone managed successfully to defend claims for more than 12,000 acres, but the commonwealth of Virginia levied property taxes on lands claimed, rather than land patented. The law forced him to pay taxes on thousands of acres of contested lands that yielded no income. From 1786 to 1789 alone he was party to at least ten lawsuits. Legal fees bled him dry. His sense of honor made him pay many debts a less scrupulous man could have evaded. In many cases he was also called as an expert witness, usually enraging at least one side. So often was he threatened in these controversies that "his own Kentucky was as dangerous to him as in Indian times."

In 1799 Daniel Boone moved on to Missouri. Ten years later, aged seventy-five, he did not own an acre of land. In this respect he was like many others. By the 1790s fewer than half of the households in Kentucky—the new Canaan—owned any land of their own.[43]

The Potomac Stream: George Washington as Gentleman-Frontiersman

The northwest frontier had long attracted much interest in Virginia, especially from landowning grandees of the Northern Neck. In 1749 the Ohio Company was founded to exploit this region. Among the company's members were various Lees, Washingtons, Carters, and Fairfaxes, as well as merchants in London. The company received a grant of 500,000 acres on the Ohio River, based on the old 1609 charter that had defined the boundaries of Virginia to include all lands 200 miles north and south of Old Point Comfort, extending "sea to sea, west and northwest."[44]

By the Treaty of Lancaster in 1744 the Iroquois had ceded much of the Ohio country to Britain, but France still asserted a claim. In the summer of 1749, the marquis de La Galissonière, governor-general of Canada, ordered a French officer, Captain Pierre Joseph Céloron de Blainville, to deposit six lead plates at strategic points along the Ohio River. This stroke was meant to be a bold assertion of French sovereignty over the Ohio Valley. It was intended specifically to discourage English colonization by the newly formed Ohio Company of Virginia.[45]

69. This lead plate was laid by Captain Pierre Joseph Céloron de Blainville on August 18, 1749, at the confluence of the Ohio and Great Kanawha rivers as part of a coordinated effort to claim the entire Ohio watershed for France. It is the only surviving intact example. Another was discovered in 1798 at the mouth of the Muskingum River in Ohio by hardheaded Yankees, who used it to assert their sovereignty in another way. They melted it into bullets.

Indians removed one of the French plates and sent it to Governor George Clinton of New York, who forwarded it to the Lords of Trade in London. Seeing a golden opportunity to turn the Indians against the French, Clinton informed the Indians that "it was a matter of the greatest consequence, involving the possession of their lands and hunting-grounds and that . . . the French ought immediately to be expelled."[46]

Reports of the lead plates were carried also to Williamsburg. On behalf of fellow speculators in the Ohio Land Company, Lieutenant Governor Robert Dinwiddie received authorization from London to expel the French if they encroached on English land. By the terms of early charters, Virginia claimed everything west to the Pacific Ocean. Conflict was inevitable.

An ambitious twenty-one-year-old Virginian named George Washington offered to deliver an ultimatum to the French. His proposal was accepted. Washington was guided to the forks of the Ohio (now Pittsburgh) by Christopher Gist, who was thought to be the first English-speaking American to see the Ohio Valley. The English demands were presented to the local French commander and promptly rejected.[47]

In April 1754 Washington was sent back, this time as colonel of the Virginia Regiment, a special force of red-coated provincial regulars. They had been raised because the militia were reluctant to march in defense of distant speculations by Virginia grandees.[48]

Washington's orders were to expel the French from Virginia's northwest frontier. The French commander, hearing of his approach, dispatched Ensign Coulon Jumonville with a few troops to warn him off. Fearing ambush, the Virginians attacked the small French party on May 28, 1754, killing Jumonville and several others.

Aware that a larger French force was nearby, Washington threw up a palisade aptly called Fort Necessity at the Great Meadows in present-day Pennsylvania. The French surrounded the fort and began an assault that the Virginians were unable to withstand. Washington agreed to a capitulation on what he thought were terms of honor and incautiously signed the document of surrender in a language he could not read. Then he was allowed to march home with his men.

In Europe the document caused a sensation. It referred to Jumonville's death as "l'assasinat." By signing it, Washington appeared to have confessed to the murder of a diplomatic emissary. In England, Horace Walpole wrote that "the volley of a young Virginian in the backwoods of America set the world on fire."[49]

The Ohio Valley was to the eighteenth century as the Balkans and Southeast Asia were to the nineteenth and twentieth—a cockpit of international rivalry. The actions of a twenty-two-year-old land-hungry officer on the Virginia frontier led to a world war that was fought in Europe, India, and Africa as well as North America.

For a time Washington's reputation was tarnished by this event, but it gained new luster in 1755 after General Edward Braddock's defeat. Washington helped restore order and staved off further disaster.

In 1763 the war that Washington had begun ended in a triumph for British arms. France was expelled from Canada, and its claims to the Ohio Valley were extinguished. The British government declared that the land west of the Appalachians should be reserved for the Indians. Washington regarded this Proclamation of 1763 as *"a temporary expedient to quiet the minds of the Indians."* By 1769 the Indians had, in fact, agreed to various concessions all along the line.[50]

Heavy pressures were building in Virginia for settlement of the Ohio Valley. To induce men to join Washington's 1754 expedition, Dinwiddie had issued a proclamation offering 200,000 acres in the West to those who signed up. On November 29, 1769, the Virginia House of Burgesses directed that a list be drawn up of all lands applied for in the Ohio country. On December 15 Washington made a formal petition on behalf of the officers and men of his 1754 command that the 200,000 acres promised by Dinwiddie be set aside in several places along the Ohio River. Virginia's governor Norborne Berkeley, baron de Botetourt, granted the request.

On October 5, 1770, Washington set out for the Ohio.[51] At the confluence of the Ohio and Great Kanawha rivers was a peninsula of rich bottomland that Washington reserved for himself. William Crawford, who accompanied Washington, did most of the actual surveying. Later, when the lands were allotted among the veterans, some of them were "a good deal shagereened" that Washington and Crawford had taken the best for themselves. Washington countered that not only had he borne the greatest expense for the survey, but also "if it had not been for my unremitting attention to every favorable circumstance, not a single acre of land would ever have been obtained."[52]

As an officer Washington was entitled to 15,000 acres. He also bought up some of the 400–acre allotments made to private soldiers who preferred cash to property rights in distant lands. Late in 1772 Governor Lord Dunmore approved Washington's application for four tracts along the Ohio and Great Kanawha rivers totaling 20,150 acres. The outbreak of the Revolutionary War prevented Washington from doing anything with these lands until 1784, when he ran notices offering leases to settlers.[53]

Virginians and the Opening of Ohio

The American Revolution delayed only momentarily the influx of settlers to those areas. In 1778 Virginia created Illinois County and sent George Rogers Clark of Albemarle County to that region. By 1776 he was in Kentucky, which he represented in the Virginia legislature. When the War for Independence began, Clark persuaded Governor Patrick Henry to send a military force into Kentucky to protect the settlements against the British and Indians. He was given command and proposed not merely a defensive campaign but a design for the conquest of British bases in the Old Northwest. Clark wrote to Henry: "I know the case is desperate but Sir, we must either quit the cuntrey or attact. . . . No time is to be lost. Was I shoer of a reinforcement I should not attempt it. Who knows what fortune will do for us? Great things have been affected by a few men."[54]

Patrick Henry sent secret orders to proceed. From George Wythe, George Mason, and the governor, Clark also received assurances that "if he and his associates were successful they might rely on the Assembly for grants from the conquered lands."[55] With fewer than 180 Virginians, Clark traveled by boat down the Ohio River, then marched 240 miles through the wilderness and captured Kaskaskia, Cahokia, and Vincennes. In campaigning that continued even after Yorktown, Clark's small forces drove the British back to Detroit and defeated their Shawnee allies as well. It was largely through Clark's efforts that the Northwest became part of the United States at the end of the Revolutionary War. But in 1781 Virginia had decided to cede its claims north of the Ohio River to the national government and refused to reimburse Clark for his expenses.

Virginia's cession, which formally took place on March 1, 1784, was part of a coordinated effort among the states to promote national unity. Virginia ceded to the national government its claims north of the Ohio River with

70. In 1778–79 George Rogers Clark's small band of Virginians successively captured the British posts of Kaskaskia, Cahokia, and Vincennes, in the Illinois country. His victories helped to ensure that the Old Northwest became part of the United States. The portrait is by John Wesley Jarvis.

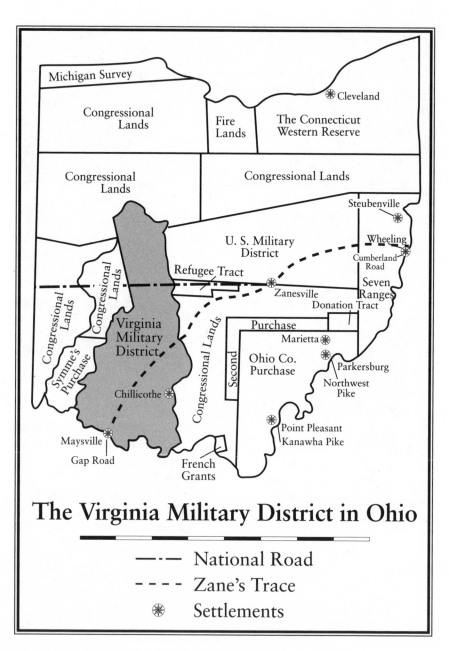

The Virginia Military District in Ohio

—·— National Road

- - - - Zane's Trace

✳ Settlements

Labels on map:

Michigan Survey

Congressional Lands

Fire Lands

The Connecticut Western Reserve

✳ Cleveland

Congressional Lands

Congressional Lands

Steubenville ✳

U. S. Military District

Wheeling ✳

Refugee Tract

Cumberland Road

Congressional Lands

Congressional Lands

Seven Ranges

Zanesville ✳

Donation Tract

Virginia Military District

Purchase

Marietta ✳

Symme's Purchase

Congressional Lands

Second

Ohio Co. Purchase

Parkersburg ✳

Northwest Pike

Chillicothe ✳

Maysville

✳ Point Pleasant Kanawha Pike

Gap Road

French Grants

71

the proviso that all previous private purchases of land therein, being unauthorized by Virginia, would be considered null and void. Virginia also stipulated that a tract between the Scioto and Little Miami rivers, in what became Ohio, be set aside as land with which Virginia would compensate its Revolutionary War veterans for their enlistment bounties or as pay for their wartime services. The area was called the Virginia Military District. Although some veterans preferred cash to distant land grants and therefore sold their land warrants at deep discounts to land speculators, who thereby amassed huge holdings, others disdained inflated paper money and settled in the military district, giving the area to this day a strong Virginia flavor.

The Indians strongly resisted until their defeat at Fallen Timbers in 1794. The Treaty of Greenville in 1795 opened much of the territory to settlement. A flood of migrants followed, as families converged on Ohio from many parts of the United States. Emigrants from Connecticut carried the folkways of New England into the Western Reserve in the northeastern corner of Ohio. Farmers from the Delaware Valley and the Alleghenies poured into central Ohio. Virginians occupied their military district in southern Ohio and founded towns with names such as Williamsburg and New Richmond.

A Virginia Clique in Ohio: The Chillicothe Junto

In the vanguard of the Virginia migration, once again, was a small elite who came to be known in Ohio as the Virginia Clique or the Chillicothe Junto.[56] Prominent among its leaders was Thomas Worthington (1773–1827). The son of a rich landowner in Charleston, Virginia (now West Virginia), Worthington moved across the Ohio River in 1798 and settled near Chillicothe, where he "set up the establishment of a country gentleman after the Virginia fashion."[57] Living nearby was his brother-in-law, Edward Tiffin (1766–1829), an energetic immigrant from Carlisle in the British borderlands who was a physician and landowner. Worthington and Tiffin brought slaves into Ohio, manumitted them, and continued to employ them as free labor in their fields. Also part of the junto were Charles Byrd and William Henry Harrison, both Virginians. Half a century later, when Harrison ran for president, he was presented as a humble "log cabin" candidate. In fact, he had been born in Charles City County at Berkeley, one of the most opulent tidewater estates in old Virginia. He was the son of Governor Benjamin Harrison, a great-grandson of Robert "King" Carter, the largest planter in colonial Virginia, and a descendant of Sir William Berkeley's cavalier elite.

Ohio's Virginia Clique was small in numbers, but it was rich, powerful, and exceptionally able. It broke the power of a rival group from the free states and dominated the early political history of the state. The first governor was Edward Tiffin. One of its first U.S. senators was Thomas Worthington, who later became governor as well. William Henry Harrison became the first governor of the Indiana Territory.

From long experience in their home state, other Virginians such as Simon Kenton, Nathaniel Massie, and Duncan MacArthur became leading land surveyors and controlled access to some of the best lands in southern Ohio. Together these Virginians did much to guide the Northwest Territory through its formative years.[58]

Indiana and Illinois

The migration stream that flowed from Virginia to Ohio continued across southern Indiana and Illinois to the Mississippi. Together, those two states attracted nearly as many Virginians as Ohio itself. Patterns of settlement were similar to those in the Buckeye State, and the cultural results were much the same. A distinctive subregion formed in the southern reaches of the Old Northwest. Language, architecture, and land use all had a distinctively southern flavor.

There was, however, much mixing with other cultures on the edges of this migration stream. The ancestors of Adlai Stevenson, the Democratic candidate for president in 1952 and 1956, were good examples. Stevenson remembered that "my father's family moved to Kentucky from Virginia and North Carolina, and a generation or so later they moved on to Bloomington, Illinois, before the Civil War. They were Scotch-Irish Presbyterians and Democrats, and strong in the faith, both political and religious. Miraculously, Grandfather Stevenson flourished politically in Republican Illinois and was elected Vice-President with Grover Cleveland in 1892. . . . My father's Democratic allegiance and activity ended only with his death in 1929." Adlai Stevenson's mother descended from Pennsylvania Quakers. The two regional cultures came together in his household, a common event in the Old Northwest.[59]

Beyond the Mississippi: Virginia and the Acquisition of Louisiana

In January 1803 Thomas Jefferson was chief executive of the largest republic in world history—an "empire of freedom" that was already larger than all the major monarchies of western Europe combined. Many American citizens—New Englanders especially—thought that the country was quite large enough. Virginians did not agree. For many generations they had been expansionists, hungry for fresh supplies of what they liked to call virgin land. Their culture consumed land at a prodigious rate. The Old Dominion had become a vast agrarian growth machine.

In the month of January 1803, Jefferson threw his intellect and energies into the task of making the great Republic even greater in its physical dimensions. He and Governor William C. C. Claiborne of the Mississippi Territory (also a Virginian) seriously discussed the forcible annexation of Louisiana and the Floridas. With Governor William Henry Harrison of the Indiana Territory (another Virginian), Jefferson simultaneously planned the acquisition of Indian lands east of the Mississippi River.

On January 18, 1803, the president sent a confidential message to Congress, asking a secret appropriation of $2,500 for a covert mission to explore the western lands from the Mississippi River to the Pacific. Democratic-Republican leaders in Congress (many of whom were Virginians) agreed.

This was before the purchase of Louisiana. As early as 1792 Jefferson, as secretary of state, had proposed a transcontinental expedition under the auspices of the American Philosophical Society, which he then headed. Eighteen-year-old Meriwether Lewis asked to head the expedition but was turned down. The plan miscarried, but Jefferson was convinced that America's destiny lay to the west, and he never lost interest in the project. Now, as president, he was able to act.

To head the expedition Jefferson appointed Virginians Meriwether Lewis and William Clark. He knew their families in Albemarle County. The Jeffersons, Randolphs, Meriwethers, Lewises, and Clarks had been part of Virginia's westward movement from the tidewater to Albemarle County for as many as five generations before 1803. The Louisiana expedition of 1804–6 was the culmination of a long historical process of expansion in Virginia.

Meriwether Lewis was born at Locust Hill, Albemarle County, within sight of Monticello, whose owner Thomas Jefferson became Lewis's mentor.

72. Meriwether Lewis (1774–1809), shown here in a profile portrait by St. Mémin, headed the Corps of Volunteers for Northwestern Discovery, now called the Lewis and Clark Expedition. Besides Lewis and his deputy William Clark, seven other Virginians were among the thirty-four soldiers and ten civilians who constituted the party.

73. William Clark (1770–1838), shown here in a copy of a portrait by John Wesley Jarvis, was the younger brother of George Rogers Clark. Meriwether Lewis treated him as an equal, and they complemented each other. Clark was the more outgoing, assertive, and experienced in frontier living. Lewis was the organizer and scientist.

As a boy his family moved to the Broad River in Georgia, an area that attracted many Virginians. There he learned woodcraft and took an interest in natural history. Later he continued his education in Virginia. He served with distinction in the army at several western posts. A week after Jefferson's election, Lewis was invited to become the president's private secretary. The president wrote, "Your knowledge of the Western country, of the Army, and of all it's interests and relations has rendered it desireable for public as well as private purposes that you should be engaged in that office."[60]

The younger brother of George Rogers Clark, William Clark had been born in Caroline County, Virginia. His great-grandfather had settled on the James River about 1630. The family moved westward to Albemarle County and then returned east in 1755 to Caroline. In the autumn of 1784, the family migrated by flatboat to Kentucky, where General George Rogers Clark already was established. They settled at Mulberry Hill near Louisville, which was William's home until he and Meriwether Lewis set out on their transcontinental journey.

By 1789 at the latest, Clark had become an Indian fighter, and by 1792 he was in the regular army as a lieutenant of infantry. For four years he served under General "Mad" Anthony Wayne. In the Fallen Timbers campaign he served in the same unit with Meriwether Lewis. In 1796 Clark resigned his commission and returned to Mulberry Hill, where in 1803 he was invited to serve as Lewis's deputy in the expedition that President Jefferson was sending across the continent to find a convenient route to the Pacific Ocean.

Lewis and Clark complemented each other. The former was quiet, imbued with a spirit of inquiry, and a superb organizer. The extroverted Clark had a bravura that impressed the Indians, and he proved to be a natural diplomat.[61] As they traversed the continent, they named various features for Virginia acquaintances. Clark named a tributary of the Missouri Judith's Creek after a friend from Virginia, and Lewis named the north branch of the Missouri River Maria's River after his Virginia cousin Maria Wood. Of the three streams that formed the headwaters of the Missouri, two were named for Jefferson and Madison.[62]

Before Lewis and Clark and about fifty other frontiersmen set out on their expedition, they received word that R. R. Livingston and Virginia's James Monroe had succeeded in purchasing the entire Louisiana Territory for the United States. This vast and unexpected windfall doubled the area of the nation in a single transaction. New England Federalists were so unhappy at the potential dilution of their power that some talked of secession.

The Louisiana Purchase posed several major problems for a president of Jeffersonian principles. A strict construction of the U.S. Constitution did not allow such an act. Worse, the diverse people who lived in Louisiana did not wish to be purchased.

The Virginia dynasty was undeterred. A proclamation was circulated in Louisiana. "Nature designed the inhabitants of the Mississippi and those of New Orleans to be one single people. It is your peculiar happiness that nature's decrees are fulfilled under the auspices of a philosopher who prefers justice to conquest, whose glory it is to make man free and not a slave. . . . Although he is careful of your happiness, he will not permit you to destroy it by obstructing our rights. . . . Would you try to prevent New Orleans from fulfilling its destiny?"[63]

Thus was born a vision of America's manifest destiny to liberate the people of the world, whether they wished to be or not. In 1803 that doctrine was a new-modeled version of Virginia's old idea of hegemonic freedom. Old Sir William Berkeley, who also spoke of liberty even as he denied it to others, would have understood. The people of Louisiana (and soon of Florida, Texas, and California) could only sigh.[64]

Virginians in Missouri:
The Development of Little Dixie

When the United States purchased Louisiana in 1803, Thomas Jefferson did not at first view the region as an area for European settlers but as a place to which the Indians east of the Mississippi River might be moved.[65] His constituents, however, no more liked the idea of reserving the Louisiana Territory for the Indians than their forebears had approved George III's Proclamation of 1763 on the trans-Appalachian West.

Settlement began at once, particularly in what is now the state of Missouri. Even before the Louisiana Purchase, a few Virginians were already living there. Moses Austin moved to Missouri from Virginia in 1798, drawn by generous land grants, religious toleration, and no taxes. He was also prospecting for lead deposits because his mines in Southwest Virginia had proved disappointing.[66]

Others followed soon after the Louisiana Purchase. By 1820 Missouri had enough inhabitants—more than 70,000—to become a state. From long experience Virginians were particularly drawn to the rich bottomlands along the Mississippi and Missouri rivers. A thirteen-county area of central Missouri came to be called Little Dixie but was more akin to Virginia than to the Deep South.

Many of the settlers in Little Dixie are known to us today through portraits by a leading American artist who grew up in this region. In the year before Missouri became a state, Henry Bingham, a Virginian down on his luck, took his family to Franklin, Missouri, where he bought a tobacco farm near Arrow Rock in Saline County. Henry Bingham died suddenly at the age of thirty-eight. His widow kept the family together and encouraged the artistic aspirations of their second son, George Caleb Bingham, who had been born in Augusta County, Virginia, in 1811.[67]

Before he made his reputation as a genre painter, George Caleb Bingham was a local portraitist. A high percentage of his sitters were, like himself, Virginians. A few were from the tidewater and Southside. Meredith Miles Marmaduke (1791–1864), whom Bingham painted at Arrow Rock, had come from Westmoreland County, Virginia, by 1819. In the same period arrived Dr. and Mrs. John Sappington, whom Bingham painted at Arrow Rock as well. Also in 1819 came Judge Henry Lewis (1782–1873) of Buckingham and Prince Edward counties. Most of Bingham's Virginia sitters, however, came from the western parts of the Old Dominion. The dates of their migration describe a continuing flow across the Mississippi. Brigadier General Robert Wilson (1800–1870), a native of Staunton, was on the scene by 1820. General Thomas Lawson Price of Danville arrived by 1829. Lewis Bumgardner (1806–1890) came to Howard County from Augusta County before 1830. Captain William Daniel Swinney (1797–1863) left Lynchburg in 1832 and settled on a Howard County tobacco plantation. William Joseph Eddins, Jr. (1814–1886), of Fauquier came to Howard County in 1833. Madison Miller (1811–1871), a boyhood friend of Bingham, moved to Missouri in 1836. Mary Jane Royall of Halifax County came with her family to Boone, another county in Little Dixie, in 1840.

Others among Bingham's sitters, though native Virginians, had lived in Kentucky before moving on to Missouri. Among these migrants were Captain William Johnston (1776–1850) of Culpeper, Virginia, and Bourbon,

Missouri's
Little Dixie

74

Kentucky, and Judge Warren Woodson (1796–1868), who moved with his family at age nine from Goochland to Kentucky, then in 1818 to Boone County, Missouri.[68]

Many of these Virginians brought with them large numbers of African-American slaves. Among the 87,000 slaves in Missouri by 1850 was Dred Scott, who had arrived from Virginia by way of Alabama. The complexity of Scott's many movements in the West and his temporary sojourns with his owner on the free soil of the North raised legal questions of national significance concerning the expansion of slavery and the rights of black Americans.

The Virginians who moved to Missouri included not only slave owners and slaves but also of opponents of slavery. Edward Bates was lured from Virginia by his brother Frederick, secretary of the Missouri Territory. The Bates family were Quakers, deeply hostile to the peculiar institution. Edward Bates joined the Republican party and became Abraham Lincoln's attorney general. Other Virginians were Henry Taylor Blow, an abolitionist, and John Brooks Henderson, who left Pittsylvania County for Missouri in 1832. The latter introduced in the U.S. Senate the Thirteenth Amendment, which abolished slavery.

Other Missouri Virginians fought these men in the political campaigns of the 1850s and in the military campaigns of the Civil War. James S. Green (1817–1870) was a states' rights Democrat who served as U.S. senator. John Wimer, mayor of St. Louis in 1843–44 and later a secessionist, was born in Virginia in 1810. Sterling Price, governor in 1852 and afterward Confederate general, was born in Virginia in 1809.[69]

Altogether, Missouri in 1850 was home to 40,777 native white Virginians. Besides Virginia, only four states had more. By 1860 only one state had more—Ohio. Even these numbers underrepresented the contribution of Virginia to the peopling of Missouri. In 1850 about two-thirds of Missourians were from Virginia, Tennessee, or Kentucky, and many of the Tennesseans and Kentuckians were from families with Virginia roots.

Some were strongly supportive of the Confederacy in 1861. Others sided with the Union.[70] The Civil War in Missouri was bitter because these groups did not merge into a single frontier culture, as Turner believed, but rather clung to traditional beliefs and ways that brought them into conflict.

One of the most interesting products of the Missouri-Virginia culture of Little Dixie was Mark Twain, born Samuel Langhorne Clemens. His father, of Virginia stock, moved to Kentucky, Tennessee, and then Missouri. Mark Twain's Clemens and Langhorne forebears were both old Virginia families who asserted they had an earldom in their ancestry and cherished a connection to Sir William Berkeley's cavalier elite. Mark Twain populated his fiction with figures from his past. In his dress, his manners, and his conversation, he combined the style of a Virginia gentleman with the folkways of the western rivers.

Gone to Texas: Virginians in the Lone Star State

Texas in the 1840s exerted the appeal that Kentucky had possessed in the 1780s and 1790s and Missouri in the 1810s and 1820s. Many Virginians became founders and leaders of Texas. Prominent among them was Moses Austin of Richmond. He headed a branch office of Stephen Austin & Company, an importing firm headquartered in Austin's native Connecticut and later in Philadelphia. Austin quickly expanded his interests in Virginia. He leased and later bought lead mines on the New River in Wythe County in Southwest Virginia. He told the government in Richmond that he intended to build a "Shott Manufactory" at Richmond to process his lead into shot to lessen American dependence on foreign munitions. Austin received a contract to provide lead for the roof of the new Capitol at Richmond, and he helped to persuade Congress to impose a duty on imported lead. The town that arose around Austin's mines was called Austinville, and there his son Stephen Fuller Austin was born in 1793.[71]

Despite the town's initial success, Moses Austin and his partners became overextended and heavily mortgaged. Then Congress refused to renew the protective tariff against foreign lead, thus lowering domestic lead prices. In 1796 Austin obtained a Spanish passport to visit the lead-mining region near Ste. Genevieve, Missouri, then part of Spanish Louisiana. Believing that his future lay in the West and induced by the liberal terms offered by the Spanish governor, Austin, his brother-in-law, their wives, slaves, and some workmen—forty people altogether—set out for Missouri in nine wagons and a coach in 1798.[72]

After the Louisiana Purchase his lands increased in value, and Austin became a major stockholder in the Bank of St. Louis. The bank failed in the panic of 1819, and again Austin looked westward to recoup his fortune.

In 1820 Austin solicited Spanish authorities at San Antonio, Texas, for permission to settle 300 American families, who were supposed to become Roman Catholics and Spanish citizens. Through influential friends Austin succeeded in his request, and he rushed with the news back to Little Rock, Arkansas, where his son Stephen had established a stronghold after the family left St. Louis. But before he could undertake to move, Moses Austin died of pneumonia in June 1821.

In January 1822 Stephen Austin fulfilled his father's dream by settling 300 families in a fertile but largely uninhabited area of east Texas in the Colorado and Brazos River valleys. Its principal town was called San Felipe de Austin.

One of the "Old Three Hundred" (as they later were known) was Horatio Chriesman (1792–1878), who, though a native Virginian, came to Texas by a circuitous route through Kentucky and Missouri. Another was Jared Groce (b. 1782), a Virginian who had moved to Lincoln County, Georgia, in 1804 and to Alabama in 1814. He was another "portable planter," to use Marion Nelson Winship's phrase, who arrived in Texas with his family, slaves, a train of livestock, and more than fifty wagons of movables—the whole stock of his plantation. As further evidence that the southern frontier was not an engine of equality, Mexico gave Groce eighty acres for each slave he brought in. Later, Mexico outlawed slavery, an act that may have fueled independence sentiment among Anglo-Texans, who were mostly immigrants from slave states. A Virginian of more humble condition was Samuel Wolfenberger (1804–1860), a wheelwright and wagon maker who left Virginia at age twenty-one for Tennessee, moved to Missouri in 1830, and arrived in Texas in 1831. He became a cotton farmer and served on the local Committee of Safety when the independence movement began to grow.[73]

For many years Stephen Austin remained firmly loyal to the new Mexican state that had thrown off Spanish rule, but in 1833 he petitioned that Texas be separated from the state of Coatuila and was imprisoned as an insurrectionist. When he was finally released in July 1835, Texas was on the verge of revolt against Mexico. Austin was offered command of the Texas volunteer army but declined, instead soliciting credit and support for the aspiring republic in the United States. In a letter to Philadelphia banker Nicholas Biddle, Austin wrote, "I consider that the cause of Texas is the cause of freemen & of Mankind, but more emphatically of the people of the United States, than of any other."[74]

At least twelve Virginians were among the fifty-nine signers of the Texas Declaration of Independence, including convention president Richard Ellis (1781–1846), who had served in the Alabama constitutional convention of 1819 and had moved in 1834 to an area in dispute between Texas and Arkansas.[75] News of their apparently unequal struggle fired the hearts of young Virginians. Peter Hansborough Bell (b. 1812), a Petersburg businessman, dashed off to fight for Texas independence. He was elected the state's governor in 1849 and 1851. William G. Cook of Fredericksburg (1808–1849)

75. Stephen Austin contested with his fellow Virginian Sam Houston (fig. 77) for the Texas presidency in 1836.

and Moses Albert Levy of Richmond both joined the New Orleans Grays to fight for Texan independence. The altruistic and practical motives of these men were conveyed in Levy's letter to his sister, noting that "they offer large grants of land in addition to pay as regular soldiers to all who will come and enroll themselves in the ranks of freemen assembled to oppose tyranny and oppression like our forefathers of imperishable memory."

Another attitude appeared in "Bigfoot" Wallace, from Lexington, a descendant of William Wallace and Robert the Bruce. This borderer-turned-backsettler believed in *lex talionis,* the rule of retribution. News that a cousin had been killed in the massacre at Goliad prompted him to go to Texas "to take pay out of the Mexicans."[76] At least 17 of the 180 defenders of the Alamo in 1836 were native Virginians. Many others had more distant roots in the Old Dominion.[77]

The commander of the Texas army that sought revenge with the cry "Remember the Alamo" was Sam Houston of Rockbridge County, Virginia. The American founder of the Houston family was John Houston, who arrived with his wife and six children in 1730. He signed himself "John Houston, gent.," and was of a family of border baronets. He did not come penniless to the New World. According to family legend he carried with him a small keg of gold sovereigns. When the captain and crew tried to steal it, Houston organized the passengers, seized the ship, and sailed her himself to America. He acquired large holdings in the Valley of Virginia, settled on Timber Ridge in Rockbridge County, and at the age of sixty-five was killed by a falling tree.

Among his descendants was Samuel Houston, Sr., who joined Daniel Morgan's riflemen in the Revolution and afterward became a professional soldier. He married Elizabeth Paxton, daughter of the richest man in Rockbridge County, and their son, Sam Houston, Jr., of Texas fame, was born March 2, 1793.

By 1807 the family faced bankruptcy because of constant overspending, some of it associated with Samuel Houston's position as inspector of Virginia militia. The elder Houston planned to move his family to East Tennessee, where some relatives already were prospering, but he died on a tour of military posts before the move was accomplished. It remained for Elizabeth Houston to take the family across the mountains to a 420–acre tract in Blount County, Tennessee. Relatively speaking, the Houstons still went in some style, with nine horses and two Conestoga wagons. They were accompanied by several slaves.

76. This buckskin coat was worn by Bigfoot Wallace (1817–1899), a backsettler of border descent born in the Valley of Virginia. In 1836 he moved to Texas, where his career as a scout, Indian fighter, mail carrier, and Texas ranger made him the subject of countless tall tales. Also called "The King of the Lariat," he was a prototype of the cowboy in penny dreadfuls.

Young Sam Houston had some exposure to learning at Liberty Hall Academy in Lexington and another year of formal schooling in Tennessee. Then he went for a time to live among the Cherokees, who gave him the name of "The Raven." In March 1814 Houston enlisted in the U.S. Army. His bravery at the battle of Horseshoe Bend during the Creek War was noticed by the American commander, Andrew Jackson. In 1818 Houston moved to Nashville, studied and practiced law, and entered politics as a protégé of Old Hickory. He served in Congress in 1823–27 and was elected governor in 1827. In 1829 he married Eliza Allen, but she deserted him after three months. The ensuing scandal caused Houston to resign the governorship and leave the state. He joined the Cherokees already west of the Mississippi River and became their spokesman to the whites.

Houston first went to Texas in 1832. On March 2, 1836, he signed the Declaration of Independence from Mexico. He was appointed commander in chief of the Texas armies and on April 21, 1836, defeated and captured the Mexican president, General Antonio López Santa Anna, thus ensuring Texas's independence. Houston became president of the Republic of Texas in 1836–38 and 1841–44. After Texas entered the Union, he served as U.S. senator, 1846–59. He was governor of Texas in 1859–61 but was deposed for refusing to take the Confederate oath of allegiance. He died in Huntsville on July 26, 1863.[78]

Mexico did not passively accept Texas independence. In 1842 George William Brown, a Henrico County lawyer, answered the call for volunteers for a proposed expedition against Mexico following Rafael Vasquez's invasion of San Antonio. Ben Ficklin (1827–1871) of Albemarle County took a leave of absence from Virginia Military Institute to serve in the Mexican War in 1846–47. After his belated graduation in 1849, he began operating stagecoach lines in the Southwest and in 1859 helped organize the Pony Express. He returned to Virginia at the outbreak of the Civil War, served the Confederate cause there, and is buried at Charlottesville.

Such return migrations were not unusual. William Byrd, son of Richard Evelyn Byrd and Anne Harrison Byrd, was born in Winchester, Virginia, in 1828. Like Ficklin, he graduated from VMI in 1849. After attending law school at the University of Virginia, he left for Texas in 1853. After the Civil War he returned to Winchester to practice law and became the grandfather of Senator Harry F. Byrd, Sr., and Admiral Richard E. Byrd, the polar explorer.[79]

Another graduate of the University of Virginia Law School was William Lewis Moody, who moved to Texas in 1852, a year before Byrd. He decided that prosperity was beyond his reach in Virginia: "What my two or three dryed up negroes could make me in a year, would be consumed by me long before it was due." He settled at Fairfield, Freestone County, Texas, according to tradition because his horse died there. He enticed two of his broth-

77. Virginian Sam Houston opposed Stephen Austin (fig. 75) for the presidency of Texas in 1836.

ers to Texas, and they formed W. L. Moody & Brothers, cotton merchants. By 1860 the firm was worth $100,000, and the Moodys were among the wealthiest 1 percent of Texans, according to the federal census. When Texas seceded, he wrote a brother, "It gratifies our inmost heart to hear now from old Virginia—God bless her—as soon as she can grease her machinery I am confident she will perform as in days of yore."[80] After the war he summered for many years in Lexington, Virginia, sent his son to Hollins Institute in Roanoke and Virginia Military Institute, and in 1898 the elder Moody returned to Tappahannock to study the genealogy of his family. He never returned to Virginia to live but asked to be buried among the graves of his ancestors in Chesterfield, Virginia.[81]

Oregon and California: Virginia's Pacific Argonauts

After Texas the next mecca was Oregon. Virginians were among the many settlers who rode 2,000 miles in four-by-ten-foot wagons from Independence, Missouri, to the Pacific coast. One traveler named his prairie schooner "Old Dominion."[82] At one point the Oregon Trail divides. One branch leads to Oregon, the other to California. An old joke maintained that the north branch was marked by a sign; those who could not read headed south.

But even before there was a trail, Virginians found their way to Oregon and California. Joseph and Stephen Meek, mountain men and brothers, were in California in 1833, when it was still Mexican territory. Joel P. Walker, his wife Mary Young Walker, and his brother Joseph arrived in California from Oregon in 1841. Born in Goochland County, Virginia, in 1797, Walker died in 1879 at Santa Rosa, Sonoma County, California, having traveled coast to coast.[83]

Many others followed after the opening of the Oregon Trail. Among them was William Blackburn (1814–1867), a native of Harpers Ferry who came with the Swasey-Todd party. He became alcalde (mayor) of Santa Cruz in 1847–49 and later a county judge. The first brick house in California was constructed in Santa Cruz by Virginia bricklayer Gallant Duncan Dickensen, who arrived in 1846 with his wife Isabella McCray Dickensen, four sons, and two daughters. William Isaac Tustin came with his wife and son as a member of the Grigsby-Ide party of overland immigrants. Also in 1846 James Clymer, surveyor and trapper, came to California from Oregon with the McMahon-Clymer party.[84]

In 1848 escaped Virginia slave Robert Owen settled in Los Angeles. Also arriving that year was Charles T. Botts, whose brother John was a politician in Virginia. Charles Botts was a naval storekeeper in Monterey, a member of the constitutional convention of 1849 that led to statehood in 1850, a lawyer, and publisher of the Sacramento *Standard* beginning in 1858.[85]

In January 1848 Henry Bigler of Virginia was present at John Sutter's Coloma Mill when gold was discovered. His *Diary of a Mormon* is among the most reliable accounts of the discovery. In the ensuing year several of the major gold fields were found by James H. Carson, a native of Warren County, Virginia, who listed his hometown in 1851 as Alexandria, D.C. (Alexandria reverted to Virginia in 1846–47). He had come in 1847 with the first military detachment ordered to California after the declaration of war with Mexico. He was in the mines by 1848, and Carson's Hill, a rich lode, bears his name, but duplicitous business partners kept him from becoming rich. In 1852 he published *Early Recollections of the Mines,* in which he waxed nostalgic for the early heady days of 1848–49. The Whigs of Calaveras County tendered him their nomination to the state legislature, "but he being a democrat, of the Virginia school," he declined and ran successfully instead as a Democrat. Soon afterward he died of rheumatism. A month later his wife and child arrived, unaware of his death. Generous subscription to a fund enabled them to return east.[86]

The gold rush made San Francisco a boomtown in 1849. Its mayor that year was a Virginian, Dr. John Townsend, a physician who nonetheless headed for the mines with the others. He and his wife died of cholera during the winter of 1850–51. The first important commercial building in San Francisco, indeed in California, was the Parrott Building, completed in 1852 at a cost of $117,000 by John Parrott, a Virginian. Worth $60,000 in 1851, he was a millionaire four times over by 1871.[87]

Dreams of comparable wealth fired the imagination of Virginians at home. In 1849 newspapers in the Old Dominion were filled with announcements by ad hoc companies that proposed to transport men to the gold rush for an investment of $300.

These emigrants called themselves the Virginia argonauts, because like the argonauts of Greek legend, they sought the Golden Fleece. One of them was Dr. George Colbert Tyler of the Eastern Shore. He did not intend to mine for gold but hoped to pay off his debts by a flourishing medical practice. He was speedily disillusioned. After a few months he wrote home that he had made a mistake, though "I was being ruined in Pungoteague, and I thought such a trip necessary to break the spell from me. I thought I should be better off from that place and its habits." It was "a most painfull thought to me to have to return home without money, and though continual disappointments have met me, yet I have always maintained a hope, sometimes barely the skeleton of a hope of a turning tide." His tide of fortune did not turn, and he returned to Virginia worse off than before.[88] In a similar state of disillusion was Richmonder C. H. West, who wrote home, "If you are doing anything at home worth pursuing, remain where you are."[89] On the other hand, John F. Farnsworth of Brooke County, Virginia, was lured west in 1849 by a letter from his eldest brother "filled with the wonders of California's ideal climate, beautiful scenery, and . . . financial security for all."[90]

Other Virginia argonauts did better than Dr. Tyler, though seldom by mining. A colorful example was Charles Snowden Fairfax. He was entitled by inheritance to the Scottish title Baron Cameron, which had been held by his ancestor, Lord Fairfax, owner of the Northern Neck of Virginia in the eighteenth century, but Charles Snowden Fairfax never became a British subject, and the title remained dormant until it was claimed two generations later by another member of the family.

On April 6, 1849, at City Point, the twenty-year-old Fairfax and other members of the ad hoc Madison Mining Company stepped aboard the *Glenmore,* a ship laden with tobacco, soap, machinery, appliances, and other wares, bound for the gold fields of California. When the *Glenmore* arrived in San Francisco on October 6, 1849, the members of the Madison Mining Company sold the ship's contents to finance their mining ventures. Unfortunately, in the glutted market they recovered only $12,000 of their $36,000 investment. While members of the company raced to the mines, their tobacco rotted on the wharf.

Fairfax spent his first winter in Grass Valley, a mining center, but like many others he quickly realized he would not find his fortune there. He entered politics as a Democrat and became a delegate to the Democratic state convention in July 1851. In 1853 he became a member of the California General Assembly from Yuba and Sierra counties, and in 1854 he became speaker of the house. In 1857 he won the remunerative post of clerk of the California Supreme Court. From 1865 to 1867 he was a supervisor of Marin County.

78. Charles Snowden Fairfax (c. 1828–1868) was heir to the title Baron Cameron
through his ancestor Lord Fairfax, owner of the Northern Neck of Virginia in the
eighteenth century. Charlie Fairfax, as he liked to be called, was a Virginia forty-niner
who became Speaker of the California House of Assembly.

In 1855 Fairfax married Ada Benham, a newly arrived Cincinnati belle. As a wedding gift from Dr. Alfred W. Taliaferro, they received a Marin County estate that they called Bird's Nest Glen. There they built a house "surrounded by porches" that resembled Greenway Court, the sixth Lord Fairfax's commodious house on the Northern Neck of Virginia. They entertained lavishly in the old Virginia style. Fairfax was known to his many friends as Charlie. His wife, however, liked to be called Lady Fairfax.

Like many Virginia gentlemen of his time, Fairfax was addicted to gambling and was a firm believer in the *code duello.* His reputation as a crack shot secured him some immunity from conventional affairs of honor, but he was wounded in an informal encounter in 1858. While walking down a Sacramento street, Fairfax was accosted by a court reporter, a former employee, who snapped his fingers in Fairfax's face and made accusations no gentleman could accept. Anger flashed in Fairfax's eyes, but at once his assailant drew a sword from his cane and stabbed Fairfax, who coolly drew his derringer, cocked it, aimed it at his opponent's head, then put it back in his pocket and walked away contemptuously.

Fairfax died on April 4, 1868, while returning from the Democratic National Convention, where he had chaired the California delegation. He was only forty. His widow attributed his death to the stab wound that never healed properly. He was buried among his ancestors in Virginia, but his name remained in California, where a town called Fairfax rose on the ruins of Charlie Fairfax's Bird's Nest Glen estate.[91]

Another Virginia argonaut was Alfred W. Taliaferro (1825–1885), a physician from Mathews in Essex County. Like Fairfax, he was among the seventy-five members of the Madison Mining or Virginia Company who left Virginia aboard the *Glenmore* on April 6, 1849, bound for San Francisco and arrived six months later. Taliaferro seems never to have engaged in mining, but he formed a company to engage in agriculture in San Rafael, Marin County, north of the Golden Gate. By December 1849 he had leased land from Don Timoteo Murphy. Later he bought the land and built a house on it.

Taliaferro also was a physician and surgeon who, because he nearly monopolized the practice of the county, might have become rich, but, as a friend observed, he "had no regard for money." Like many Virginia gentlemen of the period, Taliaferro was fond of gambling, "used cuss words like a trooper," was quick to take offense, and was a fine dancer and an ardent Democrat.

79. This bronze bust is inscribed "Alfred Walker Taliaferro, M.D. / 'A Good Samaritan.'" An Essex County physician, Taliaferro was one of seventy-five forty-niners who left Richmond for San Francisco on April 6, 1849, aboard the *Glenmore*.

He was elected to the state assembly in 1853 and to the state Senate in 1854, serving until 1858. He was elected to the San Rafael Board of Trustees in 1874.

For a time Dr. Taliaferro was prison doctor at San Quentin. His generosity and service to the community of Marin County made him a beloved figure in later years. At his death he lay in state at the San Rafael Opera House. A newspaper obituary observed that "the fact of a patient being impecunious acted as a stimulus rather than the reverse. He would jump out of bed at any time of night or in any kind of weather."[92]

Another Virginia forty-niner was Joseph E. N. Lewis (1826–1869), a native of Jefferson County, who settled in Butte County, California, which he helped to organize. He represented Butte and Shasta counties in the California Senate. Another politician was Edmund Randolph (1819–1861), a descendant of Virginia's Adam and Eve, who came to California from New Orleans, where he was clerk of the U.S. Circuit Court. He became a member of the first California legislature. Though a gifted orator, his aloofness and eccentricity held back his political ascent. He died denouncing Abraham Lincoln.[93]

The argonauts of Virginia did not strike it rich in the gold fields, but some achieved success in politics and the professions. These forty-niners helped to form a new elite, which several students have found to be similar to those in the East.

Typical of this Pacific gentry was the family of General George S. Patton, a Californian who was descended from Virginians on both sides of his family. His ancestors were the Pattons who led Scotch-Irish settlers into the southern Shenandoah Valley. His grandfather, Colonel George S. Patton, was killed fighting at Winchester in the Civil War.

After the war Colonel Patton's son, George S. Patton, Jr., went with his widowed mother to California. He returned to attend the Virginia Military Institute, then went back to California and became district attorney of Los Angeles. He married Ruth Wilson, the daughter of a Richmond belle and Don Benito Wilson, a tough Tennessee Indian trader who was one of the largest landowners in southern California.

From this union the future general George S. Patton was born. In the arid hills of sunny California, he was raised to think of himself as a Virginian and to measure his conduct against the honor of his ancestors. When he went into battle for the first time in World War I, Patton was pinned down by German machine guns. He later remembered,

I was lying flat on my belly and scared to death, hardly daring to lift my head. But finally I did, and looked up to a bank of clouds glowing reddish in the almost setting sun. And then, just as clear as clear can be, I saw their heads, the heads of my grandfather and his brothers. Their mouths weren't moving; they weren't saying anything to me, but they were looking, looking not so much in anger as with unhappy scowls. I could read their eyes and they said to me, "Georgie, Georgie, you're a disappointment to us lying low down there. Just remember lots of Pattons have been killed, but there never was one who was a coward." So I got up, drew my gun, and gave commands. And at last Colonel George and the others were still there, but smiling.[94]

Thus the ghosts of Virginians past also migrated to California and took up residence on the Pacific slope.

Virginians in the Rocky Mountains

Many men and women sought to reach California by land rather than by sea. Virginians had a role in this migration, too. James Pierson Beckwourth (1798–c. 1866) was a mountain man who discovered the pass that bears his name in the High Sierra. He was born in Fredericksburg, Virginia, the son of Revolutionary War veteran Jennings Beckwourth and a mulatto slave woman. In 1810 the family moved to the vicinity of St. Louis in the Louisiana Territory. James Beckwourth was apprenticed to a blacksmith but at age eighteen ran away. From 1823 to 1826 he was employed as a blacksmith and groom by the Rocky Mountain Fur Company. The company undertook expeditions along the Yellowstone, Big Horn, Platte, Green, Bear, and Beaver rivers in Montana, Wyoming, Colorado, and Utah, during which Beckwourth met frontiersmen such as Jim Bridger.

From 1826 to 1837 Beckwourth lived among the Crow. He became a chief and married Still Water, daughter of Chief Black Lodge. Later he also became a member of the Blackfoot tribe and married into it.

When gold was discovered in California, Beckwourth was among several scouts who sought to discover routes through the Sierra Nevada. In 1852 he discovered a new pass, since called Beckwourth Pass, about twenty miles northwest of present-day Reno, Nevada, in Plumas County, California. There Beckwourth established a trading post and an inn. In 1859 he moved back to Denver, where he had a ranch and store. In the early 1860s he served as a guide for army patrols in the Colorado country. In 1864 he was guide for

80. James P. Beckwourth (1798 c. 1866), who ranged the Rocky Mountains as a fur trader, Crow chief, and guide, was the son of a Fredericksburg, Virginia, Revolutionary War veteran and his slave. In 1851 he discovered the lowest pass through the Sierra Nevada into California.

81. This 1859 photograph taken in St. Louis shows Jim Bridger (1804–1881), son of tavern keepers in Richmond, Virginia. Bridger was a trapper, fur trader, and later scout for the U.S. Army.

the Chivington Expedition that massacred Cheyenne Indians. In 1866 he was sent with Jim Bridger and Hank Williams to pacify the Crow tribe. Beckwourth never returned. Some say he was poisoned.[95]

Jim Bridger was the son of James and Chloe Bridger, tavern keepers in Richmond, Virginia. He moved to St. Louis about 1812. Orphaned at an early age, he was apprenticed to a blacksmith. At nineteen Bridger joined William Henry Ashley's expedition to the Rocky Mountains. He was a trapper and fur trader until 1843. Seeing the fur trade in decline, he established Fort Bridger in southwestern Wyoming, along the Oregon Trail, as a supply post for immigrants. John C. Frémont, Brigham Young, the Donner party, and others wrote of the assistance that Bridger gave them. In 1853 the Mormons destroyed Fort Bridger. After removing his family to the safety of a farm near Kansas City, Bridger entered government employ as a scout. On one expedition he had the satisfaction of guiding the U.S. Army in its campaign against the Mormons. He marked the Bozeman Trail from Nebraska to the Montana gold fields and continued active until arthritis and failing eyesight compelled him to retire in 1866.[96]

The richest mineral deposits in the Far West were not in California but Nevada—the Comstock Lode. A group of shacks sprang up around the mines. According to Henry Comstock, in 1859 James Fennimore, known as "Old Virginia" because he was a native of the Old Dominion, "was out one night with a lot of the 'boys' on a drunk, when he fell down and broke his whiskey bottle. On rising he said 'I baptize this ground Virginia.'" The first documentation of the name appears in October 1859. The following month the site was called Virginia City, perhaps because Wells Fargo only set up offices in cities.[97]

The Northern Stream: Virginians and the Cities

Most Virginians moved south and west, but it is important to remember that another stream of migration flowed in the opposite direction—northeast, toward the rising cities of America. Many Virginians were drawn from the tidewater to Baltimore, which in the early Republic became the metropolis of the Chesapeake region and the fastest-growing city in the United States.

Among these urban migrants was Robert Carter (1728–1804) of Nomini Hall, grandson of "King" Carter and owner of nearly 500 slaves in 1790. Like many gentry in the Northern Neck, he formed a Maryland connection through his marriage to Frances Tasker. His motives for moving to Baltimore were both material and moral. In the 1780s Carter found that he was not making enough from his plantation and slaves to pay his taxes. At the same time he was growing increasingly uneasy about the keeping of slaves. In 1790 he established a scheme of manumission for 483 slaves and divided his lands among his children. He was deeply religious in a restless, seeking way and became in succession an Anglican, Deist, Baptist, and Arminian. Finally he found his faith in Swedenborgianism, a movement that was attractive to other gentlemen of Virginia. Several Fairfaxes joined the same sect. The nearest Swedenborgian reading group was in Baltimore. To be near it, Carter moved to that city in 1793, joined the Swedenborgian New Church, and published its liturgy and hymnbook at his own expense. He remained in Baltimore for the rest of his life.[98]

Another Virginian who moved north was General Henry Lee, who had studied at Princeton and formed many northern friendships. He distinguished himself in the Revolution as "Light-Horse Harry Lee." After the war he married his cousin Matilda Lee, heiress to Stratford Hall in Westmoreland County, and became master of that great estate. Lee was three times elected governor of Virginia. Following the death of his first wife, he married Anne Hill Carter. One of their children was Robert E. Lee.

The great windows of Stratford looked north across the Potomac, and after the Revolutionary War that was the direction Lee's ambition took him. He proposed many ventures for the development of the Potomac, made large purchases of land in the West, and planned a great commercial city named Matildaville. Lee was a staunch Federalist and an American nationalist. He hated slavery and wished to free his own slaves.

Before he could act decisively on any of these plans, however, his investments collapsed, and in 1809 he went to jail as a debtor in Spotsylvania County. He deeded over Stratford to a son and in 1811 moved to a rented house in Alexandria. Lee shuttled back and forth to Baltimore, where he tried to salvage his fortune by publishing a memoir of his military career. While in Baltimore in 1812 he tried to defend an outspoken Federalist editor from a Jeffersonian mob and was himself viciously attacked by the rioters, who called him "a d—d old tory general" and tried to gouge out his eyes and cut off his nose. The Jeffersonian mob left him bleeding, maimed, and presumed dead. He survived but for months wore a black cloth over his face to hide his terrible wounds. In 1813 his physicians advised him to travel to the West In-

82. Robert Carter of Nomini Hall (1728–1804) freed more than five hundred slaves in 1791—the largest single emancipation in Virginia history—and sought spiritual solace among the Swedenborgians in Baltimore. This portrait of him as a carefree youth was done in London by Thomas Hudson about 1750.

dies for his health, but he never recovered from the attack. As death approached, he tried to sail home to Virginia but got only as far as Cumberland Island, Georgia, where he died in 1818, far from his beloved home.[99]

Through the next two centuries other Virginians moved north to Baltimore and Washington. The children of prominent planting families found their way to both cities, as did many of their former slaves. A large part of the present African-American population of both cities is descended from Virginia slaves. Many poor whites also migrated from Virginia to the cities in search of work and for a century made up a significant portion of the population of Baltimore in particular. After the Civil War the size of these flows greatly increased. This exodus to the north was antebellum Virginia's forgotten emigration.

Conclusion

Altogether, the movement beyond Virginia was one of the largest migrations in American history. No other state could match it, in terms of magnitude, duration, range, variety, and complexity.

The great migration beyond Virginia began in the seventeenth century and continued through four centuries. It carried in many different directions—south along the Atlantic coast; southwest through the piedmont and the valleys of Tennessee and Alabama; west into Kentucky; northwest to Ohio, Indiana, and Illinois; north into the great American cities.

Virginians took the lead in opening the great western valleys: George Washington in the Ohio and Thomas Jefferson in the Mississippi Valley. Two land-hungry gentlemen of Virginia, Jefferson and James Monroe, purchased Louisiana and annexed West Florida, nearly doubling the lands of the new nation. Two other Virginia gentlemen, Lewis and Clark, were the leading explorers of this vast domain.

Virginians were quick to plant colonies on the best soil that lay beyond the Mississippi. They peopled the fine planting land of Missouri's Little Dixie. They took leading roles in Texas, California, and the opening of the Rocky Mountains, where cities bear the names of such Virginians as James Denver and Jesse Reno.

One must ask what was the cause of this activity, and what its cultural consequences may have been. Those questions are the next business of this inquiry.

4

Problems of Cause and Consequence

Emigration, Economics, and Slavery

From 1789 to 1825 four of America's five presidents were Virginians. Their elections seemed to confirm the Old Dominion's status as the most powerful and populous state in the new nation.

These appearances were deceiving. In the moment of its greatest eminence, Virginia had already entered into a process of steep decline. A long agricultural depression devastated Virginia's planters. Three presidents of the Virginia dynasty—Jefferson, Madison, and Monroe—all had their final years clouded by the specter of insolvency.

This decline began not later than 1770. Thereafter, the tidewater could not support a growing population. Soil exhaustion in the tidewater became chronic, and a British traveler said that Jefferson's piedmont county of Albemarle was "worn out, washed and gullied" so that rivers "appeared like a torrent of blood" carrying off the topsoil. John J. Ambler, Jr., thought that Virginia was "one wide waste of desolation." He reported that a once prosperous neighbor was now too poor to "pay his postage."[1]

Even planters who bought additional land found themselves becoming not richer but more extended. There was not much prime real estate left in Virginia to which one could move. Land values in the Old Dominion plummeted from $207 million in 1817 to merely $90 million in 1829.

In 1816 a legislative committee concluded of the state that "a very large proportion of her western territory is yet unimproved, while a considerable part of her eastern has receded from its former opulence. How many sad spectacles do her lowlands present of wasted and deserted fields, of dwellings abandoned . . . of churches in ruins."[2]

The problem seemed all the worse by comparison with the northern states. Virginian Lucian Minor wrote from Massachusetts, "Here is not a hundredth part of the abject, squalid poverty that our state presents."[3]

For many, the only option was to leave the state. In a two-year period 25 percent of the white landowners in Sussex County disappeared from the tax rolls.[4] "The times are dreadful," wrote Elizabeth Trist, "if we may judge from the numbers that are migrating to different parts of the continent. Scarce a day passes that families are not going to the Alabama, Missoura or some of those places."[5]

Families saw the nation's future, and their own, in the West. More than a third of the white children born in Virginia about 1800 left the state,[6] and

83. *The Ruins of Jamestown, Virginia, America,* by John Gadsby Chapman (1834). The old church at Jamestown was the best known of many ruined churches and mansions in the tidewater. Even its tombs were shattered by the growth of a giant sycamore. These fallen monuments to Virginia's former glory captured the climate of despair that was spreading through the state.

slaves stood a 30 percent chance of being removed by slave traders.[7] Between 1790 and 1800 twenty-six Virginia counties actually lost population. Through a later, longer period from 1810 to 1840, twenty-eight of sixty-two counties east of the Blue Ridge were declining in the number of their inhabitants, while the nation as a whole was growing rapidly. In 1845, toward the end of the downward cycle, Governor James McDowell spoke of "the ruinous process of depopulation and impoverishment now at work."[8] Three years later Branch T. Archer declared, more succinctly, "Virginia is waning fast."[9]

The French traveler Alexis de Tocqueville perceived that the problem was not one of stagnation but of actual decline. Many native Virginians agreed, even those most loyal to their state. As early as 1813 John Randolph of Roanoke wrote: "In a few years more, those of us who are alive will have to move off to *Kaintuck,* or the *Mississippi,* where corn can be had for sixpence a bushel, and pork for a penny a pound. I do not wonder at the rage for emigration. What do the bulk of the people get here, that they cannot have for one-fifth of the labor in the western country?"[10]

By 1830 Randolph was convinced that with "soil and staples both worn out," Virginia had an incurable "galloping consumption."[11] He compared Virginia to King Lear, "an old and feeble monarch," abandoned by its children.[12]

John Hartwell Cocke believed that nothing could redeem Virginia "from the *curses* (for there are many) which in the wisdom and justice of Providence he has imposed upon it."[13] Essex County planter James Mercer Garnett lamented in 1827: "Virginia, poor Virginia, furnishes a spectacle at present which is enough to make the heart of her real friends sick to the very core . . . her agriculture nearly gone to ruin from a course of policy which could not well have been worse destructive if destruction had been its sole objective. . . . Hope is nearly dead, and I can see nothing in the perspective of the times calculated to renew it, or at least nothing which is not too slow in the operation to affect much in our times."[14]

The next year Francis Eppes, one of Thomas Jefferson's grandchildren, echoed Garnett: "I see no ties which should bind any descendants of our grandfather to this state. The people are cold to his memory, the soil is exhausted, the staple reduced almost to the prime cost of the materials—a level to which it is fast progressing. What inducement is there to remain! Our children may grow rich under a different system, but *we* will never witness better times—here."[15]

William M. Bridges wrote wistfully from Ohio, "Well may poor, poverty-stricken Virginia, whose sons have to leave her side for good, mourn over the loss of [this] Territory of inexhaustible wealth." Of Illinois he wrote similarly: "Just to think that Va, in a spirit of magnanimity, gave away this Territory [in 1784]; and yet, strange to say, has received no return for the bread thus cast upon the waters—The money thus given to private citizens of Illinois would pay the whole debt of Virginia and leave enough to complete every line of internal improvement in the State."

Of course, no such redress was in the offing. Bridges concluded that "the vast number of young men in Richmond, who are living on salaries barely sufficient to keep them out of the poor-house, and others, who are constantly on the qui vive for employment, ready to go any where or do any thing for a bare existence, are infernal fools for not packing up duds, and bidding the skinflints of Richmond farewell, and flying hence in pursuit of happiness and prosperity."[16]

His pessimism was contagious. A literature of declension developed in Virginia during the early nineteenth century. In Nathaniel Beverley Tucker's novel *George Balcombe,* the owner of Raby Hall, Essex County, lives in poverty on his dilapidated plantation.[17] In George Tucker's *Valley of Shenandoah,* Edward Grayson returns to the family home in Charles City County, where "the sight of this venerable seat of his ancestors reminded him of the fall of his family from their former opulence and consequence to the most absolute poverty; and the tender and not unpleasing melancholy he had formerly experienced, was exchanged for a bitterness of feelings, and soreness of heart, which had nothing in it consolatory or agreeable." Grayson was a fictional character, but the bitterness was real enough.[18]

Searching for the Cause: Agriculture and Economics

Most Virginians recognized the problem, but they were not of one mind about its cause. Many thought that the root of the matter was the reliance on mistaken agricultural methods. Thomas Jefferson lamented the dependence on tobacco and slavery, calling it a "culture productive of infinite wretchedness. . . . Men and animals on those farms are barely fed, and the earth is rapidly impoverished."[19] In 1847 the president of Washington College in Lexington wrote that Virginia was not alone: "In the older parts of the slave states . . . are . . . too evident signs of stagnation or of positive decay—a sparse population—a slovenly cultivation spread over vast fields that are wearing out."[20]

To many modern historians and to contemporaries such as Henry Ruffner, the problem lay elsewhere—in Virginia's lack of communications, marketing centers, canals, and especially railroads, which exacerbated the state's troubles. Virginia, they believed, was not connected to the growing West.

But others took the opposite view. One character in John Pendleton Kennedy's 1832 novel *Swallow Barn* says: "Things are getting worse and worse. I can see how it's going. What's the use of states if they are all going to be cut up with canals and railroads and tariffs. NO. NO. Gentlemen! You may depend. Old Virginny's not going to let Congress carry on in her day."[21]

The search for scapegoats inevitably turned north. Many of the delegates to the Virginia convention of 1829–30 blamed the state's troubles on "Yankee greed." John Randolph deplored northern control of Congress because of "King Numbers." William Leigh orated that "the influenza—the small

84. Many of the delegates to the Virginia Constitutional Convention of 1829–30 blamed the state's troubles on "Yankee greed." A year later many of the same men founded the Virginia Historical Society to preserve the memory of Virginia's greatness, which they believed had passed. This painting is by George Catlin, later famous for his portrayals of Indians of the Great Plains.

pox—the varioloid—the Hessian fly—the Circuit Court system—Universal Suffrage—all come from the North."[22] Philip N. Nicholas thought Virginia was a "victim to her honour."[23] James Mercer Garnett prefaced his 1827 lament by saying, "We have made ourselves a tributary to the North and East—every day is augmenting our dependence."[24] Francis Eppes agreed. Within months of the death of his grandfather Thomas Jefferson, Eppes wrote: "Many circumstances of late have induced me to believe that the liberality and generosity, and patriotism of the old Dominion, is on the wane. The noxious exhalations from the eastern states, have poisoned our atmosphere. Yankee notions and Yankee practices, have wrought a thorough change in the public mind. The maxim now is to take care of number one." These and "the more equal distribution of property, has smothered the flame which once burnt in our bosoms."[25]

What these men were regretting was the passing of what some scholars call "the Jeffersonian moment." According to this argument the election of Thomas Jefferson in 1800 seemed to fuse "the virtues of republicanism and eighteenth-century liberalism into a cohesive political philosophy offering the bright promise of equal social and economic advancement for all in a land of abundance" under the rule of enlightened liberal gentlemen or, in Jefferson's phrase, "natural aristocrats."[26]

Many of these men believed that the virtuous republicanism of the eighteenth century had been supplanted by rampant materialism and unbridled individualism—what Eppes deplored when he noted that "the maxim now is to take care of number one." No wonder that Thomas Jefferson, confronting the new fashions of the next generation, died in a state of disillusionment, if not despair.[27]

Slavery and Emigration

While some blamed Yankees, others thought that slavery was the root of the problem. After the Revolution there was a gradual realization of the incompatibility of the Declaration of Independence with the institution of slavery. Antislavery sentiment grew in Virginia, but nothing was done because of the lack of a practical scheme of emancipation that met with general approval. Colonization to Liberia was too expensive, considering the size of Virginia's black population, and even Virginians who thought themselves as progressive and hostile to slavery were unwilling to accept blacks as equals.

Even as some Virginians became convinced that slavery should be abolished, there was increasing fear of armed slave rebellion. The enthusiastic response of slaves to Lord Dunmore's call for revolt disillusioned many who thought their slaves were happy and content. Fear grew greatly after the massacre of the master class in Santo Domingo.

In 1800 Gabriel Prosser organized a black revolt that was to begin on the Henrico County plantation of Thomas Prosser. According to the plan all whites in the area were to be killed except for the French, Quakers, Methodists, and poor whites without slaves. Then General Gabriel was to march on Richmond and be installed as king of Virginia. Two of the many slaves who joined Gabriel betrayed him. Governor James Monroe took immediate action. Gabriel was arrested, tried, and executed.

Five days after Gabriel Prosser's execution, Nat Turner (1800–1831) was born in Southampton County in Southside Virginia. In 1831 he began hearing voices and having visions that convinced him that he was a divine instrument. He planned a slave insurrection to begin, appropriately as he thought, on July 4, but illness forced a postponement. It finally started on August 11, when Nat Turner and his recruits killed the Turner family to whom he had been leased. They went from house to house in rural Southampton County, killing between fifty-five and sixty-five whites in the first two days. The number of Turner's followers grew to sixty or seventy, but whites rose instantly against him, his followers were taken, and Nat Turner was driven into hiding. He was discovered on October 30 and taken to Jerusalem, the county seat, where he was tried, convicted, and executed.

A spasm of fear pulsed through Virginia and the South. Increased emphasis was put on sending free blacks to Liberia. The ship *James Perkins,* which sailed for Africa on December 9, 1831, carried 276 free blacks from Southampton County alone. At least 41 followed in 1832. Many were happy to leave. The voyage was compared to climbing Jacob's ladder and the destination to Canaan, Heaven, or Jerusalem.[28]

Many who stayed also sang of Jerusalem, but with a double meaning. They referred not only to the place where Christ was condemned and crucified but also to the seat of Southampton County (later called Courtland) where Nat Turner was convicted and executed. These songs were carried south and west by Virginia slaves bound away to distant lands.[29]

Some white Virginians responded to the Turner affair by calling for the end of slavery. On November 11, 1831, Governor John Floyd wrote in his

HORRID MASSACRE IN VIRGINIA.

The Scenes which the above Plate is designed to represent, are---Figure 1. a Mother intreating for the lives of her children.
---2. Mr. Travis, cruelly murdered by his own Slaves.---3. Mrs. Barrow, who bravely defended himself until his wife escaped.
----4. A company of mounted Dragoons in pursuit of the Blacks.

Just Published, an Authentic and Interesting

NARRATIVE

OF THE

TRAGICAL SCENE

Which was witnessed in Southampton county (Virginia) on Monday the 22d of August last, when FIFTY FIVE of its inhabitants (mostly women and children) were inhumanly massacred by the Blacks!

Short and imperfect sketches of the horrid massacre above mentioned have appeared in the public Journals, but the public are now presented with every particular relative thereto, communicated by those who were eye witnesses of the bloody scene, and confirmed by the confessions of several of the Blacks while under sentence of death.

A more shocking instance of human butchery has seldom occurred in any country, and never before in this—the merciless wretches carried destruction to every white person they found in the houses, whether the hoary head, the lovely virgin, or the sleeping infant in the cradle! they spared none!—a widow (Mrs. Whitehead) and her 10 children were murdered in one house! among the slain on that fatal night, was an amiable young lady but 17 years of age, who the day following was to have been united in marriage to a young gentleman of North-Carolina, who had left home the evening preceding with the expectation of conveying there the succeeding day the object of his affections! but, alas! how sad was his disappointment! he was the third person who entered the house after the horrid massacre, to witness the mangled remains of her whom he was so shortly to espouse! The Blacks after having completed their work of death, attempted to evade the pursuit of those who had collected to oppose them, by secreting themselves in a neighboring swamp, to the borders of which they were pursued by a company of mounted dragoons. Of the fifty five slain nearly two thirds of the number were children, not exceeding twelve years of age! and it was truly a melancholly scene (as was observed to the writer by one who witnessed it) to behold on the day of their interment so great a number of coffins collected, surrounded by the weeping relatives!

While the friends of humanity however or wherever situated, cannot but sincerely and deeply lament the awful destruction of so many innocent lives, yet, the humane and philanthopic citizens of New-England, and of the middle States, cannot feel too thankful for the repose and peace of conscience which they enjoy, by wisely and humanely abolishing laws dooming a free born fellow being (without fault or crime) to perpetual bondage!---an example truly worthy of imitation by our brethren at the South.

The Narrative (which contains every important particular relating to the horrid massacre) is afforded for the trifling sum of 12 1-2 Cents. ☞ This paper left for perusal, and to be returned when called for.

85. Nat Turner's slave revolt resulted in the deaths of between fifty-five and sixty-five whites, may have doomed the close vote on gradual emancipation in 1832, and fostered greater repression of slaves and of dissenters on the slavery issue.

diary, "Before I leave this Government I will have contrived to have a law passed gradually abolishing slavery in this State, or at all events to begin the work by prohibiting slavery on the west side of the Blue Ridge Mts."[30]

At the next session of the General Assembly, in January 1832, two sets of Virginia leaders came together and fought for emancipation. One group were old Whigs. The other were young liberals—Thomas Jefferson Randolph, the president's oldest grandson; Charles James Faulkner; and James McDowell.

They rested their arguments not on human rights but on economic interest. Noting the westward movement of Virginians (the 1830 census showed that the white population west of the Blue Ridge was 90,000 greater than that eastward of the mountains), they argued that the slavery system, its concurrent depletion of the soil, its degradation of manual labor, and its promotion of indolence and sensuality among whites prevented Virginia from making the internal improvements needed to arrest the flow of its population to the West.[31]

A vote was taken on January 25, 1832, on the strongest of the antislavery measures. It was rejected, 73 to 58. A shift of eight votes would have changed the outcome. The old Whigs and new liberals, despite their eloquence and statistics, failed mainly because they were unable to offer an acceptable plan for emancipation.

The argument continued in print. In September 1832 Thomas Roderick Dew made the case for slavery as a positive good in the *American Quarterly Review.*

Other Virginians took the opposite side. Among them was Jesse Burton Harrison, son of a tobacco merchant and an acquaintance of former presidents Jefferson and Madison. Harrison studied at Harvard and Göttingen in Germany (where Dew had been one of his friends and fellow students). With remarkable foresight Harrison had spent time in Europe interviewing members of the Russian court on serfdom "in view of reasoning upon it in relation to that of our African slaves."[32]

Harrison returned home to Lynchburg and began a law career. In 1833 he published anonymously his *Review of the Slave Question* "by a Virginian." He argued that "we shall never believe that Virginia would not have a thousand temptations for different sorts of emigrants, for capitalists, for free labourers, and for her own sons who meditate emigration, were but measures resorted to take the whole labour of the State out of the hands of slaves."[33] Harrison took his stand as a moderate reformer who asked that the state encourage voluntary emancipation and buy young slaves and annually deport them to Africa.

After the vote in 1832, the tide of reform sentiment quickly ebbed. More Virginians favored repression than emancipation. Fear of slave rebellion subsided, and so also did desire for change. The growth of the interstate slave trade seemed to solve the problem for many. Progressive Virginians, who had demanded the end of slavery, responded to the problem by leaving the state. Jesse Burton Harrison joined them and moved to New Orleans.

A Sense of Loss

In 1847 Dr. Henry Ruffner, president of Washington College in Lexington, studied the great migration from Virginia with a sense of sadness and loss. Ruffner believed that eastern Virginia would forever be in the thralldom of slavery. He advocated a division of Virginia so that the western part of the state might emancipate its slaves and deport them to Africa. Like Jesse Burton Harrison in 1833, Ruffner also believed that slavery was the cause of the continued hemorrhaging of Virginia's population. "It is a truth, a certain truth, that slavery drives free laborers—farmers, mechanics, and, all, and some of the best of them too—out of the country, and fills their places with negroes."[34]

Ruffner noted that from 1790 to 1840 Virginia had lost more people by emigration than all of the original free states combined. He wrote:

> It appears that in the ten years from 1830 to 1840, Virginia lost by emigration no fewer than 375,000 of her people, of whom East Virginia lost 304,000 and West Virginia lost 71,000. At this rate Virginia supplies the West every ten years with a population equal in number to the population of the State of Mississippi in 1840! Some Virginia politicians proudly—yes, proudly,—fellow citizens,—call our old Commonwealth, The Mother of States! These enlightened patriots might pay her a still higher compliment, by calling her The Grandmother of States. For our part, we are grieved and mortified, to think of the lean and haggard condition of our venerable mother. Her black children have sucked her so dry, that now, for a long time past, she has not milk enough for her offspring, either black or white.[35]

As in 1832, nothing was done. Two generations of Virginians had only one practical response to Virginia's problems—to move away from them.

Individual Motives for Migration

As one might expect in such a massive movement, individual motives for migration were extremely diverse and often mixed. In 1836, for example, a young lawyer named Joseph Glover Baldwin (1815–1864) packed a few possessions in his saddlebags and left Winchester, Virginia, bound for the frontier. He went first to East Tennessee, then to De Kalb, Mississippi, and to Gainesville, Alabama. In 1854 he moved to California, where his incessant wandering finally ended.

Baldwin wrote that as a lawyer he was drawn to the frontier mainly by the "most cheering and exhilarating prospects of fussing, quarrelling, murdering, violation of contracts, and the whole catalogue of *crimen falsi.*" He thought of the frontier as a lawyer's utopia. "What country could boast more largely of its crimes? What more splendid role of felonies! What more terrific murders! What more gorgeous bank robberies! What more magnificent operations in the land offices! . . . And in Indian affairs! — the very mention is suggestive of the poetry of theft — the romance of a wild and weird larceny! . . . Swindling Indians by the nation!" In another voice Baldwin added that he was also "urged by hunger and request of friends."[36]

Many another young Virginian shared Baldwin's purposes while describing them in more decorous ways. Henry Clay hoped that competition for legal clients would be easier in Kentucky than in Richmond. Indeed, all the professions were drawn to the West in numbers that the new settlements could not readily support. Clergymen migrated in the expectation of finding empty pulpits; some of them found no pulpits at all. Budding politicians dreamed of elections and offices in new places that promised to be more open to talent, not realizing until they arrived that many other promising young men had precisely the same ideas.

Physicians, too, were attracted to the Southwest by the hope of business. One of them was Dr. James Somerville, who, in moving his family from Virginia to Alabama, was carrying on a family tradition. A great-uncle, the first of the family to come to America, had settled at Fredericksburg, Virginia, before the American Revolution. He invited a nephew, sixteen-year-old James Somerville, the father of Dr. James Somerville, to move from Scotland to Fredericksburg in 1790 to take over his property and be his heir. This James Somerville became a successful merchant who, about 1812, moved to a large estate in Culpeper County and built Somervilla.

THE

FLUSH TIMES

OF

ALABAMA AND MISSISSIPPI.

𝔄 Series of Sketches.

BY

JOSEPH G. BALDWIN.

NEW-YORK:
D. APPLETON AND COMPANY,
200 BROADWAY.
LONDON: 16 LITTLE BRITAIN.
M.DCCC.LIII.

86. James Somerville observed in 1837 that "there are opportunities for making money in the S. West which though not so great as a few years ago are still astonishing to Virginians." In 1853 Joseph G. Baldwin took a more jaundiced view, but still the idea of opportunity flourished.

In the fall of 1835 Dr. Somerville ventured west to investigate the public sale of former Indian lands in western Alabama and Mississippi. Despite the survival of a large body of letters, his motive for leaving Virginia never is given explicitly, but like so many migrants he already had a relative—his wife's uncle—living in the region to which he was contemplating moving. From Huntsville, Alabama, he wrote his wife that "the country around here is the handsomest and richest I have ever seen," and at Tuscaloosa he wrote that "in coming South no one ought to pass through Huntsville and from thence by Decatur, Carolton, and Tuscumbia for the country there so far surpasses in richness, beauty and fertility that he becomes too hard to please." He noted, however, that "there is scarcely a good section of land unsold."

Not finding suitable land to buy, Somerville returned to Virginia but late in 1836 set out again for the Southwest. From Greensborough, Alabama, he wrote home that "if I had brought my negroes here I could hire them for more money . . . but they would not have been so well treated and would have been placed in a part of the country I cannot think healthy." On this second journey Somerville seems not to have been seeking land but a place to reestablish his medical practice. Of Tuscaloosa, where he ultimately settled, Somerville wrote that "there is no professional talent there engaged in the practice of medicine" and "there are opportunities in the S. West for making money which though not so great as a few years ago are still astonishing to Virginians."[37]

Others were not drawn to the West by dreams of prosperity but driven from the East by problems at home. Simon Kenton was on the run from a murder charge. Others sought to escape prosecution for debt. Many unserved writs in Virginia were endorsed on the back, "Gone to Kentucky." Later, so many people fled their creditors to the Rio Grande that Virginia sheriffs resorted merely to the initials "G.T.T."—Gone to Texas.

Other young Virginians, the spiritual descendants of Gilbert and Ralegh, were attracted by dreams of honor, glory, and adventure. Thomas Brown went to Florida with sixty slaves and "about twenty young men, who desired to adventure with me."[38]

One motive, however, was mentioned more than any other. Most observers agreed that Virginia's great migration was drawn by one great magnetic attraction: land. Thomas Hardeman despaired of ever being more than a tenant in Virginia and moved to Tennessee in hope of getting a farm of his own. Newlyweds James and Elizabeth McClure went to Texas because they could not find good land in Virginia. Moses Austin wrote generally of all the people he met on the roads to the West: "Ask these Pilgrims what they expect when they git to Kentuckey the Answer is Land. have you any. No, but I expect I can git it. have you any thing to pay for land, No. did you Ever see the Country. No but Every Body says its good land." Austin asked himself, "Can any thing be more Absurd than the Conduct of man, here is hundreds Travelling hundreds of Miles, they Know not for what Nor Whither, except its to Kentucky, passing land almost as good and easy obtained, the Proprietors of which would gladly give on any terms, but it will not do its not Kentuckey its not the Promis.d land its not the goodly inheratance the Land of Milk and Honey."[39]

References to western lands were often cast in paradisical terms. William Byrd II had called part of his western domain "the land of Eden," an image that often recurred in the westward movement. John Donelson told fellow Virginian William Preston that he had seen "that western world *that land of promise, that Terrestrial Paradice and garden of Eden.*"[40] In his 1784 book *The Discovery, Settlement, and Present State of Kentucky,* John Filson extolled Kentucky as "the most extraordinary country that the sun enlightens with its celestial beams."[41]

Some of Moses Austin's "Pilgrims" were former servants and laborers. Many travelers described migrants in rags, working their way west with a few battered possessions in a desperate struggle against their poverty. Most, however, were at least in middling circumstances, and some had been prosperous in the East. Harry Toulmin wrote of Virginia, "Here persons who have but four or five hundred acres and a large family think it time to begin to make a provision for them, by going to Washington County, Nelson, or Kentucky in order to exchange their five hundred for five thousand."[42]

Family Purposes

The hunger for land was indeed at the heart of this great migration. For most people, however, land was merely a means to another end, which for many movers was the welfare of their families. In a society where kin connections were exceptionally strong and important to one's identity, many were thinking not about themselves alone but about their relations. In 1784 Alexander Breckinridge wrote from Kentucky to his half brother in Virginia that if he could secure a house "that would contain us all," he would do it, "let it be in whatever part of the Globe was most agreeable, I care not where it is, so we could all be together."[43] Breckinridge's half brother came out nine years later. By then his mother, four adult siblings and their families, and two aunts and uncles, along with assorted cousins and their children, had preceded him.

This family-centered thinking shaped the structure of migration. Virginians tended to move west in family groups. If they traveled individually, they settled in a place where they already had relatives. Chain migration was common in this great hegira. There were exceptions of solitary travelers. The Virginia argonauts who went to California during the gold rush were almost all alone and unmarried. But family ties and family purposes were strong in the westward movement. John Brown moved to Kentucky in search of economic opportunity. He hoped that litigation arising from land speculation would be lucrative for lawyers such as he, but he was not bent solely on individual aggrandizement. His purpose was to transplant his family, which he did with high success. By the time he brought his parents to Kentucky a few years later, his six brothers and sisters already had settled there.[44]

Many others did something similar. David Meade specifically asked that his letters be passed around the family to entice its members to join him in Kentucky. Once the threat of his indictment for murder was removed, Simon Kenton brought his father's family to Maysville, Kentucky. James Somerville looked to Alabama because his wife's uncle lived there. James and Elizabeth McClure had no relatives in Texas, but when they were disappointed with it, they went to Missouri because her brother had moved there. William Lewis Moody, who liked Texas better than the McClures had, enticed his brothers to join him in business.

Family letters were a major element in the flow of information that led to the decision to move. Branch Archer wrote from Texas in 1848, "Tell Uncle Powel . . . to quit her [Virginia] as rats quit sinking vessels, and take a house in this land of promise; where he will find what he found in Virginia forty years past, in her halcyon days of Liberty, quiet, and defiance." These appeals did not always succeed. Archer failed to persuade his sisters to leave Cumberland Court House. Sometimes news from the West discouraged migration. The McClures and a woman identified only as Sallie F. expressed disappointment with Texas, and one Virginian recounted the deaths of a neighboring family that had moved to Texas and been murdered by thieves.[45]

Francis Eppes, Thomas Jefferson's grandson, wrote Nicholas Trist: "What say you to a *general* move to a more southern latitude[?] I want to go where

87. Two large demographic movements are reflected in the life of Ann Mary Wetzel Aulick Booker (1759–1834), shown here in a 1805 painting by Jacob Frymire. As a child she came from Germany to Winchester, at the head of the Shenandoah Valley. In 1818, after marrying a second time, she moved on to Indiana, like many other Germans who flowed from the northern Shenandoah into the Midwest.

I can make more money. . . . What say you to Florida, — or Kentuckie; or Tenessee; or Missouri? I will go any where so that we may all settle together: but from accounts lately received should greatly prefer E. Florida. . . . Here lies the road to wealth! bundle up, and let us leave our gullies to the Yankee pedlars, who covet them so much."[46] Elizabeth Randolph Eppes confided to Virginia Randolph Trist that she and her husband were comfortable in Virginia but that other family members were not: "Our own affairs, considered separate from my family's are what the world would call comfortable enough, & the world I dare say (the little world of Bedford at any rate) contemns as ill-judged the step we meditate," but "No, our interests are inseparably united, and as they cannot live here, we must seek together some more favoured spot."[47] Based on glowing reports from his father-in-law, Francis Eppes sold his home, Thomas Jefferson's retreat at Poplar Forest in Bedford County, and settled in Tallahassee, where he later became mayor.

Another sort of motivational pattern also arose from the same strong familial ties of Virginia society. Historian Joan Cashin argues that in the aftermath of the struggle for national independence, an ethos of personal independence emerged (earlier, independence had meant freedom from manual labor). Young men went west to achieve this personal independence. There are many examples to support this view. John J. Allen left because of a dispute with his father. Burton Carr departed after quarreling with his older brothers and thereafter corresponded only with his youngest brother. Branch Archer went to Texas after killing a cousin in a duel, fought for the independence of Texas, and settled in Velasco, where he practiced medicine.[48]

Women tended to think about moving in different ways from men. By and large, they were not happy about leaving home. The letters from Kentucky of Patrick Henry's sister Annie Christian were a litany of woe. She wrote, "This Country has Sufferd much by the Indians this Summer, I must give my oppinion to you of this place now, which is, if we had trade & a Peace with the Indians we might live very well, but at present it is the most expensive part of the world I ever lived in, every thing being excessive high, & little & no Credit, however I hope for an alteration to take place some time hence, Your Brother seems to be much displeased with Kentucky generally & I fear to have to move again."

Annie Christian urged her "disgusted" husband to give Kentucky more time, but he was unmoved. She wrote, "So it Seems as if we were to wander stil farthur. but I pray, to have grace not to murmur."[49] Five months later

My Dear Sister Dec.r 15 1785

We rec'd yours & had the pleasure of seeing my
Cousin Dorcy at the same time, He is well & gone
up to Fyatte, We are all well here thank the
Lord, we now have peace since the winter Sets
in, which seems a great Satisfaction to me,
This Country has Suffered much by ~~them~~ the Indians this
Summer, I must give my oppinion to you of
this place now, which is, if we had trade & a
Peace with the Indians we meight live very
well, but at present it is the most expensive
part of the world I ever lived in, every thing
being excessive high, & little & no Credit,
however I hope for an alteration to take peace
some time hence, Your Brother seems to
be much displeas'd with Kentucky generally
& I fear to have to move again, I shall
take all care of your dear Son while
with us, & am in haste with my best duty
to your dear Mother, & kindest love to Col'
Fleming & your dear little Children
                    I remain my dear Sister
                        your ever aff.t
                                A. Christian

88. Letter from Annie Christian, Patrick Henry's sister, to her sister-in-law
in Virginia. She wrote that her husband is displeased with Kentucky and "I
fear to have to move again."

Colonel William Christian (1732–1786) was killed by Indians. Although he had laid claim to large tracts of land, these rights did not automatically translate into cash, and he left an estate encumbered by £2,000 in debt. Annie Christian took on the heavy responsibilities of supervising the estate and running her family. For two years she stayed in Kentucky managing her property and slaves and setting the estate in order, but by 1788 she had had enough. That year she returned to Virginia, where she died two years later.

Cashin finds evidence in her research that Annie Christian's attitude toward the West was common among Virginia women. Men could hope to create new networks in business, politics, or the militia after migration, but women were devastated by breaking home ties. In view of the circumscribed role of women in that period, their sense of identity depended more than men's on kinship and neighborhood networks. The sundering of these bonds was traumatic, both for those who went and for others who stayed behind. Elizabeth Ambler tried to persuade her son not to go to Alabama—"Heaven forbid"—but he went anyway. John J. Ambler, Sr., knowing several of his sons were meditating migration because of displeasure with the bequests intended for them, made generous provisions for the youngest son so that he would stay in Virginia and assist his father. That Elizabeth Otey's son left for Tennessee was a source of "great grief." "Would to God you had never gone" was what Sarah Irby wrote her son who had migrated to Mississippi.[50]

Even here, however, evidence is mixed. James Breckinridge decided against moving to Kentucky in 1792 largely because of his wife's reluctance.[51] Elizabeth McClure went west with some trepidation, but so did her husband. The story of the McClures' migration began in what historian Bernard DeVoto called the year of decision, 1846, as Elizabeth Ann Cooley prepared to marry James McClure. Her father was a man of means in Carroll County, Virginia, but the young couple had searched in vain for good, affordable land in the Old Dominion. On February 15 she wrote in her journal, "Texas is the motto with me now." Ten days later she married. By March 8 they "had looked at all the land that were for sale, and tired and weary of the pursuit concluded that we would go to *Texas*. . . . I am fixed to go to Texas, a country to which I had rather go than anywhere else, and to leave my *dear* old native land." On April 9 they set out but heard on the road disquieting news: "War in Texas . . . a heap [of] trouble going on." On May 19 she expressed her reservations: "I fear to go to Texas, dread to go back—hope we will like it." They did not. Hardly had they arrived when McClure observed: "A stern, heartless people, no sympathy. . . . I think we had better go to Missouri. . . . I rue the day we ever thought of *Texas*. . . . Oh! ambition how hast thou led me astray." Her brother lived in Missouri. "I believe I will like Missouri," she wrote. Once there, she and her husband became schoolteachers, but on September 13 she wrote, "I wish I was back in Va., I am not happy here," and a few days later, "I want once more to visit my native land before I die if the Lord will." The Lord did not. In March 1848 she contracted typhoid fever. On March 29 her husband closed out her journal: "This Journal is done! The author being Elizabeth A. McClure died March 28, 1848. . . . She was 22 years 7 months and 12 days old."[52]

Social Class and Emigration

How did these emigrants from Virginia fare? Generally, the elites did well. David Meade chronically pleaded a shortage of cash, but he was better off in Kentucky than in Virginia. John Breckinridge gained political eminence in Kentucky, but in Virginia he had been elected to Congress without campaigning. John Brown achieved his political ambitions. Henry Clay missed the ultimate prize of the presidency (though not for lack of effort), but no Virginian who went west had a larger influence on the nation's affairs. Edward Coles became governor of Illinois three years after arriving there but ended up in Philadelphia. Within a few years of arrival, W. L. Moody and his brothers were among the wealthiest 1 percent of Texans. Henry Tayloe purchased 1,620 acres in Alabama in 1834 and soon added many more. He lent money at high interest and declared unashamedly: "I have no scruples toward the Alabamians. . . . I came here to make money." After two poor harvests he considered returning to Virginia. O. G. Murrell went to Tennessee in the 1830s, but debts forced him on to Mississippi in the late 1840s. He was beset by insect infestation, bad weather, and sick slaves. Admitting that he could not handle money, he turned his affairs over to a brother. A. W. Taliaferro, who arrived in California in 1849, might have become rich through his medical practice but was careless with money. He died beloved in his community for his generosity. Branch T. Archer, son of a Powhatan County planter, did moderately well in Texas. He owned $4,400 in property, but no slaves, in 1850. He never approached his father's Virginia holdings in 1820. He left a son, Powhatan, a common name among Virginia expatriates. J. W. Calvert made and lost lots of money but remarked, "I always felt independent."[53]

The middling sort of people had more varied experiences than the gentry. Simon Kenton, like his friend Daniel Boone, was careless with land titles and lived in poverty until relieved by a small government pension. "Bigfoot" Wallace became a folk legend in his own time but on a smaller scale than Daniel Boone or David Crockett. Cyrus McCormick demonstrated his mechanical reaper at Steele's Tavern, Virginia, in 1831, but he became commercially successful only after moving in 1847 to Chicago, the heart of a vast area where farmers were not constrained by acreage but by the ability to work it. Artist George Caleb Bingham had a moment of fame before dying in obscurity. Thomas Hardeman, who had left Virginia as a tenant in 1778, became a large landowner in Middle Tennessee, but late in life wanderlust pushed him on to Missouri. Within two generations his descendants had explored the Rockies, traded in Texas and Santa Fe, and gone to Oregon, California, and even Mexico. Jim Beckwourth was briefly famous, too, but died under mysterious circumstances. Abraham Lincoln and Thomas Lincoln, the grandfather and the father of the future president, had headed for Kentucky after the Revolution, but they lived very near the margin there, as they had in Virginia.

In general, however, most studies suggest that for free migrants, moving out did indeed mean moving up. Even as inequality persisted on the southern frontier, social mobility increased. Wealth and class continued to be as highly stratified in the West as in the East, but the lines could be crossed more easily by an ambitious young Virginian who traveled over the mountains. The westward movement became an avenue of upward striving that many followed with success. Individuals changed their positions, even as the system remained the same.[54]

It was rarely a matter of rags to riches. There were always a few success stories of that sort—the steamboat fireman whom W. L. Moody wrote in 1853 was worth $150,000—enough to inspire many others, but the usual experience of emigrants was modest improvement in their way of life. Motives made a difference in this great migration. Large public purposes were less important than small private ambitions for prosperity of a family or profit in a career.

These emigrants had no quarrel with their own society. They wished only to flourish in it. They were Tocqueville's "venturous conservatives." That attitude made a difference for the culture they created in the West.

Getting There: The Process of Westward Movement

The knowledge that the immigrants and those they left behind might never meet again made departure a heart-wrenching affair. Of the day she left home, Elizabeth McClure wrote, "We arose early . . . and busily prepared for leaving. Many of our friends came there to see us start, and oh, how solemn was the scene. His dearest friends taking him by the hand bidding him farewell, and perhaps forever. Oh! how hard it was to part, next to death, but yet we tore away." The Friday before they left Virginia, the Eppes family visited Mrs. Eppes's father's home in Lynchburg and attended a prayer service where all sang "Blest Be the Tie That Binds." In 1836 Sarah Ann Quarles Chandler left Green Spring Valley, Louisa County, for Cooper County, Missouri. In her diary she wrote, "Nothing of consequence occurred except that we have left Virginia and this makes me feel sorrowful enough."[55]

After leave-taking came the journey. Most traveled by road or river. The roads followed game trails and buffalo traces through the forest. Travel was extremely dangerous. The Indians in the Southwest strongly resisted invasion; there was much bloodshed in Kentucky and Tennessee especially. Bandit gangs infested the western roads and preyed on lone travelers. People traveled together, and most of them were armed. Even Quaker women and children over twelve carried weapons on western roads.[56]

The early overland movement commonly took place on foot or horse, with women riding on pillions behind their husbands. Later came two-wheeled carts and two-horse wagons. Another reason for travel in groups was mutual assistance in getting over the mountains—the teams doubled or trebled, and the men worked together four behind and two to chock.[57]

The game traces were gradually improved into a network of roads, of which several were especially important in the migration from Virginia. A branch of the Great Philadelphia Wagon Road reached the Long Island of the Holston River (now East Tennessee) by 1775. From there Daniel Boone and thirty men blazed the Wilderness Trail through the Cumberland Gap into central Kentucky. It was thought to deserve its name. In 1785 Annie

Henry Christian wrote from Kentucky to her sister-in-law in Virginia about the Wilderness Road, "Had I any Idea of its being half as bad as I found it no inducement on this earth, woud have encouraged me to attempt it, So that my weak advice to your Mother yourself, & Sister Madison is never to think of coming thro' the wilderness to this country."[58] The first wagons traveled on the Wilderness Road in 1795. In 1796 David Meade expected that it would be improved. In 1836 Sarah Ann Quarles Chandler, migrating from Louisa County to Missouri, noted that a macadamized road was being built from Cumberland Gap to Louisville.[59]

The boatyard in Sullivan County, Tennessee, where the Wilderness Road began, was the starting point for both the overland journey and the river voyage that resulted in settling Nashville. In 1779 James Robertson led a party, mostly men, through Cumberland Gap into central Kentucky, then south to the Cumberland Basin. John Donelson led a flotilla of flatboats that carried most of the women and children on what was erroneously believed to be the safer, easier route, down the Tennessee River and back up the Cumberland via the connecting Ohio River. By 1789 the Avery Trace connected Nashville with East Tennessee and Virginia.

Another route, the Kanawha Road, ran through rugged country. Levi Coffin described it: "Crossing Dan River, it led by Patrick Court House, Virginia to Marberry's Gap in the Blue Ridge Mountains, thence across Clinch mountain by way of Pack's Ferry on New River, thence over white oak mountain to the falls of the Kanawha and down that river to the Ohio, crossing at Gallipolis."[60] Another way west was the Maggodee Route—the Virginia turnpike from Richmond, Lynchburg, and Fincastle to the confluence of the Ohio and Kanawha.[61]

In 1806 work began on the National Road from Cumberland, Maryland, to Wheeling, Virginia, and over the Ohio River. It was finished to Wheeling in 1821, Columbus in 1827, and Indianapolis in 1830. Further extensions reached Illinois. Many Virginians traveled far north to take this route. Rapid progress could be made along it because it featured a twenty-foot-wide gravel bed crowned for drainage.

The vehicles commonly used were Conestoga-type wagons, which were developed by German immigrants in the Conestoga Valley of Pennsylvania. These wagons had a distinctive boat shape and muslin or linen covers stretched over hoops. "Some had no paint, but were pitched with tar instead, while the horses were hitched to them with huck collars and rawhide traces."[62] These vehicles were much in use by Virginia migrants from the western regions of the state. Most Conestoga wagons, however, never were taken west but were used for hauling freight and tobacco. Cigars came to be called stogies because the tobacco used to make them was hauled in Conestoga wagons.

When used as emigrant wagons, as by young Sam Houston and family, who moved from Rockbridge County to East Tennessee in 1809 in two Conestoga wagons, the people rode separately (the Houstons had nine horses and several slaves) or walked alongside.[63] At night they slept on the ground or

89. The classic emigrant wagon of the American frontier originated near Conestoga, Pennsylvania, in the eighteenth century. These vehicles were much in use by Virginia migrants, especially those from the western regions of the state. Today at least twelve such wagons survive that probably were made in Virginia. This one, made by J. B. Kiger of Sperryville, is the only signed example extant. It still preserves his maker's marks and the original blue and red paint.

at an inn. The wagon sheltered the household goods. The prairie schooner that developed in the 1800s lacked the boat shape of the Conestoga wagon because it was designed to traverse flat land, and consequently it had a driver's bench that Conestoga wagons lacked.

Some traveled in high state. David Meade's cavalcade consisted of "the coachee, my chair, our baggage waggon, two hired waggons," and "about fifty souls" in all. They traveled north from Virginia through Maryland and Pennsylvania to Red Stone Fort, making twelve to twenty miles a day. "Repeated disasters of the baggage wagon were really disheartening," wrote Meade, but his wife Sarah exulted that the Blue Ridge Mountains were no terror, and they found "no Howling wolves — croaking Ravens — or growling Bears" but rather many signs of civilization.[64]

At the Monongahela River they took "Kentucky boats," or flatboats, downriver. Below Pittsburgh, Meade wrote of the Ohio River valley that "the most indifferent part of it is better than the best upon James River below the Falls has ever been." But the cost of moving was higher than he had anticipated. Wagon hire from the Blue Ridge to Red Stone Fort was £100. Once across the Blue Ridge they had to pay "tavern prices" for all provisions. Four slaves escaped.[65] In contrast to Meade, Robert Lewis went scouting for western land with only one slave, Spencer, and a one-horse sulky. Even so, he was a Virginia gentleman, a nephew of George Washington, and expected to be treated as such. On his way to the Scioto River valley in Ohio, he deplored the lack of hospitality at many establishments, but of one he wrote, "I breakfasted quite in the old Virginia stile — loaf bread, corn pone, and delightful coffee and tea." Of course it did not surprise him to find that his hostess was a Virginian, the daughter of Robert Pollard of King William County and a cousin of his brother's wife. On a humbler plane was David Barrow, a Baptist preacher who boasted of the simplicity of his hosts, "who served him with their own hands for they despise hereditary slavery."[66]

Most written travel accounts come from people in comfortable circumstances, but occasionally these narratives reveal the plight of less fortunate travelers. In 1836 James Somerville wrote of groups leaving Virginia for the Southwest, including "a party of about fourteen in number, 10 of whom were children under 12 years of age without horse, cart, or any means of conveyance and all the children barefooted and some of them almost naked."[67]

Among these various emigrants there was a great disparity in the quantity of goods taken west. Francis Eppes wrote before leaving Poplar Forest,

"Among other perishables I shall be obliged to sell the clock which I purchased at Monticello. My reasons are simply want of money, the impossibility of taking it with me, and the impossibility of having it repaired in the savage wilderness to which I shall go."[68] The McClures did take a clock to Texas. The works have survived, but not the case, which perhaps was damaged on the road. William Keys, who left Rockbridge County in 1805, reported that "we sometimes passed the fragments of broken wagon beds, broken furniture and remnants of broken boxes and other marks of damage."[69] A large corner cupboard, now in the lieutenant governor's mansion, survived the trip to Kentucky, as did a painted dower chest from Wythe County, Virginia. John Donelson took his small writing desk from Virginia to Nashville on his flagship *Adventure*. It survives at the Tennessee State Museum on loan from descendants.

90. The interior of a flatboat was sketched by French naturalist Charles-Alexandre Lesueur, who traveled widely in the Ohio Valley during the second quarter of the nineteenth century.

One Kentucky settler recalled that "almost every housekeeper had some bowl or dish she had brought from the old states, that was kept carefully along with perhaps, a few silver spoons, as proof of her primitive gentility."[70] James McBride and his wife brought a complete china tea service by pack mules to Kentucky. It was used on special occasions, such as to entertain the Reverend David Rice (1733–1816), a Virginian who made an exploratory trip to Kentucky in 1783 in the hope of creating an inheritance for his children. He found land titles uncertain and society unstable and returned to Virginia, but he was lured back to Kentucky by some who had heard him preach. Family in tow, he arrived at the widow McBride's and was served from her elegant tea service lovingly brought from the old state. In 1832 Garrett Minor Quarles of Louisa County took to Kentucky a ceramic mug that by then was an heirloom supposedly used to drink a toast upon receiving news of Cornwallis's surrender at Yorktown.

Men such as David Meade and Thomas Jones have been called "portable planters" because they "believed that they could detach from that . . . eighteenth-century Chesapeake social system . . . a cohesive unit consisting of the planter, his family, his genteel accoutrements, his black 'family' and the portable wealth they embodied and could spin it off or float it down the Ohio River to trans-Appalachian lands."[71] A visitor to Meade's Kentucky home, La Chaumière des Prairies, noted the portraits brought from England, probably including one of Meade himself done in London and an English-looking portrait of Sarah Meade, perhaps done by Cosmo Alexander in Virginia. Meade's "massive silver" probably was English also, although there were silversmiths in Kentucky from the 1780s, including Edward West, Jr., father of portrait artist William Edward West, and Samuel Ayres, who left Essex County, Virginia, not later than 1786.[72] In 1810 Thomas Jones and his wife Elizabeth, on their way to Kentucky, left their goods temporarily at the boatyard in Sullivan County, Tennessee (now Kingsport). Their receipt reveals china tea sets, bed curtains figured with peacocks and vines, and fifty-five volumes of history.[73]

5

African-American Migration

Emigrants in Chains

AT THE SAME TIME that emigrants of European descent were moving out of the Old Dominion, there was also another great migration—of African-American Virginians. The magnitude of this movement was great. One scholar has reckoned that, on the average, about 10,000 Virginia slaves were sold every year to southern and western states during the three decades from 1830 to 1860, a total of 300,000 in that period alone. This number, large as it is, takes no account of slaves who were sold before 1830, nor does it include African-American emigrants who left Virginia in other ways.[1]

Black migration from Virginia, like its white counterpart, was vast and varied. There were many roads from the Old Dominion, and African Americans traveled them in different ways. Large numbers were carried south and west by slave traders; many others emigrated with their masters. For most African Americans migration from Virginia was a movement into a bondage more severe than what they had known before. For many others this was a movement to freedom. Altogether, the magnitude of African-American emigration from Virginia to other parts of the United States was much larger than immigration from Africa to British America. It was a process of great importance in its cultural consequences. The African slave trade led to the creation of new African-American cultures in the coastal colonies of early America. The black migration out of Virginia, along with that from other eastern states, created a system of slavery that was of continental dimensions. At the same time migration transformed African-American culture into a system of enormous diversity—as pluralistic as the culture of European Americans.

The Domestic Slave Trade

The emigration of slaves from Virginia began in a small way during the eighteenth century. By 1790 at least 13,000 African Americans were living in Kentucky. Nearly all of them came from Virginia.[2] The magnitude of this trade increased rapidly during the early Republic. Some of it went overland, across the same western roads that free emigrants used. In 1836 James Somerville was told by a tavern keeper in Knoxville, Tennessee, that 40,000 slaves had been marched by his establishment from Virginia, bound away to the Cotton South. Much of this movement was by sea, in a large coastal trade from the Chesapeake and its tributary rivers to the Carolinas, Georgia, and the Gulf coast. During the last thirty years of slavery, an increasing proportion went by the new railroads, which gave a new spirit of modernity to this ancient commerce in human flesh. An article in a Petersburg newspaper that was reprinted in a Texas paper on February 12, 1859, read: "SLAVE EXODUS—An almost endless outgoing of slaves from Virginia to the South has continued for more than two weeks past. On Tuesday morning the car allotted to servants on the Richmond and Petersburg Railroad was filled to such an extent that one of the spring bars over the track broke down, without, however, producing any harm."[3]

A former slave, Lorenzo Ivy of Danville, Virginia, vividly remembered from his childhood the sight of long lines of slaves moving to the railroad for shipment farther south. "Dey sol' slaves heah an everywhere," he recalled. "I've seen droves of Negroes brought in heah on foot goin' Souf to be sol'. Each one have an old tow sack on his back wif everythin' he's got in it. Over de hills dey come in lines reachin' as far as you kin see. Dey walk in double lines chained tergether in twos. Dey walk 'em heah to de railroad an' ship 'em Souf lak cattle. Truely, son, de haf has never been tol'."[4]

Ivy had been born about 1850 and was in his eighties when his recollections were recorded. One might think that his memory of slaves going to market "in lines reachin' as far as you kin see" was exaggerated. Quantitative research, however, suggests that it may have been accurate.

Virginia was by far the most important participant in the interstate slave trade. One historian has estimated that in the decade of 1800–1809 there was a total net emigration of 66,000 slaves from one state to another. Of that number at least 41,000 (63 percent) came from Virginia and the remainder mostly from Maryland and Delaware.[5] Other states gradually became net exporters of slaves at a later date: North Carolina from the 1810s, South Carolina from the 1820s, Tennessee and Kentucky from the 1850s. Throughout the history of American slavery, however, by far the largest slave exporter was Virginia, which even as late as the 1850s nearly equaled the next two largest slave-exporting states combined. Furthermore, much of the slave trade from other states consisted of the children of emigrants from Virginia.[6] A slave in the Upper South had a 30 percent chance of being sold to a slave trader during the first forty years of life. Many sales were at slave marts in Alexandria and Richmond, but most were made directly by planters in rural areas. More than half of these sales broke up families.

For most slaves the journey from Virginia was arduous in the extreme. Many who were sold south had experiences that were comparable in some ways to those of the Middle Passage. In 1834 Englishman George Featherstonhaugh saw 300 slaves on the New River being marched to Tennessee. There were nine wagons and single-horse carriages for the whites and lame slaves, but the 200 black men were *"manacled and chained to each other."*[7] He saw the slave coffle crossing the New River in Southwest Virginia. Noting that escapes sometimes were made during the confusion of a crossing, Featherstonhaugh reported that "the slave drivers, aware of this disposition in the unfortunate negroes, endeavor to mitigate their discontent by feeding them well, and by encouraging them to sing 'Oh Virginia, never tire' on the banjo."[8]

A recent study suggests that half of slave sales broke up families.[9] Some masters, however, leased out slaves rather than separate families. Others consulted slaves about their willingness to be sold. In 1849 John McCalley of Spotsylvania County refused to sell the slave Tom to a relative in Huntsville, Alabama, because "when I consulted him the other day," he "was unwilling to go."[10] Elizabeth Ambler, who remained in Virginia while her husband settled in Alabama, asked for the return of Adam, her favorite slave, before he was stricken with the epidemic sweeping the plantation.[11]

The slaves themselves often told a different tale. One former slave recalled: "Now, you want to know how slaves were sold. Um, um, um, sad, sad times. Slaves were sold off of blocks, rasselled [raffled?] off. . . . There was young gals an' dey were marched down to the train—baby, baby! I can recollect it—a terrible time too, it wuz. Dar was a great crying and carrying on mongst the slaves who had been sold. Two or three of dem gals had young babies taking with 'em. Poor little things. As soon as dey got on de train dis ol' new mas-

91. Lewis Miller, a folk artist from York, Pennsylvania, sketched this slave coffle being marched from Virginia to Tennessee in 1853.

ter had train stopped an' made dem poor gal mothers take babies off."[12] Another Virginia slave, Samuel Chilton, remembered: "Oh, yes, I done seen 'em sel niggers sell 'em like cattle. Make you stan' up on a block. Yes, zamine you like you was a hoss. Sometimes take an' sell you in groups. . . . You would see gangs of slaves chained together un, un, setch a cryin' an' screamin' you ain't nebber heard like dem pitiful cries of dem po' slaves. Dat was a sad partin'

92. Clara Brown was born a slave in Virginia. In 1809 her owner moved to Kentucky where Brown married a slave carpenter. She had four children, but her family was broken up by sale. Once freed, Brown made a lifelong search for her daughter Eliza Jane that took her to several states in the Midwest and Far West.

time. Little babies was taken from deir mothers breast while nursin' some time dat little mouth would be holin' tight but dey snatched him away."[13]

Traveling with Masters

Even this enormous traffic was only a part of African-American emigration from Virginia. One recent study indicates that the slave trade accounted for only about 60 percent of forced interregional migration of slaves. Another 40 percent accompanied their masters to the West.[14] Many examples of such migration appear in plantation records. John Breckinridge took eighteen slaves to Kentucky in 1793; more followed later. Thomas Jones left with eighteen in 1810. In 1796 David Meade took even more.

For John Breckinridge, the trek to Kentucky was "a pleasant journey," but for his slaves who had been sent ahead it was a winter hell. They were kept going only by hourly breaks for whiskey. Once there, the slaves were taken to the plantation of Breckinridge's brother-in-law, where the slaves visited friends and family to assuage the disorientation of the journey. When Lettice Breckinridge failed to consider slave family ties when moving to Kentucky, her slave Jack abandoned the party.[15] One of Thomas Jones's slaves miscarried on the trip to Kentucky. Four of David Meade's bondspeople escaped during the journey. Keeping marriage partners together reduced the risk of slaves running away. Sometimes a slave owner divided slave families among his children. A few of these families reassembled in the West, and some slave reunions occurred. But most slaves lacked the consolation of being able to correspond with or visit kin, activities that eased the pain of separation for many white migrants.[16]

Black experiences of emigration were as diverse as those of whites, but in general slaves dreaded the thought of moving west and especially of being sent into the Deep South. "Child, it makes me shudder when I hear talk of dat cotton country," one Virginia slave remembered. "I ain't never seen dar an' I don't wanta!"[17] They feared the Lower South with good reason. Of eleven slaves Richard Ambler took to Alabama in 1835, eight died of disease or were killed by Indians who lived in nearly forests.[18]

Others were put to work in gangs on cotton and sugar plantations that were very different from the smaller units in Virginia. Cotton and sugar slavery was far more profitable than Virginia's peculiar institution. That disparity was one of the major determinants of the slave trade.

The agricultural decline in Virginia and the growth of cotton and sugar planting in the Southwest made slavery unprofitable in Virginia but profitable outside it. Just as the African slave trade arose in the late seventeenth century to supply labor for tobacco culture, so an internal slave trade emerged to supply labor to the Cotton South. In 1834 George Featherstonhaugh wrote: "This land traffic, in fact, has grown out of the wide-spreading population of the United States, the annexation of Louisiana, and the increased cultivation of cotton and sugar. . . . Hence negroes have risen greatly in price, from 500 to 1000 dollars, according to their capacity. . . . The soil of Virginia has gradually become exhausted with repeated crops of tobacco and Indian corn; and when to this is added the constant subdivision of property . . . small proprietors . . . have become embarrassed in their circumstances, and, when they are pinched, are compelled to sell a negro or two."[19] It made no economic sense to use high-priced slaves to grow low-priced crops in Virginia. In large numbers bondspeople were sold or leased out in Virginia or elsewhere.[20]

Opportunities for masters beckoned in the West. W. L. Moody, who came to Fairfield, Texas, from Chesterfield, Virginia, in 1852, wrote his brother James the next year: "If you will come out and go to planting cotton on some of the bottom lands of our navigable rivers you can in the course of a few years make a fortune. If you will invest all your money in negroes and come out I can get you as much money as you want to buy a place and provisions for a start. One of our planters fifteen years ago was fireman on a steamboat; now he owns two plantations, works in the field 76 negroes, and is worth $150,000."[21]

Such profits overcame many scruples. William Macon Waller, an Amherst County planter, and neighbor James Taliaferro went down the Great Wagon Road of the Valley of Virginia in 1847 to sell slaves in the Southwest. Compassion for his slaves, concerns about the morality of his actions, and a large dose of self-pity caused him to brood over the matter. He wrote to his wife, "I have already seen and felt enough to make me loath the vocation of slave trading."[22] Yet he felt so oppressed by his debts that he executed the unpleasant task of selling them in Mississippi and New Orleans. He received $12,600 for twenty slaves. For these and hundreds of thousands of other slaves, the words "I'm bound away" from the ballad "Shenandoah" had a tragic double meaning.

Emancipation and Emigration

Other slaves left Virginia because they were emancipated by their masters. Edward Coles (1786–1868) attended Hampden-Sydney College and the College of William and Mary. He wrote later, "While attending the political course of studies in the class at William and Mary, I had my attention first awakened to the state of master & slave." The undergraduate asked his teacher James Madison, president of the college and bishop of Virginia, how the owning of men could be justified. Coles remembered that Madison "frankly admitted it could not be rightfully done and that Slavery was a state of thing that could not be justified on principle and could only be tolerated in our Country, by our finding it in existence and the difficulty of getting rid of it."[23]

In 1808 Coles inherited a plantation of 782 acres on Rockfish River twenty miles from his parents' home Enniscorthy in Albemarle County. Along with it came twenty slaves, of whom nine were children. Soon he began to think of emancipating them, but his plans were delayed by his acceptance of an offer to be President-elect James Madison's private secretary, a post he held from 1809 to 1815. In 1816 Madison sent Coles, who was a cousin of Dolley Madison, on a diplomatic mission to Russia.

After his return he explored various possibilities for settling his slaves on free soil and at length decided to take them to Edwardsville, Illinois, and help them get started. On the first of April 1819, having sold his Virginia lands, Coles set out by covered wagon with his slaves. Their destination was not revealed to them. When they reached the Ohio River, they were transferred to flatboats. Coles later wrote that as they floated downriver,

> I called on the deck of the Boats, which were lashed together, all the negroes, and made them a short address, in which I commenced by saying it was time for me to make known to them what I intended to do with them. . . . I proclaimed in the shortest and fullest manner possible, that they were no longer Slaves, but free—free as I was, and were at liberty to proceed with me, or to go ashore at their pleasure. The effect on them was electrical. In breathless silence they stood before me, unable to utter a word, but with countenances beaming with expression which no words could convey, and which no language can now describe.[24]

They were further delighted when Coles promised each family 160 acres, and "soon after reaching Edwardsville, I executed and delivered to them

93. Edward Coles became convinced of the immorality of slavery while a student at the College of William and Mary. This painting depicts his announcement to his slaves of their emancipation while headed to Illinois on flatboats.

Deeds to the lands promised them. . . . the lands I intended to give them were unimproved lands. . . . they would have to hire themselves out till they could acquire by their labour the necessary means to commence cultivating and residing on their own lands." Some he offered jobs, others he told that "labour was much in demand in that new Country, and highly paid for."[25]

Coles himself settled in Illinois and three years later was elected governor of the state. He found that though slavery was prohibited in Illinois, the peculiar institution existed in everything but name. Cole led a campaign to suppress it. Some historians believe that he played a major, even decisive role in stopping a movement toward the expansion of slavery into the Old Northwest.[26]

One of the most remarkable sagas is that of the Randolph slaves. When John Randolph of Roanoke died in 1833, he left three wills. The earliest freed his slaves. The second provided for the purchase of land for their resettlement. The third stipulated that they should be sold, though he repudiated this document on his deathbed. A court ruled that the last will was invalid because Randolph was insane when he made it and validated the second will, but the decision was not rendered until 1844, and the slaves were not freed until May 4, 1846. The second will provided $38,000 "to transport and settle the said slaves in some other state, . . . giving to all above the age of 40 not less than ten acres of land each."[27] Randolph's executor employed an agent, who bought 3,200 acres in Mercer County, Ohio, along the Indiana border. Other blacks had lived there since 1835.

The former Randolph slaves set out for Ohio in June 1846. According to Clem Clay, one of the 383, they "had tents along, bought eatables along the road, sang songs in the evening, [and] came on boat to Cincinnati from Kanawa [River]."[28] At Cincinnati they boarded boats for the 100-mile journey to their promised land. The white inhabitants of Mercer County, mostly recently arrived German peasants, adopted a set of resolutions: the Randolph party must leave the county by March 1, 1847; and after January 1, 1847, no one would employ or trade with them. Words being deemed not strong enough, an armed mob met the blacks when they docked at New Bremen, and the Randolph party's agent hastily hired boats to take them away. They made a temporary camp near Piqua in Miami County. Some were taken in by white or black farmers; others stayed on in nearby towns and villages. One, who had been John Randolph's personal servant, returned to Virginia, thereby forfeiting his freedom. Even today the former Randolph slaves are seeking compensation for the loss of their lands. The government has declined to offer any settlement on the grounds that it was private, not governmental, action that deprived them of their property.[29]

Many of the 383 slaves of John Randolph of Roanoke who moved to Ohio still have descendants in the vicinity of Rossville. On the anniversary of their ancestors' freedom, they come together for Randolph Freedom Day. They retain a strong sense of community that their ancestors shared on the plantation and on their trek westward.

Virginia's African Frontier: Liberia

One of the most interesting chapters in the history of Virginia's great emigration was the flow of former slaves to Africa. The idea of African colonization by former slaves had great appeal to Virginians. As early as 1777 a legislative committee chaired by Thomas Jefferson worked out a scheme for gradual emancipation and colonization, though it was not voted on or even debated by the full assembly. Resolutions in support of colonization were passed by the Virginia General Assembly in 1800, 1802, 1805, and 1816.

After a pioneering voyage by black merchant Paul Cuffe, who supported a colonizing voyage of thirty-eight former slaves out of his own pocket, the American Colonization Society was founded in 1816. A large part of its leadership was Virginian. The society's first president was Supreme Court Justice Bushrod Washington, nephew of George Washington and heir to Mount Vernon. Other early officers of the colonization society included James Madison and James Monroe. The two leading towns in Africa were named Monrovia and Harper, the latter after another native Virginian, Robert Goodloe Harper (1765–1825), who had been born near Fredericksburg and later moved to the Carolinas and settled in Maryland. It was Harper who coined the name Liberia, from the Latin noun *liber,* freeman.

The first emigrant vessel departed from New York. The ship *Elizabeth* carried eighty-six colonists, accompanied by three white agents of the colonization society, and was escorted by the USS *Cyane.* Many shiploads of African Virginians followed, sailing directly from Norfolk and City Point: the brig *Nautilus* (1821), chartered by the federal government; the *Oswego* (1823); the brig *Hunter* (1825); the *Indian Chief* (1826); the brig *Doris* (1827); *Harriet* (1829); the brig *Valador* (1831); the *Roanoke* (1833); and the brig *Luna* (1835).[30]

Altogether, approximately 15,000 former slaves were sent to Liberia, many from Virginia. The first president of the colony was Joseph Jenkins Roberts (1809–1876), born in Petersburg and called a free black, though he was seven-eighths white. He was described by W. E. B. Du Bois as "a man of intelligence and poise, slight and handsome, with olive skin and crisp hair . . . [and] the manners of a gentleman."[31]

An extraordinary file of correspondence survives from Roberts's friend Peyton Skipwith, a former Virginia slave who in 1833 went to Liberia with his wife Lydia and six children. He and his children wrote regularly to their former master, John Hartwell Cocke of Bremo, for thirty years. Cocke was a progressive planter who combined the dash and color of the cavalier with the moral rigor of a modern reformer. The master of Bremo plantation in Fluvanna County, he was a Virginia slaveholder who hated slavery and became a strong believer in scientific farming, temperance, and universal emancipation.

Cocke was convinced that Virginia could not halt its decline unless slavery was abolished. With many of his contemporaries, however, he also doubted that blacks and whites could ever live together in peace and harmony on a footing of equality. For that reason he launched a major experiment in gradual emancipation on his own plantations and in 1816 became a founder of the American Colonization Society, which sought to return freed slaves to Africa.

Cocke allocated a portion of his profits toward his scheme, and he allowed his slaves to work overtime to earn money to purchase their freedom. By this means he hoped to make the slaves hardworking and self-reliant and to create a model for gradual, compensated emancipation. He conducted daily religious devotions among his slaves, and his wife Louisa taught them to read and write even after it became illegal. Cocke would not release anyone he thought unfit for the responsibilities of freedom. He thought it better "that they remain under the care of humane masters rather than be turned loose on civilization to embarrass colonization and their race."[32]

One slave who met Cocke's exacting standards was Peyton Skipwith, who at the age of thirty-three was sent to Liberia with his wife and six children. The former slave and his old master corresponded across the ocean.

Cocke also experimented with another scheme for emancipation. In 1840 he acquired a plantation in Greene County, Alabama, and named it Hopewell. Forty-nine slaves whom Cocke thought prime candidates for manumission were sent there and arrived after a seven-week march. Their earnings from cotton, less the cost of maintaining them, were to be set aside for the purchase of their freedom. The overseers were very lenient by the standards of that day, and self-motivation was encouraged.

Cocke told the slaves that the cost of their freedom would be about $1,400 each, which he estimated they could save in five to seven years. A central figure was Lucy Skipwith, who was the slave teacher at Hopewell. As shown by her letter of 1857 inquiring whether the slave Solom "is gune to Africa," she had been taught to read and write in Virginia.

The Alabama experiment did not fulfill the high hopes of the master or the expectations of the slaves. Cocke complained that education and family cohesion broke down at Hopewell. The slaves protested that they were unable to gain their freedom under the terms that had been given them. By 1850 few were eligible for freedom under Cocke's terms. In the end emancipation came to Hopewell in the violence of the Civil War and was followed by the half freedom of tenancy and racial oppression.[33]

In Liberia a remarkable story unfolded—a vivid example of cultural persistence in a new environment. Liberia patterned its institutions closely on those of America. Its flag was red, white, and blue, but with a single white star and eleven stripes for the signers of the country's declaration of independence. Its constitution followed the Constitution of the United States, exactly as Kentucky copied the laws of Virginia. The culture of the members of Liberia's ruling elite closely resembled that of their masters and mistresses in early America. As late as 1952–53 American writer John Gunther visited Liberia and found its leaders living in "old-style mansions, built in the manner of the American South," complete even to the porches and stately white columns. Gunther remarked that in the drawing rooms of Monrovia, the tone of society was what the American South "might have been in the old days. . . . Everybody knows everybody else, and people have an easy courtesy, with a sense of dignified tradition." At one social gathering Gunther watched in amazement as the leaders of Liberia danced a Virginia reel. A woman explained to him, "We took our dances with us to America, and now we have brought them back here."[34]

The Liberian elite also reintroduced de facto slavery and the slave trade. They farmed their own plantations with forced labor and exported the workers from their country to other African colonies as late as the 1930s. So strong were these cultural patterns that Liberia's West African natives called Monrovia "the American place" and referred to the freed slaves who lived there as "white men."[35]

These patterns were not unique to Liberia. They were part of a powerful process that appeared in most new settlements—a process that stood the frontier thesis on its head. Anxiety and nostalgia, altruism and material interest all conspired to create a powerful cultural conservatism. Nowhere was it possible to replicate the old ways, but even that fact reinforced a determination to try—not merely in superficial aspects of culture but in fundamental values and in the structure of rank, wealth, and power.

The American Colonization Society failed in its larger purposes, and its founders did not consistently support their own settlement in Africa. Bushrod Washington in 1821 sent fifty-four Mount Vernon slaves not to Liberia but to Louisiana, after selling them at a handsome profit and severing close family ties. When a scandal broke in American gazettes because of the violation of George Washington's injunction that slaves not be sold out of the state, Bushrod Washington issued a defiant public letter, insisting, "I do not admit the right of any person to decide for me on this point."[36] The fact that Washington was simultaneously demanding the right to decide for his slaves never occurred to him as an inconsistency. Virginia's hegemonic freedom ways were deeply ingrained in that respect. Few gentlemen of Virginia would admit the right of any external body to determine their affairs, especially in regard to slavery. The colonization movement in Virginia foundered on that rock.

In Africa the abandoned colonists struggled heroically against heavy odds. Many were homesick for Virginia. Harry Jarvis (b. 1832) of Northampton County escaped during the Civil War and caught a ship bound for Liberia. He later returned to the United States. In the 1870s an interviewer asked him, "Didn't you feel like staying in Africa when you were there?" He replied, "No, madam. I went 'shore in Liberia, an' looked about, but I 'cluded I'd rudder come home."[37]

These black Virginians in Africa were as vulnerable to the climate as European immigrants. As large a proportion of the founders of Liberia died as did the Jamestown colonists. With inadequate support and facing serious obstacles, they succeeded in building a new nation. Like the process that began at Jamestown, however, it was colony building by conquest. The former slaves invaded a land and ruled over an existing population. The long rule of their descendants ended bloodily in 1980, when the government was overthrown and its leaders were killed by Liberians with no links to the colonizationist past.

Slaves Who Freed Themselves

For many African Americans in the Old Dominion, migration carried them to a system of bondage more cruel than that they had known in Virginia. Others moved in a different direction—toward freedom and independence. They did so in different ways. Some bought their freedom and moved away.

One such person was Sully Watson, who was born in Virginia in 1772. His mother was the daughter of an African chief from Guinea. He was owned by William Moncure, who held a 500-acre farm near the District of Columbia. Watson was allowed to marry Susan Custelo, a free woman of color who lived in Richmond. He remained with his master in northern Virginia but

94. Sully Watson, a slave in northern Virginia, was freed by his master's will. He moved first to Ohio and later to Milwaukee, where his freedom papers and family photographs recently were found at a flea market.

was permitted frequent visits to his family. In 1827 Moncure agreed to let Watson buy his freedom for $500. When Moncure died in 1831, half the sum had been paid, and Watson was freed by his master's will. He emigrated with his family to Columbus, Ohio, and in 1850, when nearly eighty, moved again to Milwaukee, Wisconsin, to be with his son and daughter. The family's papers were recently discovered in an antique shop.[38]

In 1806 the Virginia assembly passed legislation that required emancipated slaves to leave the state within twelve months or forfeit their freedom. Some did not want to go. Patty Barrett petitioned the state in 1827 for permission to remain, so she could be with her husband, who was a slave, and her mother, who was too old to move. The General Assembly refused her request, just as they denied many others.[39]

Some who had been freed earlier did not wish to emigrate but felt compelled to leave. In 1838 a group of property-owning free blacks in Fredericksburg petitioned the legislature for a school for their children, implying that otherwise they would be infected with radical notions from northern schools. They were refused on the basis of a law adopted in the repressive aftermath of the Nat Turner revolt. Over several years they left Virginia; most settled in Michigan.[40]

Among these free black families who left Fredericksburg were Lees, Cooks, Williamses, DeBaptistes, and Pelhams. The Williamses continued as bricklayers and the DeBaptistes as carpenters. Fannie M. Richards, who was only ten when her family left Virginia, was educated in Detroit and Toronto, operated a private school, and taught in the public schools for half a century.[41]

Some of Virginia's slaves freed themselves and found their own way out of the state. A group of slaves escaped northern Virginia when the British occupied Washington in the War of 1812 and went to New Brunswick in Canada.[42] Others fled alone. Madison Jefferson was a slave on a tobacco, corn, and hemp farm on the Ohio River near Parkersburg. He first escaped at age sixteen but was captured and received 39 lashes. After his sister was sold south, he made a second effort, also unsuccessful, which got him 50 lashes. On his third attempt he reached Cleveland, only to be retaken and given 150 lashes. On his fourth try he reached sympathetic Quakers and abolitionists, who spirited him off to Canada. Even there he feared being kidnapped because there was a price on his head, so he moved to England.[43]

Austin Steward, another escaped Virginia slave, became a leader of free black communities in New York and Canada. He had been a slave on Captain William Helm's plantation in Prince William County, Virginia, and escaped to New York in the winter of 1814. In freedom, Steward bought books and learned to read, write, and do arithmetic. He established a meat and produce market in Rochester,[44] prospered, bought a lot, built a house, and briefly taught a Sabbath school for black children. He married in 1825.

Steward learned of a colony of African Americans living in Canada 200 miles from Buffalo, New York, on a tract purchased for them by the Society of Friends. There were 1,100 inhabitants. Some had fled antiblack riots in the northern United States. Others were escaped slaves from the South who feared recapture. Steward moved to Canada in 1831 and assumed the presidency of the community, which adopted at his suggestion the name of Wilberforce, in honor of English abolitionist William Wilberforce.[45]

In 1860 Sara Lucy Bagby escaped from her master, William S. Goshorn of Wheeling, Virginia, and made her way to Cleveland. Her flight gave rise to one of the last fugitive slave cases before the outbreak of the Civil War. Bagby, described by the press as "about twenty-eight years of age," maintained that she had been told that she ought to be free because she had accompanied Goshorn's daughter Isabella on a short trip to the free soil of Pennsylvania. Her argument was not supported by the courts. The Supreme Court had ruled in the Dred Scott decision that temporary residence on free soil did not make one free. Her master also pointed out that as in the Dred Scott case, the slave had returned to slave soil, escaped from there, and should be returned in accord with the Fugitive Slave Act of 1850. Cleveland and the Western Reserve of Ohio generally had been settled by New Englanders and were hotbeds of abolitionism. Judge Daniel R. Tilden acknowledged this in his remarks on January 21, 1861: "It has been said in all quarters of the country that this city is disloyal to law and order. . . . I don't believe there is a section of this country where a feeling against the Fugitive Slave Law prevails to the extent it does here, where so much regard is felt for the dignity of the law. Let us in this instance testify to the country that we are a law-abiding as well as liberty-loving community."[46]

The *Cleveland Herald*, a moderate Republican newspaper, conceded that William Goshorn had complied with all the forms of the law and that, consequently, the people of Cleveland should acquiesce in Bagby's return, "not that they hate slavery less, but because they love obedience to law more." An article in the *Plain Dealer*, however, noted the irony that if Lucy had escaped from one of the states that already had seceded, she would be free, as those

95. Sara Lucy Bagby in 1860 escaped from her master, William S. Goshorn, in Wheeling, Virginia. She was arrested in Cleveland, returned to the Wheeling jail, and "punished severely." A few months later the Civil War began. Her master became a prisoner of war and was locked in the same jail that had held his slave.

states, maintaining to be foreign countries, could not invoke the Fugitive Slave Act of 1850 or any other U.S. statute.[47] But Virginia had not then seceded. The case was open and shut. Sara Lucy Bagby was returned to Wheeling, "where she was lodged in the jail and severely punished."[48] A few months later Virginia seceded, and the Union army entered Wheeling. William Goshorn was impounded as a prisoner of war and lodged in the same jail where his slave had been imprisoned.[49]

One of the most famous escapes from bondage was that of Anthony Burns, a slave of Colonel Charles F. Suttle of Alexandria, Virginia. In February 1854 Burns fled to Boston, Massachusetts, where he worked in a clothing store. His master invoked the Fugitive Slave Act to secure his return. An Alexandria court record for May 16, 1854, reads:

> On the application of Charles F. Suttle, who this day appeared in Court and made satisfactory proof to the Court that Anthony Burns was held to service and labor by him in the State of Virginia, and service and labor are due to him from the said Anthony, and that the said Anthony has escaped. Anthony is a man of dark complexion, about six feet high, with a scar on one of his cheeks, and also a scar on the back of his right hand, and about twenty-three or four years of age—it is therefore ordered, in persuance of an act of Congress, "An Act respecting fugitives from Justice and Persons escaping from the Service of their master" that the matter set forth be entered on the record of this Court.[50]

Eight days later Anthony Burns was apprehended in Boston by slave catchers. Suttle refused an offer of $1,200 by Boston citizens to buy Burns's freedom. On June 3, 1854, Burns was escorted through Boston by two thousand federal troops and put on a government vessel that returned him to slavery in Virginia. He was imprisoned in Richmond and given only one meal a day for four months. From his cell he wrote a letter to Richard Henry Dana, Jr., of Boston. It reads in part: "But I am yet Bound In Jail and are waring My Chings [chains] Night and day. . . . they told My oner to Not Let you all have Me But I am for Sale. . . . And if you will get Sum of your friends to come to Alexandra and not to Say that he come from Boston . . . he wood take $800h dollars for Me Now."[51]

Burns was bought by a North Carolinian who sold him to Boston abolitionists, led by black minister Leonard A. Grimes. Subscribers to the fund freed Burns, who then attended Oberlin College and Fairmount Theological Seminary in Cincinnati. He died in Canada in 1862, only twenty-eight years old.[52]

THE
BOSTON SLAVE RIOT,

AND

TRIAL

OF

Anthony Burns,

CONTAINING THE

REPORT OF THE FANEUIL HALL MEETING; THE MURDER OF
BACHELDER; THEODORE PARKER'S LESSON FOR THE DAY;
SPEECHES OF COUNSEL ON BOTH SIDES, CORRECTED
BY THEMSELVES; VERBATIM REPORT OF JUDGE
LORING'S DECISION; AND, A DETAILED AC-
COUNT OF THE EMBARKATION.

BOSTON:
FETRIDGE AND COMPANY.
1854.

Press of J. S. Potter & Co., 2 Spring Lane and 130 Washington Street.

96. Two thousand federal soldiers were needed to escort fugitive slave Anthony Burns from the Boston jail to the ship that returned him to slavery in Virginia. Although this title page purports to depict Burns, the same image was used elsewhere to portray Henry "Box" Brown.

The extradition of Anthony Burns led Massachusetts to enact a law in 1855 nullifying the federal Fugitive Slave Act, which became virtually unenforceable in that state. Burns was the last known fugitive slave to be seized on its soil.

Another slave who made a celebrated bid for freedom was Henry "Box" Brown, who worked in a Richmond factory. According to his autobiography, ghostwritten by Charles Stearns, Brown had been allowed to marry and to earn his own money, but in August 1848 his wife and children were sold south.

Henry Brown observed the largest boxes commonly sent from the freight depot and made a mental note of the size. A carpenter built such a box for him with three small airholes. Arrangements were made with an abolitionist society in Philadelphia to receive the container of human cargo. Brown climbed in with some biscuits and a bladder of water, and a friend nailed down the lid.

The box was marked "this side up," but nonetheless it was stood upside down at the express office. At the depot it was tossed into a baggage car,

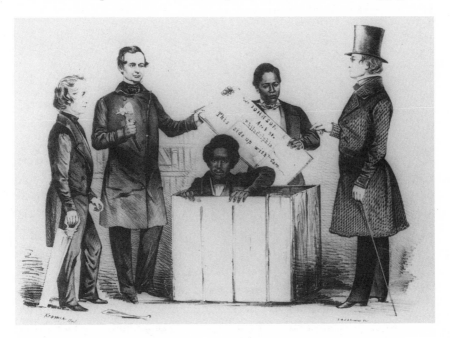

97. Henry "Box" Brown escaped from slavery by having himself shipped in a box from Richmond to an abolitionist group in Philadelphia.

where it fell right side up. When transferred to a steamboat, however, it again turned upside down, and Brown nearly died after two hours head down. Fortunately some workmen turned it over to sit on during a break.

When the box finally reached Philadelphia, a wagon was sent to the depot to retrieve it. One of the recipients tapped on the box and said tremulously, "Is all right within?" Brown replied, "All right." One of those present, William Still, an escaped slave from Maryland, later wrote that Brown emerged from the box saying, "How do you do, gentlemen?" Henry Brown's own account says simply that he stood up and fainted.[53]

Freedom could be a lonely road, accompanied sometimes by much suffering. Madison Henderson, another escapee, lived a life of crime, dictated his *Confessions,* and died on the gallows. The disruption of family ties was also wrenching. There were instances of newly freed blacks returning to servitude to be near their families, rather than being forced to leave Virginia as required by law. Others responded in another way. Dangerfield Newby became free but was unable to procure freedom for his wife, a slave who lived in Brentville, Prince William County. In desperation he joined John Brown's raid on the arsenal at Harpers Ferry and was killed there.[54]

The Travels of Dred Scott

The expansion of slavery became a political issue, and the movements of one Virginia slave, Southampton County native Dred Scott, had national implications. Scott was born a slave in Southampton County, Virginia. His migration to the West gave rise to a controversy of national importance. Sometime after his birth he was taken from Virginia to Missouri and sold in 1832 or 1833 to Dr. John Emerson, an army surgeon. His new master took Scott to Fort Armstrong in Illinois and then to Fort Snelling near the site of St. Paul, Minnesota. Illinois was a free state, and slavery was banned in what is now Minnesota under the terms of the Missouri Compromise of 1820, which prohibited it in the part of the Louisiana Purchase north of 36° 30′. At Fort Snelling, Dred Scott met and married a slave named Harriet Robinson. Four children were born of this union. They moved with Dr. Emerson many times, south to Louisiana and Texas and possibly Florida and north again to the free soil of Minnesota and perhaps Iowa. At various times

98. The travels of Dred Scott were a microcosm of slave migration from Virginia. This posthumous painting from a photograph was commissioned by the black citizens of St. Louis.

Scott and his family were lent to another army officer and leased to a civilian master. In 1846, three years after Dr. Emerson's death, Dred Scott and his wife were living in the slave state of Missouri. The executor of Emerson's estate, John F. A. Sanford, leased them out yet again. The Scott family sued for their freedom in a St. Louis court, arguing that his residence in free states and territories had made them free.

After ten years of litigation, the case was taken to the U.S. Supreme Court, which on March 6, 1857, handed down its decision. It ruled that the Missouri Compromise was unconstitutional because Congress had no right to restrict slavery anywhere. Even if Scott had been entitled to his freedom, they ruled, he had forfeited it by returning with his master to the slave state of Missouri.

Chief Justice Roger B. Taney wrote that being a slave, "Dred Scott was not a citizen of Missouri within the meaning of the Constitution of the United States, and not entitled as such to sue in its courts." Moreover, he noted "that neither the . . . slaves, nor their descendants, whether they had become free or not, were . . . intended to be included" in the body politic. In other words, even free blacks were not citizens. African Americans, he ruled, "had for more than a century been regarded as beings of an inferior order . . . so far inferior that they had no rights which the white man was bound to respect."[55]

By permitting the introduction of slavery into hitherto free territories, the decision elated many southerners but caused an angry outcry in the North and contributed powerfully to the growth of the Republican party. The decision of Chief Justice Taney has been called "the most frequently overturned case in history."[56]

After the trial was over, Scott and his family were transferred by fictitious sale back to previous Virginia owners, who promptly manumitted them in May 1857. They were free at last and took up residence in St. Louis. The state of Missouri required them to post bond of $1,000 for "good behavior," and Dred Scott was in poor health. He died of consumption on September 17, 1858. His descendants lived on, and some attended the centennial observation of the Dred Scott case in 1957.

The travels of Dred Scott had major consequences for the institution of slavery. The migration of black Virginians had a profound impact on the future of their nation.

6

The Cultural Legacy

W HEN VIRGINIANS traveled beyond their native state, they took their folk-ways with them. More important than their wagons and flatboats, crammed with material things, was the cultural baggage that they carried in their heads. Wherever Virginians settled, they planted ideas and institutions in the American ground. The westward movement became a process of cultural enlargement. The old culture was renewed by its expansion, in the range of its territory and the reach of its ideas. The story of its growth was not a simple Turnerian tale of transformation, nor was it an anti-Turnerian process of replication. What happened was an intricate combination of change and continuity, in which elements of persistence were very strong. The results remain highly visible on the cultural landscape of a nation.

Fields and Fences: Patterns of Land Use

When one flies in a modern aircraft above the Mississippi Valley, it is possible to identify the origins of early settlers, even from a height of 35,000 feet. The historical evidence is written across the face of the country in the geometry of field systems on the land below.

The pattern is especially clear in Ohio, where several streams of cultural migration passed close together to create a striking contrast. Where New Englanders settled in the West, rectangular land surveys were imposed on the land. Virginians did things differently. After acquiring a right to land on the frontier by grant, purchase, or reward for military service, a Virginian selected his tract by the "metes-and-bounds" method. He carried his warrant into the wilderness and marked or "tomahawked" the land he wanted by blazing trees or marking other features at the corners of his tract. These points of reference were called "metes," and the lines connecting them became the "bounds" of the property. By stepping off the bounds, the claimant determined whether the tract matched the approximate acreage to which he was entitled. Then a surveyor was engaged to take more precise measurements. Once the surveyor signed the settler's land warrant, it could be exchanged for a deed.

This metes-and-bounds method had been used in Virginia for many years. It was introduced throughout Kentucky, Tennessee, and Ohio's Virginia Military District. The result, wherever it appeared, was a crazy-quilt pattern of irregularly shaped tracts that may be seen today throughout the area of Virginia settlement. In Ross County, Ohio, for example, the west bank of the Scioto River lay within the Virginia Military District. Its land system re-

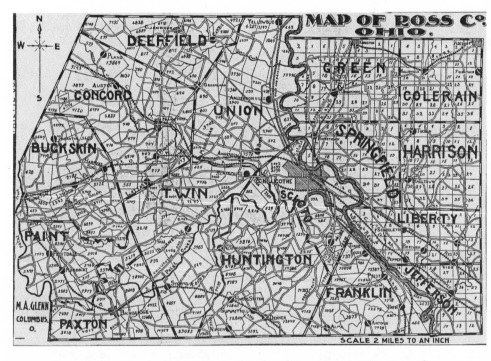

99. Two systems of land taking appear in this plat of Ross County, Ohio. East of the Scioto River, congressional land was distributed in neat rectangular holdings. To the west was the Virginia Military District, where land was surveyed in irregular lots under Virginia's metes-and-bounds system that allowed first takers an advantage.

sembled a patchwork of irregular parcels. The east bank is very different in its appearance. This was congressional land, laid out as a grid in neat rectangles with firm right angles.

The Virginia system represented an individuated ethos that imposed minimal constraints on large landowners and allowed them to survey their holdings for maximum advantage. It had been used in the tidewater and the piedmont. The congressional and New England methods tended to give more weight to ideas of community, regularity, and equality.[1]

These different ways of imposing cultural order on the landscape had social consequences. By comparison with other patterns of land use, the Virginia system created a tangle of overlapping claims, based on ephemeral markers. It greatly encouraged litigation. Areas such as Kentucky and Tennessee and Ohio's Virginia Military District became havens for hungry lawyers. In his 1848 history of Ohio, Henry Howe wrote: "Any individual holding a Virginia military land warrant may locate it, wherever he chooses, within the district, and in such shape as he pleases. . . . The irregularities with which the several locations have been made; and the consequent interference and encroachment of some locations upon others, more than double the litigation . . . than there has been in any other part of the state, of equal extent."[2]

The Virginia system was also distinctive in the size of its land grants. Individual allocations in Ohio's Virginia Military District were nearly ten times the size of holdings in other parts of Ohio. Something of that disparity still survives two centuries later. In Madison County, Ohio, the core of the Virginia Military District, geographer Hubert H. G. Wilhelm found that the size of an average farm is 364 acres, more than double the average for the state (167 acres).[3]

Cultural differences were also evident in the manner of enclosing fields—a major problem for a farmer. New Englanders and Pennsylvanians preferred straight walls, hedges, and post-and-rail fences. Virginians threw up zig-zag "worm" fences of crudely split rails, stacked one above the another. "New Englanders have a saying," wrote one early nineteenth-century traveler, "that when man is in liquor he is making Virginia fences." The result may not have pleased a Yankee eye, but it was an efficient way of enclosing a southern space with a minimum of technology, capital, and labor.[4]

Roads and Towns: Patterns of Settlement

Roads also were laid out differently in the American West according to the origins of settlers. Virginians ran their roads from point to point across the landscape, conforming to the terrain but cutting across survey lines. In other areas where rectangular surveys had been used, roads ran in straight lines from one right angle to another, closely conforming to survey boundaries. A study by Norman J. W. Thrower finds that in the Virginia military district, only 8 percent of road mileage followed land survey lines. In other parts of Ohio where rectangular surveys were used, the proportion was 77 percent. Virginia's land system engendered conflicts between public rights of way and private ownership of fields, which were more often at odds than in a rectangular system.[5]

Yet another pattern of cultural distinctiveness appeared in town founding. Hubert Wilhelm observes from long study of the Ohio landscape that New Englanders "laid out the land to create centrally located, compact settlements. The large number of small towns in the New England settlement area is indicative of their intention to have settlers live in the communities. Even farmers lived in town, going out each day to work in their fields or outlots."[6]

Very different were the Virginians, whose system of settlement had less need for towns. These differences derived from cultural values, social purposes, economic systems, and earlier environmental adaptations. They were especially visible in Ohio, where three migration streams flowed side by side. Similar patterns also appeared in other states, wherever Virginians settled.

These processes should not be understood as evidence of cultural replication, which never happened in any migratory movement. But one does find a distinctive pattern of cultural persistence.

Cabins, Cottages, and Virginia
I-Houses: Vernacular Architecture

To travel a western highway is to discover another legacy of early settlement in the houses that stand by the side of the road. Emigrants tended to use building plans and methods they had known at home. In the process they introduced building traditions that continued long after the founding generation was gone.[7]

100. The tidewater cottage was often rebuilt in the West by emigrant Virginians. This is the eighteenth-century Walnut Valley plantation, Surry County, Virginia.

101. Bride's Hill plantation, Lawrence County, Alabama, c. 1830, replicates the tidewater Virginia cottage.

These patterns of cultural persistence appeared even in the most humble shelters. Simple log cabins of one or two rooms tended to conform to sub-regional folk styles in their floor plans and chimneys. An example was the southern variation of the log cabin called a "dogtrot," in which two single-room cabins were built side by side and separated by a covered passage that was suited to the warm climate of the South. Techniques of log notching and finishing were also regional in their distribution and have been mapped in close detail by cultural geographers. Methods of cabin construction throughout the West reveal the regional origins of the families who built them. The pattern of their diffusion becomes a map of migration fields and streams.[8]

The more elaborate houses of yeoman farmers and middling planters also betrayed the origins of their builders. Virginians had a fondness for story-and-a-half tidewater cottages, which are familiar to any visitor to Williamsburg. The tidewater cottage had developed from English models into an efficient building that was well suited to the southern environment. The most common type was a single-pile, two-room, hall-and-parlor structure, to which a central passage was later added for privacy and ventilation. Set on

102. The Virginia I-house was carried throughout the Old Northwest and Old Southwest. This is a Madison County, Virginia, example.

posts or masonry foundations, the tidewater cottage could be built of wood or brick. It was simple to construct and pleasing to the eye. A typical example of the type is Walnut Valley plantation in Surry County, Virginia.

The tidewater cottage was easily exportable, and it adapted well to frontier conditions far from home. A case in point is a plantation house called Sunnybrook in Lawrence County, Alabama. It is one of a group of surviving Virginia tidewater cottages constructed in the Tennessee Valley during the early years of settlement. The first owner was Robert Dandridge, a Virginia emigrant from a tidewater family prominent in the colonial era.[9] The builder may have been Daniel Wade, also a Virginian, who had lived in Chesterfield and Nottoway counties and for a short while in Botetourt County. He emigrated to Alabama with a colony of relatives and neighbors and built houses for the group.[10]

Another house type much favored by farmers of middling estate was the "I-house." It was a simple, straightforward structure of distinctive proportions—one room deep, two stories high, and three bays wide in its purest form. A central hall or passage commonly separated the rooms on each

103. An I-house in Lawrence County, Ohio.

floor.[11] The I-house was an American invention that spread through many parts of the United States. Virginians favored a variant form that had a low-pitched roof (because snow accumulation was not a major problem), a raised foundation (to deter dry rot), and chimneys on the gable ends. A long porch often spanned the front, to catch the western breezes on a summer day. Later examples added to the facade a small central pediment or even a grand two-story portico, strengthening the vertical axis of the entry and enhancing a sense of pride that comported well with a culture that valued honor and dignity. The Virginia I-house was carried west to Alabama, Tennessee, Kentucky, and Ohio.[12]

The migration of vernacular architecture from Virginia was a process of high complexity, compounded by many regional and ethnic variations. An example was a highly distinctive T-plan favored throughout Southside Virginia. The two-story center block extended beyond the flanking one-story wings. This form was carried to North Carolina and marked a regional migration stream.[13]

Ethnic styles also were part of the architectural migration from Virginia. Emigrants from the Shenandoah Valley perpetuated the stone and brick building traditions of German settlers. A favorite Germanic type was the *Flurkuchenhaus:* a massive structure with three rooms, a kitchen on the main floor, and bold interior carving and painting. Its decoration was akin to the flamboyant expression of Valley fraktur, ceramics, and furniture.

The *Flurkuchenhaus* migrated from Germany to Pennsylvania and into the Valley of Virginia. There it was combined with English building traditions that had been carried west from the tidewater. The result was a distinctive architectural hybrid that developed in Virginia and was carried farther west to the Mississippi Valley. An example is Sportsman's Hill, built in Kentucky about 1790 by William Whitley and his wife Esther, who emigrated from Augusta County, Virginia. Their initials proudly appear on the facade, set with glazed headers in Flemish-bond brickwork.

Sportsman's Hill is a classic example of the Valley hybrid. The exterior decoration is English, with brickwork laid in a lively diamond pattern inspired by seventeenth-century tidewater models. The building plan is a German *Flurkuchenhaus* with a bold, massive form and a three-room plan with the kitchen on the main floor. The interior embellishments are both German and English. A stair newel carved in the form of a console and a unique

104. Sportsman's Hill, built in Lincoln County, Kentucky, before 1794, combines English Georgian and traditional German elements in a hybrid form that developed in the Valley of Virginia and was carried west.

chimneypiece combine the motifs of Germanic folk traditions with classical triglyphs and metopes of English Georgian architecture. Sportsman's Hill is a hybrid not merely of English and German forms but also of continuity and creativity. It is a paradigm example of cultural memory at work in the western movement.[14]

Barns and Outbuildings: Virginia Farmyards

Houses built by Virginians in the West were usually at the center of a working farm. Close by them stood barns and outbuildings that became prominent features of the cultural landscape in both Virginia and the West.

In response to specific material needs and cultural tastes, the Virginia barn developed into a distinctive type. The soil and climate favored corn as a principal crop, and self-sufficient Virginians raised livestock as well. Their barns, built on level ground, usually were entered on the narrow gable end, with cribs provided for corn on both long sides. Fodder to feed their animals was stored in the building's loft, through an outer door protected by a hood above the fodder lift. Sheds were sometimes added to each long expanse to provide room for animals, who were easily fed with fodder dropped through openings in the loft above.

The Virginia barn was carried to the military district of southern Ohio. There, along the Ohio and Scioto rivers, Virginia emigrants continued their practice of raising cattle and corn-fed hogs. They built distinctive Virginia-style barns—very different in appearance from the Pennsylvania barn, a European form recognized by its overhanging upper floor and little changed in America. New Englanders had a taste for barns of yet another type, connected to their houses. The origins of settlers on the Ohio frontier have been mapped by the distribution of this farmyard architecture.[15]

105. Typical Virginia barns had a main door and loft hood on their gable end and sheds on either side. This one is in Albemarle County. They differed from the barns of Pennsylvania and New England that were also built in the West.

The Big House: The Virginia Style in High Architecture

The most striking examples of Virginia's cultural legacy were the great plantation houses that gentlemen of the Old Dominion constructed throughout a vast area from Ohio to Alabama. A case in point is the Carter mansion in Elizabethton, Tennessee. It was probably built by John Carter (1737–1781), who with his son Landon Carter (1760–1800) migrated about 1769 from Amherst County, Virginia. The house would have seemed more appropriate in the old English countryside than on the edge of new settlement in America. Its opulent interiors are decorated with elaborate floor-to-ceiling wood paneling in the deep-cut early Georgian style. Even the closets are fully wainscoted with woodwork of an old-fashioned design. At the time when the house was built, this style of carving had passed out of vogue in the East. To fresh eyes on a frontier, however, the work was impressive in a way that was important to its builder. It was inspired by the memory of grand Virginia houses such as Tuckahoe in Goochland County or Marmion in King George County and carried to the frontier an association with the oligarchy of old Virginia.[16]

106. The Virginia barn as built in Vinton County, Ohio.

107. Deep-cut Georgian wainscoting was used in Tuckahoe, Goochland County, Virginia, c. 1720–30.

The great house was both an ornament and a cultural instrument. Its builders had been bred to a style of life modeled on that of English gentry and transplanted to the American West. In areas that might have been developed in other ways, the Virginia great house set an architectural example and deeply influenced the building traditions of the South and Midwest.

An example is the great house called Grouseland, built in 1803–4 north of the Ohio River in Vincennes, Indiana, by William Henry Harrison (1773–1841), the first governor of the territory and later ninth president of the United States. Harrison's reputation as the "log cabin president" is one of the ironies of American history. Descended from Virginia's cavalier elite, he was born and lived as a child in the great house called Berkeley on the banks of the James River.[17]

Next to Berkeley was an even greater house called Shirley, which was much admired in the tidewater for its handsome two-tier portico, added in a ren-

108. The Carter mansion in Elizabethton, Tennessee, c. 1770–1800, also was decorated with deep-cut Georgian wainscoting.

ovation after 1771. When Harrison built his house in Indiana Territory, he was guided by the memory of the great houses he had known in his youth. His new home in Indiana followed the conventions of Virginia's high Georgian architecture in the heavy mass of the building, the strict symmetry of the facade, and its pronounced sense of grandeur, although the curved side is a Federal touch. On the front of Grouseland, Harrison included a two-tier classical portico similar to that of Shirley.

A design so impressive in a location so remote and at a date so early must have been an extraordinary sight. Grouseland is in that way akin to Virginia's first great plantation house, Green Spring, built by Sir William Berkeley near Jamestown two centuries earlier. Grouseland, like Green Spring, established an architectural standard for its region.[18]

Equally striking was another type of Virginia architecture that was favored in the canebrake region of west central Alabama. This was the five-part Palladian country house, very grand and handsome. Its lofty space was perfectly suited to the ambition and to the household needs of expatriate Virginia gen-

109. Shirley plantation, Charles City County, Virginia, 1738, porticoes after 1771.

110. Grouseland, Vincennes, Indiana, 1803–4.

III. Chatham, Stafford County, Virginia, c. 1769.

II2. Weyanoke, Marengo County, Alabama, after 1835 (destroyed in the 1930s).

try, and its high Georgian symmetry expressed that group's understanding of the world. An example was the house called Weyanoke in Marengo County, Alabama. It was built by George W. H. Minge, whose family had owned lands in Weyanoke Parish, Charles City County, Virginia, from the mid–seventeenth century.[19] George Minge was a fifth-generation Virginian. The seventh of eleven children, he emigrated to Alabama in 1835. In the name of his new residence and also in its design, Minge commemorated his roots in Virginia.[20]

Also carried west was the highly inventive architecture that Thomas Jefferson designed for both private and public buildings in Virginia. The Jeffersonian style was much admired and put to work on the frontier in ways that might have surprised their creator.

Jefferson regarded the problem of proportion in classical orders as integral to high architecture. For public buildings he designed the portico on a giant scale. In domestic buildings he kept the form but carefully reduced its scale.

113. Three-part houses, as exemplified by Jefferson's first version of Monticello, were much admired by emigrant Virginians.

114. Belle Mont is a three-part house built c. 1830 in Tuscumbia, Alabama, and was the home of Dr. Alexander Mitchell, a native of Louisa County, Virginia. It incorporated several exterior features and interior details of Jefferson's first Monticello.

115. Jefferson's second design for Monticello, c. 1793–1809.

That subtlety was lost on some of his admirers, who happily applied to their plantation houses the porticoes that Jefferson had used for the State Capitol and the University of Virginia. Thus was born the Tara style of plantation architecture in the settlements of the new South.

Other builders in the West followed Jefferson in more discriminating ways. Belle Mont in Tuscumbia, Alabama, was built c. 1830 for Dr. Alexander Mitchell, a physician and planter who emigrated from Louisa County, Virginia. The style of Belle Mont—its two-story portico, hilltop siting, and U-shaped wings—also were important elements in Jefferson's first design for Monticello. The proportions of the Alabama house and the design of its doorway were altered from Jefferson's heavy classicism to the lighter Federal style, but the fundamental design remained very close to Jefferson's plan. The copying extended even to small details such as eight-panel doors, small glazed ellipses, and shutter and door hinges set deep into beading to cause a tight opening against a frame. The brickwork of Belle Mont is very fine, and architectural historians think that the craftsman who laid it might have been a slave artisan trained on a Jeffersonian structure in Virginia.[21]

116. Jefferson's second version of Monticello was followed for Farmington, 1809–10, the home of Judge John Speed in Louisville, Kentucky.

Jefferson's second design for Monticello (the one we know today) brilliantly adapted the grandeur of a temple portico and a Roman dome to the scale of an American domestic building. This second Monticello was widely copied by Jefferson himself in other houses and imitated by his Virginia neighbors. Its influence was also carried far beyond Virginia. An example is the house called Farmington, which stands near Lexington, Kentucky. Its owner was a Virginian, Judge John Speed, whose first wife's family were Jefferson's neighbors, and whose second wife's grandfather had been Jefferson's guardian. Farmington takes its name from one Jeffersonian house and its plan from another. The proportions of Monticello were altered to achieve the lightness of the Federal style but in other ways were followed closely for their exterior form, interior plan, and details. Altogether, the reach of Virginia's high architecture was broad and deep throughout the West. Its influence continues even to our own time.[22]

Virginia Gardens in the Wilderness

Around their great houses expatriate Virginians planted country gardens that reminded them of home. Some were formal gardens in the geometric tidewater tradition. Others were informal plantings in the picturesque English style, sometimes on a vast scale.

Both of these traditions were combined in a very large forty-acre garden created by David Meade at La Chaumière des Prairies in Kentucky. It derived explicitly from the gardens at his Virginia home of Maycox in Prince George County.

On David Meade's Kentucky estate, slave laborers were put to work creating artificial lakes, picturesque hills and valleys, pleasing vistas, and romantic groves. At heavy expense the shaggy wilderness was combed and smoothed, and the American landscape was broken to the will of its new possessors.[23]

Systems of Labor

The interplay of continuity and change in cultural diffusion may be seen with even greater clarity in the history of labor systems and agricultural production. In material terms Virginians from the tidewater and piedmont, and many from the Valley as well, tried to organize their new world in the West in ways similar to those they had known in the Old Dominion.

Slavery was commonly introduced by Virginia settlers. Not all of them did so. Virginia Germans, Quakers, and others meant to move away from slavery. But most Virginians wished to continue the South's system of forced bondage on the frontier.

Nowhere did they succeed in reproducing slavery in precisely the same form as in their native state. Students of the subject have found many subtle differences between bondage in the East and West—differences in plantation size, relations between masters and slaves, the function of overseers and drivers, the intimacy of association between the races, and the content of African-American culture. But all were variations on the same labor system.

In Ohio, Virginians were unable to introduce slavery. Their peculiar institution was prohibited by Congress above the Ohio River. In its place Virginia migrants created a surrogate for slavery by introducing various forms

117. Some think that this Ohio River scene is an allegory of freedom and slavery. If so, both ideas are represented by cultural symbols from Virginia. The place and date can be inferred from the river steamboat *Washington* (left). She was launched in 1816, briefly plied the Mississippi and Ohio rivers, and blew up in 1817.

of free tenancy. In 1848 the Connecticut Yankee Henry Howe wrote in his history of Ohio, "Hence it is that the Virginia military district, much of which is held in large tracts by wealthy men, with tenants under them, does not thrive as well as some other parts of the state having a poorer soil, but cultivated by those who both hold the plow and own the land."[24]

One Virginia emigrant addressed the labor problem in another way. Cyrus Hall McCormick (1809–1884) was born in Rockbridge County, a yeoman farmer's son. He spent his childhood helping on the farm and working alongside his father, who had made several failed attempts at a mechanical reaper. Learning from his father's mistakes, McCormick invented a machine that performed the work of several farm laborers. In July 1831 the McCormick reaper was successfully demonstrated on a field of oats at Steele's Tavern near Lexington, Virginia.

McCormick was quick to recognize the opportunity presented in the American West, where farmers were not constrained by land but by want of labor sufficient to work the vast tracts available to them. With the mechanical reaper farmers could reap what they sowed. In 1847 McCormick consolidated his production in Chicago, a town not twenty years old.[25]

The preferred economic system in most areas settled by Virginia was staple agriculture. Where possible, Virginia crops were transplanted into the Mississippi. Tobacco cultivation spread through many parts of Kentucky and became the staple of that state's agriculture. Tobacco farming also was prevalent in the Virginia Military District of Ohio, as it is to this day.

Another favored crop in Kentucky was hemp. It had been a marginal crop in Virginia but did better beyond the mountains, where it flourished on the

THE TESTING OF THE FIRST REAPING MACHINE NEAR STEELE'S TAVERN.VA.A.D.1831.

118. Cyrus Hall McCormick (1809–84) demonstrated his mechanical reaper at Steele's Tavern, Virginia, in 1831, but he was not commercially successful until he moved to Chicago in 1847.

limestone and bluegrass lands of Kentucky and became a major source of income. As Virginia planters moved west, they did not hesitate to shift to other crops, in order to preserve a familiar system of slavery and staple agriculture. The staple might be cotton, sugar, grain, or other crops. But even as the cash crop changed, the system of staple agriculture, plantation farming, and slave labor remained much the same. Here was a classic example of material change that fostered cultural continuity in the westward movement.

Systems of Stratification

The story was much the same in terms of wealth distribution. Turner and his disciples believed that the frontier promoted equality. A team of highly skeptical historians at the University of Wisconsin tested this idea for westward migration from New England to Trempeleau County, Wisconsin, in the upper Northwest. They expected to disprove the Turner thesis. Instead they found to their surprise that Turner was right for the region he knew best. Equality did modestly increase on the northern frontier.[26]

The pattern was very different in Virginia's westward movement. There inequalities tended to increase. As early as the 1790s, half of all Kentuckians owned no real estate, though the promise of land had drawn them to the area. Throughout the antebellum period the West was seen as a land of opportunity, but the reality was often very different. Studies of wealth distribution indicate that inequality was greater in the southern Mississippi Valley than in the Southeast. The Virginia frontier did not serve as an engine of social and economic equality; its effect on wealth distribution was to reinforce dominant tendencies in the material culture carried into it. Mobility expanded in the westward movement from Virginia, but inequality also grew greater.

These patterns were strong on the southern frontier for those who moved from the tidewater and the piedmont and even stronger among people of north British and Scotch-Irish stock who emigrated from the Valley of Virginia.[27]

This tendency was not universal, but neither was Turner's model. The Southwest became even more inegalitarian than the Southeast had been, while the opposite tendency appeared in the migration from New England to the Northwest. The cultural dynamics of the westward movement were more complex than either Turner's frontier model or its antithesis.

Political Institutions

Most Virginians, not the gentry alone, took west a belief in the libertarian tenets of Jeffersonian Republicanism. This ideology was itself was an outgrowth of Virginia political culture as it had developed in areas such as Jefferson's Albemarle County and Madison's Orange County. The central values were personal liberty and minimal government in an expanding territory.[28]

The Jeffersonianism of the early West is not unrelated to, nor completely explained by, the massive exodus of Virginians. Many of the most talented migrants became political leaders in their adopted states. Joseph Glover Baldwin wrote in 1853, "From Cape May to Puget's Sound [Virginia] has colonized the other States . . . with her surplus talent."[29]

Some 230 men born in Virginia before 1810 became members of Congress from other states. By contrast, 147 natives of Massachusetts served other states in Congress. Eighty Pennsylvanians and only 23 South Carolinians were elected to Congress from other states. Of these expatriate Virginians one, William Henry Harrison, achieved the presidency of the United States; another, Sam Houston, became president of the Republic of Texas. Twelve held cabinet posts in Democratic administrations, and one, Edward Bates, became attorney general under Lincoln. All were from families whose names are well known in Virginia today.[30]

Most of these emigrant politicians from Virginia were Jeffersonians or Jacksonians. But there were prominent exceptions such as Henry Clay, who nonetheless began as a Jeffersonian defender of the Kentucky Resolutions and of Jefferson's Embargo Act. James H. Carson, who served in the California legislature, was described as "a Democrat of the Virginia school." W. L. Moody, a graduate of Mr. Jefferson's university, subscribed one letter "A Stronger Democrat Never Breathed."[31] By contrast, Green Rives of McKinley, Dinwiddie County, who removed to Lincoln County, Tennessee, about 1828, had a tombstone reading, "He Lived and Died a Whig. This Inscription By His Request."[32]

Laws and Constitutions

Some of these emigrant Virginians had the opportunity of writing their culture into the constitutions and laws of the western states. In Kentucky, for example, George Nicholas of Williamsburg was largely responsible for the first Kentucky constitution and John Breckinridge for the second.[33]

Western constitutions were not ahead of the eastern states, as Turner believed, but in most respects behind them. A study by political scientist Benjamin F. Wright finds that large portions of western constitutions were copied, line for line, after those of eastern states. Virginia was the leading model in the South.[34]

The same process of persistence also appeared in statute law. After the Revolution all American states faced a problem of what to do about colonial and English statutes under which they had operated for as many as 170 years before independence. Nearly all states dealt with that question by enacting an omnibus law or constitutional clause that maintained in force all English and colonial statutes and the English common law, except where specifically repealed. This practice was doubly interesting in the context of the westward movement—both for what the states did and for how they did it.

In New England the problem was solved by provisions that all laws "heretofore in force [were] to continue." That clause first appeared in the Massachusetts constitution of 1780. During the next forty years, it was copied word for word by every New England state except Vermont.

The states of the Delaware Valley dealt with the problem differently, by a provision that "the common law and British statutes were in force (or were to continue in force)." This clause was enacted by New Jersey, Delaware, and Pennsylvania.

Virginia in 1776 found a third way of solving the problem: a provision that English statutes "of a general nature" enacted before 1607 were to continue in force, and that the common law of England and British statutes "as of the first emigration" were to continue in force as well. The Virginia solution of 1776 was copied, often word for word, by more states and territories than any other: Maryland (1776), the Northwest Territory (1795), Kentucky (1792), the District of Columbia (1801), Ohio (1806), the Indiana Territory (1807), the Missouri Territory (1816), the Arkansas Territory (1819), Illinois (1819), and Florida (1822). The constitution and laws of no other state were so widely imitated as those of Virginia on this question of the continuity of common law and statute law, "as of the first emigration."[35]

Turnerian scholars have been specially interested in laws and constitutions on one question in particular—political democracy and the suffrage, which they believed to have been revolutionized on the frontier. Turner thought that "it was only as the interior of the country developed that suffrage restrictions gradually gave way in the direction of manhood suffrage." A detailed study by another historian, Chilton Williamson, found that Turner was mistaken. Eastern states moved as rapidly as those in the West, in many cases more rapidly, although Virginia waited until 1850. As late as 1812, when some eastern states had introduced what amounted to universal manhood suffrage, Williamson found that "only one state of the New West, Kentucky, had eliminated all property or taxpaying requirements." He concluded that "Turner had the western cart before the eastern horse."[36]

Turnerian writers also asserted that land law was liberalized in the western states before it changed that way in the East. Here again they were mistaken. A classic example was the law of primogeniture and entail, which had long existed in Virginia for intestate estates. Thomas Jefferson first proposed the abolition of primogeniture and entail in 1776, and the Virginia legislature did so in 1784, shifting land tenure in the state from fee tail to fee simple. The western state of Kentucky not only lagged behind. It passed new laws in support of primogeniture and entail after Virginia had done away with them. Kentucky actually reenacted entail as late as 1792 and did not abolish it until 1796. The provision was of small importance, except as another indicator that the western states followed the East in liberal reforms and did not take the lead. The Turnerian interpretation was not correct. The same pattern of cultural lag and persistence appeared in western statutes on land law as it did in the suffrage, statute law, and constitution making.[37]

Social Stratification

Virginians from the tidewater and piedmont took west a highly distinctive class system. At the top were very small, highly integrated landowning elites with lines of descent from old families, the manners of gentlemen, and an ethic of honor. Below them came a yeomanry of freehold farmers, a rural middle class, who were a minority of the population. At the bottom were two degraded proletariats, each bitterly despising the other: a class of poor whites who owned no land of their own and lived as tenants, laborers, and squatters and a teeming population of African-American slaves who did not even own themselves.

This was the social system of old Virginia. It differed from the northern states in many ways. Its elite was tighter, older, and more closed. Its middle class, from 1607 to 1860, was always a minority of the population, unlike the free states where most Americans were of middling rank. Its proletariats were very large and deeply impoverished.

Within this system of stratification, freedom was perceived in inegalitarian terms as a set of hegemonic liberties which people possessed in different degrees. Some at the top had many liberties. Others at the bottom had none. This was an idea of hegemonic freedom which coexisted with slavery. Many in Virginia and the South felt no contradiction in demanding freedom for themselves and slavery for others.

This system of stratification took root in Virginia during the seventeenth century, before it was firmly established in any other part of English-speaking America. It spread rapidly through the southern colonies and was taken into a large part of the American West. Among the leading carriers were families that had settled in Virginia and later moved to Tennessee and Kentucky and many other southern states.

As it traveled west the system changed in important ways. Sir William Berkeley had been raised in a world of impermeable orders and estates. In the migration from England to Virginia, and thence to the Mississippi Valley, social orders were transformed into the social classes. No society as deferential and hierarchical as Berkeley's ideal world was possible after the American Revolution. But in other ways it remained the same—inegalitarian, hegemonic, with a small elite, a middling minority, and two degraded proletariats.

The Ethos of Honor

Continuities also appeared in cultural values, particularly in the concept of honor and the idea of a gentleman. Sir William Berkeley and his elite lived for honor. Even Berkeley's opponent Nathaniel Bacon appealed to the same ideal. Bacon exhorted his followers, "Come on, my hearts of gold; he that dies in the field lies in the bed of honor."[38]

The ideal of honor continued to flourish in Virginia through four centuries, even to our time. Among the instruments of its persistence were formal institutions that developed in the eighteenth and nineteenth centuries.

Honor was served by the academies and colleges of Virginia. It appeared in the customs of the University of Virginia and the Virginia Military Institute. In western states many sister institutions were created on Virginia models, such as the Kentucky Military Institute and Western Military Institute, both chartered in Kentucky in 1847. The same ideas expressed themselves in the University of Virginia's honor system, which was closely copied at the University of the South (Sewanee) in Tennessee, even to the rituals and red ribbons with which young southern gentlemen were inducted and bound to the ethos of honor.

One part of Virginia's system of honor was the *code duello*. It was not as elaborately developed in the seventeenth century as it would later become, but it existed in the colony from an early date. In 1653 Captain Thomas Hackett, a gentleman of Lancaster County, sent a challenge to a justice who was sitting on the bench, specifying with elaborate courtesy the terms of the encounter and even the length of the rapier.[39]

During the late eighteenth century, dueling gained popularity from the example of British and French officers in the Revolution and became an elaborate social convention in Virginia, as it did in other southern states. The code of honor was not exclusively Virginian. The *code duello* spread through the antebellum South from several cultural hearths — South Carolina, Virginia, and Louisiana. This aspect of honor became stronger in the Mississippi Valley than in old Virginia, where gentlemen of the old school thought it an indulgent gaucherie. Many of the most avid duelists were found in the West.

But the idea of honor on which this custom rested had deep Virginia roots, and slavery provided an appropriate environment for an exalted sense of personal worth. Many of the most notorious duels in the nineteenth century involved Virginians. In 1809 Henry Clay wounded, and was wounded by, an expatriate Virginian, Humphrey Marshall. In 1826 Clay and John Randolph of Roanoke fought on Virginia soil what Senator Thomas Hart Benton called "about the last high toned duel" he had witnessed. Charlie Fairfax of California, heir to the Fairfax title, did not die in a duel, but his widow believed that his premature death in 1868 was the result of an unhealed sword wound sustained in Sacramento a decade earlier.[40] Alexander Keith McClung, of a good Virginia family, fought fourteen duels with a brace of pistols named Alpha and Omega. He killed ten men in the twenty years after he left Virginia for Mississippi. This editor and poet laureate of the Old South also gambled and drank and finally shot himself in 1855. Branch Archer had left Virginia in 1841 after killing a cousin in a duel. He invited a Virginia relation to join him in Texas, where they could live "like . . . fighting cocks."[41]

The ethos of honor and gentility had other components that were rooted in Virginia and spread throughout the South. One of them was the idea of a gentleman's hospitality. Branch Archer lamented that "the old-fashioned Virginia hospitality . . . I am sorry to say [is] rapidly going out of vogue in the old dominion." It persisted longer among Virginians who went west. A guest at La Chaumière des Prairies, David Meade's plantation in Kentucky, wrote that "for a time every day at Chaumiere was like a levee." The president of Transylvania University remarked of Meade: "No word is ever sent him that company is coming. To do so offends him. But servants are always in waiting."[42]

Another characteristic idea of honor was a cavalier attitude toward spending. When Virginia gentlemen traveled west, they took with them their habit of overspending. David Meade spent all his resources on landscaping and entertaining. Alfred W. Taliaferro, who moved to California, was a typical Virginia gentleman in his fondness for gambling, liquor, horse racing, carelessness with money, and touchiness about personal honor.

Sometimes Virginians were surprised to discover that their ideas of gentility were resented by others. A woman identified only as Sallie F. wrote from Texas in 1859 of her gentlemen callers: "They are afraid of me, & seem to think I am something extra superfine, because I am from the 'old Dominion' but 'dears' how mistaken they are."

Virginians could indeed be condescending. Sarah Ann Quarles Chandler wrote from Illinois in 1836, "The people in this country are irreconcilably filthy, and a Virginian could scarcely exist among them." Virginian Samuel Townes, however, ridiculed those who maintained they were descended from the First Families, which he thought were of questionable respectability anyway; he wrote, "Personal merit constitutes the only claim to character and consideration."[43]

Persistence, Change, and Cultural Diversity

In the westward movement Virginia's cultural legacy was complex. The Virginia heritage appeared in settlement patterns, economic systems, social stratification, political ideology, legal institutions, and cultural ethics. Patterns of cultural persistence were very strong. Nowhere, however, was Virginia exactly reproduced in the West. One does not find a pattern of cultural replication but a more dynamic process.

Many Virginians tried to preserve their old culture in a new environment, but they did so differently in various parts of the West. The result was a rapid growth of diversity in their culture—not merely in ethnic terms but in other dimensions as well.

One factor was the regional complexity of Virginia itself. Emigrants to North Carolina came mainly from the southern parts of the Old Dominion. The new society that they built in North Carolina reflected their regional origins in Virginia's Southside. Other migration streams from Virginia had their own distinctive fields of recruitment that made a difference in the same way.

Another source of diversity was the ethnic structure of old Virginia. Migration from the southern Valley of Virginia carried with it the backcountry folkways of Scotch-Irish settlers and north British borderers. Movement from the piedmont tended to draw much more heavily on the culture that had descended from Sir William Berkeley's tidewater elite. These two streams mixed in many different combinations.

Everywhere, Virginians met other ethnic groups with cultural baggage of their own. In South Carolina they intermingled with West Indian planters, in Louisiana with French creoles, in Texas with Hispanic culture, in the Northwest and Oregon with New England Yankees and Delaware Valley Pietists. The result was not homogeneity but more diversity—the growth of new hybrid cultures.

Another factor, deeply interesting to Turnerians who lived in the West, was the diversity of the American landscape. Distinct cultural adaptations developed in, for example, the bluegrass region of Kentucky and the beautiful knob country that lay just a few miles to the east. Other conditions existed in the mountains of eastern Kentucky. These geographical features made a difference; so also did the purposes and choices of individual migrants in the westward movement.

The social environment was yet another variable. When Virginians moved away, they found themselves living by different laws in some areas. The Northwest Ordinance forbade slavery. Virginians in this area preserved as much as they could of their own culture but without the peculiar institution.

All of these factors coexisted with strong imperatives for the preservation of Virginia culture. Virginians were proud of their origins. They actively worked to maintain their identities and to reenact the familiar surroundings of their early lives.

Those Who Stayed Behind:
The Impact of Emigration in Virginia

There was also another side to the westward movement: the effect of emigration on the East. Frontier historians believed that the West operated as a social safety valve for the East to release tensions that might otherwise •have caused the growth of class conflict, political instability, and an urban proletariat.

Critics of the frontier thesis have disagreed. Some argued that western land was inaccessible to those who were most in need of it and that the capital costs of getting there, buying the land, and clearing it were beyond the reach of the poor. Others added that emigration also required a large investment of mental capital and skills that were uncommon among an urban proletariat. The westward migration demanded initiative, energy, and hope for the future—qualities that do not flourish in deep poverty.

Frontier historians have answered these criticisms with the rejoinder that a western safety valve could relieve pressures in ways that had nothing to do with the poor. A journey west was an alternative to downward mobility. It could also allow a propertied majority to increase and multiply.

All of these issues refer mainly to the northern United States, the locus classicus of the Turner thesis. The same questions have not been much examined for the American South. The effects of emigration in this region are a problem much in need of further study. Nowhere can they be examined more fruitfully than in Virginia, which had the largest emigration of any American state.

The Economics of Emigration

In economic terms emigration was a heavy tax on Virginia. The Old Dominion bore the costs of raising its young people. When they were of a productive age, many left the state and contributed their skills and talents to another place. The westward movement always operated as an economic subsidy to new regions and a heavy drain on the human resources of old settlements.

Capital as well as people moved west. Savings were always scarce in the southern states, which had very high consumption habits. A large part of the small surpluses of capital in antebellum Virginia that might have been invested in local improvements and economic development at home went instead into western lands. Capital flows that came into Virginia in the slave trade drained out again in other parts of the westward movement.

There were many possibilities for economic development in Virginia during the nineteenth century. Some of them were partly realized. The state itself spent large sums to establish a railroad network. The seaports of Norfolk and Alexandria grew in the nineteenth century, partly with the expansion of the coastal slave trade. Small centers of tobacco manufacturing sprang up at Lynchburg and Petersburg. But commerce and urban development in Virginia lagged far behind the older eastern cities. A study by David R. Goldfield found that in 1790 the commerce of New York and Virginia was approximately equal in its magnitude. By 1860 Virginia's imports had declined by 85 percent, and its exports had remained the same. New York's imports had grown sixteen times greater, and its exports had multiplied fiftyfold.[44]

Politics and Migration: John Randolph and Henry Clay

The westward movement also had heavy political costs for Virginia. Many of its most able and energetic young leaders were drawn away by brighter opportunities to the west. Virginia lost a large part of two entire generations of its brightest young people. At the same time it also rapidly lost its hegemony in national politics. From 1810 to 1860 its congressional representation dropped from twenty-three to eleven.

The flow of population also changed the texture of Virginia's political leadership in important ways. Here again, migration functioned as a filtering process that screened in some people and screened out others. An example of the conservative mentality of those who stayed behind is D. H. Wright of Tappahannock, who in 1852 rebuffed the appeal of William Lewis Moody to migrate, writing that "I have always been of opinion that it is best for every young man to transplant himself in some distant land and shake off the fetters which bind him to the home of his childhood. I candidly confess I have never had the nerve to do it—I expect to live and die in the area around Essex & King and Queen, the land of my Fathers."[45]

Something of the westward movement's effect may be seen by comparing two great Virginia-born leaders who became rivals in national politics during America's silver age. One chose to remain in his native state. The other decided to leave it.

The emigrant was Henry Clay (1777–1852), a native of Hanover County, Virginia. Though he liked to call himself a "self-made" man who rose from "ignorance, and indigence," he was born to comfort and raised to be a gentleman. His father, John Clay, was a Baptist clergyman who died when Henry Clay was four and left an estate of sixteen slaves and 464 acres of prime land. Henry Clay was raised by his stepfather, Captain Henry Watkins, a gentleman planter "of good blood, and of goodly wealth." With his family's connections Clay moved to Richmond in a "'Figginy' suit . . . so stiff that [its salt-and-pepper-colored] coat tails stood out from his legs at a forty-five-degree angle." He gained an envied place as a law student in the office of Chancellor George Wythe, who had also instructed Jefferson, Monroe, and Marshall.[46]

Clay was a risk taker in public and private life. His enemies called him a "gamester in politics." In 1797 he took a chance and moved to Kentucky, where his mother and stepfather had already settled. Always he thought of himself as a Virginia gentleman and built himself a Virginia-style house that he called Ashland. At the same time he lived for the future and devoted himself to promoting economic development and national union. He gave his attention to national politics and shared the large vision of Virginia's great leaders in the early Republic.

Abraham Lincoln, who set his star by Clay's principles, thought that his "predominant sentiment, from first to last, was a deep devotion to the cause of human liberty."[47] Clay always believed that slavery was evil, and through all his career he supported a plan of gradual emancipation. He also believed

119. Henry Clay was typical of Virginians who moved west—energetic, flexible, risk taking, forward looking. He lived for the future but drew his vision from Virginia's past.

deeply in the destiny of the American nation, and three times he helped the Union to survive major crises that threatened to tear it apart. "If any man wants the key of my heart," he said in 1844, "let him take the key of the Union."[48] Liberty and Union, together, were his driving purposes. Lincoln in his darkest moments during the Civil War found strength in the example of Henry Clay. In the month before the battle of Antietam, Lincoln wrote of his hero, "I recognize his voice, speaking as it ever spoke, for the Union, the Constitution, and the freedom of mankind."[49]

One of Clay's great rivals was John Randolph of Roanoke (1773–1833), a native of Prince George County who chose to remain in the Old Dominion. He was the great-grandson of William Randolph of Turkey Island and took the epithet "of Roanoke" partly to distinguish himself from a relative whom he despised and partly to establish a claim of temporal priority and affiliation with Sir Walter Ralegh's founding dream of Virginia.

Randolph grew up at his parents' plantation, appropriately named Bizarre, in the Southside on the Appomattox River near Farmville. Later he moved to his estate, Roanoke, on the Staunton River in Charlotte County. He was a good manager. Though desperately short of capital, he built up a holding of 8,000 acres and 400 slaves and assembled a fine stable of thoroughbred Virginia horses, which were his passion. Randolph disliked slavery but did not favor a general scheme of emancipation. Like many in Virginia he was deeply torn by the question, and he changed his mind even about his own slaves.

Randolph lived by a code of honor and chivalry. Henry Adams called him a "Virginian Saint Michael."[50] He was a duelist all his life, from his student days at William and Mary in 1792 to his duel with Henry Clay in 1826. Randolph insisted that the duel with Clay had to be fought south of the Potomac because only the "chosen ground" of Virginia should "receive his blood."[51] "In his hierarchy of values," Dumas Malone has written, "Virginia came first, followed by England and the rest of 'the old thirteen states.'"[52] Randolph had no interest in the American nation or in the Union. Liberty was important to him, but in a sense very different from that of Henry Clay. "I am an aristocrat," Randolph boasted. "I love liberty, I hate equality."[53] He despised Clay's vision of national union and economic growth. Of Randolph, the poet John Greenleaf Whittier wrote:

Too honest or too proud to feign
a love he never cherished,
Beyond Virginia's border line
his patriotism perished.

In his mature years John Randolph sought a life of solitude and lived at
Roanoke in a simple log house on land that he boasted had never belonged
to anyone but the Indians and his ancestors. In 1833 he died insane of tuberculosis, tertiary syphilis, and terminal irritation with the modern world.
Randolph's remains were buried in the soil of his beloved Roanoke, but in
a typically eccentric way. He demanded to be laid in the ground facing not
east toward Jerusalem but west toward Kentucky—so that he could always
keep an eye on Henry Clay.

Emigration and the Growth of Homogeneity of Virginia

Beyond its economic and political consequences, emigration also made a difference in the culture that was left behind. Here again, the westward movement acted as a cultural filter. In general, the cultural life of countries with
heavy emigration tends to become more homogeneous, less diverse. This
growth of cultural uniformity happened in Virginia. The departure of so
many people changed the texture of the Old Dominion's cultural life in a
fundamental way.

A case in point was the departure of many Quakers from Virginia during the late eighteenth and early nineteenth centuries. These people settled
in Virginia during the seventeenth century, were driven out by Sir William
Berkeley and his cavalier elite, and returned to a new regime of toleration
in the mid–eighteenth century. After the Revolution the Quakers began to
move again, this time mostly north to what were beginning to be called the
free states.

In 1775 the distinction between slave and free states had not yet developed.
Slavery existed in every colony of British America and throughout most of
the world. Even Quakers were slaveholders, though increasingly with a sense
of deep moral doubt that led them to become the first people in the world
to forbid slavery as a violation of the Golden Rule. Those who had settled in
the South began to move away from slavery. As early as 1769 Virginia Friends
were moving north, back to Pennsylvania. By 1776 eighteen Quaker families

120. John Randolph of Roanoke, in his idiosyncratic way, represented the backward-looking values of the Virginia gentry who stayed behind.

had headed northwest across the Alleghenies and settled at Union Town on a stream that flowed into the Monongahela. By 1805, 800 families of Friends had moved to Ohio. Many others followed.[54] This migration greatly increased in the early nineteenth century. One study finds that Virginia Quakers moved mainly to Ohio, while North Carolina Friends moved through Tennessee and Kentucky into Indiana.[55] The Quaker emigration from Virginia included people of every age and condition of life. Stephen B. Weeks writes, "It is literally true to say that there were emigrants from the cradle to the grave."[56] In that regard the Quaker exodus from the South resembled earlier migrations for conscience' sake.

The first departures were Quakers in northern and western Virginia who belonged to the Baltimore Yearly Meeting and who were closer to the West. Later the emigration spread more broadly through other regions of the Old Dominion. Many Friends were not happy about leaving and were deeply divided in their hearts. A few remained and continued to hold slaves, but the majority moved away. Typical of the agony of those who went was that of Borden Stanton, who in 1802 "strove against the thoughts of moving for a considerable time." He decided, however, that a land of slavery was "Egyptian darkness," and off he went. He worried about disrupting his Quaker community that had been built in Virginia at enormous effort. With his friends he planned the move with great care and consulted with his meeting, which sent three members to find a new home. Then the entire meeting moved across the Ohio River.[57]

By 1775 many Quakers had settled below the Potomac, and their numbers had been growing rapidly. By 1830 very few Quaker meetings remained in the South. They disappeared entirely from South Carolina and Georgia. In 1844 the Virginia Yearly Meeting had so few members that it disbanded. Only a few meetings remained, mainly in Frederick and Fairfax counties.

The Quakers were only the most visible part of a larger antislavery emigration that also caused others to leave Virginia, mainly for destinations in the Old Northwest. One wonders what might have happened if they had stayed home. In 1832 the Virginia legislature came within eight votes of deciding to end slavery in the state. The margin was so narrow that emigration might have been decisive in the outcome. Whatever the effect of the westward movement on slavery, the population of Virginia tended to become more homogeneous in the period of its great migration, as dissenters moved away.

Emigration as a Safety Valve for Slavery

If the westward movement was a safety valve for free institutions in the North, it may have acted even more powerfully as a safety valve for slavery in the South. It had this effect in several ways. First, migration sustained the expansion of slavery. As John C. Calhoun powerfully observed, slavery in the southern United States had to expand or die. It was a gigantic growth machine, and the westward movement was the instrument of its enlargement. Western expansion added vast tracts of fertile lands for new plantations. Many Virginians who were strongly attached to slavery thought that their own state was changing and that they could maintain their ideal society only by transplanting it. In 1848 Branch Archer wrote from Texas that "in ten years Virginia will be an antislavery state" and invited friends and family to join him where conditions were like Virginia forty years before.[58] Five years earlier Mecklenburg County planter James Y. Jones wrote a will declaring: "I also desire & request that if the abolishment [of slavery] should succeed in Virginia," his wife was "to carry the negroes to the south or Texas."[59]

The safety valve for slavery operated in other ways as well. The westward movement tended to support the price of slaves in the East. Virginians found a ready market for their human property in the nineteenth century and did not hesitate to profit by it. Mainly because of this mechanism, slave prices continued to rise in Virginia through the antebellum period, even though Virginia's agricultural base was not flourishing.

Emigration also was used by Virginia masters to rid themselves of troublesome slaves. Those who resisted were sold south. Other slaves found their own way out. The result was to diminish the danger of rebellion within the Old Dominion. Freed slaves moved away as well, many to the border states. By 1860 half of Maryland's African-American population was free; in Virginia, however, all but 20 percent were still in bondage. White critics of slavery also were encouraged to leave the state.

In the southern states a cyclical relationship was established between migration and slavery. The existence of slavery discouraged migration into the South; at the same time the weakness of immigration sustained slavery. In 1850, 608,626 native southerners were found to be living in the North. Only 199,672 northerners were living in the South. Of that number, 29,537 lived in Virginia. They were not welcome. Small as their numbers may have been,

John M. Daniel's *Richmond Examiner* called them "the Vandal Invasion of Virginia."[60] New England's Eli Thayer in 1857 organized a scheme for introducing social change in Virginia by seeding it with Yankee immigrants. He established an industrial colony called Ceredo in western Virginia near the Ohio River and founded a printing press. Thayer's main purpose, however, was to "let Ceredo speak to her neighbors, not through pamphlets but through her steam engines." Virginians responded with fury to this enemy in their midst. The *Richmond Whig* declared that the Old Dominion would not "permit the colonizing among them of the vile and viperous set of abolitionists."[61]

On the eve of the Civil War, criticism of slavery was increasingly forbidden in Virginia. The peculiar institution gained strength within the state, at the same time that it came under more direct attack in other parts of the country. The result was an escalation of sectional unity and national conflict. Patterns of migration were closely linked to this tendency in a complex cycle of cause and consequence.

Conclusion

THE STORY OF Virginia and the westward movement spans nearly three centuries, from the founding of the Roanoke colony to the Civil War. It is a history of high complexity. For analytic purposes we have arbitrarily divided it into three overlapping parts: migration to Virginia, migration in Virginia, and migration beyond Virginia.

The first of these movements began as an extension of migration within Europe. It encompassed the founding of Roanoke (1584–87), the settlement of Jamestown (1607), the deeply troubled period when the colony was at cross-purposes with itself and its surroundings (1607–40); the pivotal era of Sir William Berkeley (c. 1640–80); the formation of a small cavalier elite, the immigration of large numbers of indentured servants, and the forced emigration of dissenting Puritans and Quakers in the same period; the arrival of African slaves and English convicts during the eighteenth century; and the emergence of a distinctive culture, dominated for nearly two centuries by descendants of Berkeley's elite.

Specially important for the cultural history of Virginia was the great migration of "distressed cavaliers" and English servants. Both groups were of the same generation. Both came from the same part of England and professed the same Anglican religion. Both cherished a common heritage of English laws and liberties. Both brought to America the English folkways that they had known in the mother country.

These folkways included an English dialect that developed into America's southern accent, a tradition of vernacular architecture that still flourishes in the South today, and a set of strongly articulated attitudes toward land and wealth, work and play, marriage and family, sex and gender, order and freedom. Tidewater Virginia was the cradle of this culture, which later spread widely through the South.

The second part of our story was about migration within Virginia. That process began when a highly mobile population expanded through the central tidewater and continued with the settlement of Virginia's many distinctive regions: the Northern Neck, the Southside, the Eastern Shore, the Chesapeake islands, and the maritime communities of Norfolk and Newport News. In the late seventeenth century, English settlers reached the piedmont, and by the early eighteenth century, they were in the Valley of Virginia.

Much of the westward movement within Virginia was dominated by Sir William Berkeley's elite. The cavalier-turned-forester, as William Byrd described himself, was the leading figure on Virginia's fall-line frontier. Great families and high officeholders controlled the avenues to the West. The Randolph family and its kin were strong in the James River valley. Fairfaxes, Washingtons, Carters, Lees, and Marshalls were dominant in the Potomac. Alexander Spotswood and his allies held sway in the upper Rappahannock Valley. The best lands were engrossed by these little groups.

In the late seventeenth and early eighteenth centuries, an important change occurred. Sir William Berkeley's Virginia had been in many ways a closed society; dissent was not allowed. After the English Revolution of 1688, a policy of toleration was forced upon the colony by British authority, at the demand of religious dissenters led by Francis Makemie on the Eastern Shore.

This new policy opened the colony to many religious and ethnic groups. The regionalization of Virginia added another dimension to that diversity. The frontier gave it room to grow and reinforced it in another way. In new settlements the pressure of anxiety and nostalgia caused settlers to cling closely to their cultural beliefs. American pluralism has derived largely from that tendency—the persistence of ethnic and religious identity in an alien and often threatening environment.

This growth of diversity promoted rapid expansion. It also encouraged a ferment of social thought during the creative period that is still remembered as Virginia's golden age. In the western piedmont and Valley especially, where settlement was most diverse, limited conceptions of English toleration gave way to more spacious ideas of American freedom. This was the context in which James Madison and Thomas Jefferson invented new models of an open society—pluralist, democratic, libertarian, expansive, confident of the future.

There were limits to these new ideas of freedom in Virginia. Having grown from the hegemonic freedom of Berkeley's cavalier elite, they continued to coexist with race slavery and other inequalities. But limited as they may have been in that way, they were genuine and very powerful ideals, open to enlargement in the future.

The third part of our story is about migration beyond Virginia. This movement began in the seventeenth century, increased rapidly in the eighteenth century, and reached its peak in the period from 1783 to 1860. It carried Virginians in many directions: south to the Carolinas and Georgia; southwest from the Valley of Virginia to Tennessee; west from the piedmont to Kentucky; and northwest from the Northern Neck to Ohio. Later in the nineteenth century, other waves of emigration carried Virginians and their offspring farther into the Deep South, Texas, the Pacific slope, the western mountains, and northern cities.

The magnitude and complexity of these migrations raise a causal question. What set them in motion? Part of the answer was to be found in Virginia's agrarian economy, which was incapable of growing as rapidly as the population that it supported. While northern states developed new industrial and commercial economies in cities and factories, Virginians chose a different kind of growth: not development of a new economy but expansion of an older one.

Another interlocking part of the explanation concerned slavery. The relationship between slavery and migration was complex. Both masters and slaves moved west in large numbers. They did so because Virginia's "peculiar institution" was incapable of developing into a different sort of system. It could only expand or die.

This great migration from Virginia was important for its cultural consequences, in both the West and the East. Virginia was by far the most populous state in the new Republic and had the largest westward movement. Its cultural institutions spread through broad areas in the Mississippi Valley.

Among those institutions was slavery, which was greatly strengthened by its expansion and flourished on the southern frontier. The emigration of masters and slaves from Virginia greatly enlarged the South's peculiar institution and probably prolonged its existence.

But at the same time there was a countertendency. A great many Virginians moved to free states where slavery was prohibited. In 1850, 204,931 native Virginians lived in other slave states, and 182,952 were in free states. More than 163,000 were in the Midwest, nearly all of them in Ohio, Indiana, and Illinois. Migration from Virginia thus enlarged and strengthened the system of free labor that was expanding in the Northwest. This migration to the free states from Virginia (and other slave states settled by Virginians) was very large. Possibly it was large enough to have made a difference in the very close-run contest of the American Civil War.

However that may have been, the westward movement beyond Virginia was part of a great historical process, in which ideas of freedom and an open society expanded yet again. The issue of slavery in the nineteenth century centered mainly on the question of whether it should be allowed to spread into the West. Virginians took both sides on that question. The state itself divided into two Virginias, one slave, the other free. In the end freedom had grown into a universal idea that embraced all humanity, in a way that it had never done before.

Frontier Thesis and Germ Theory

This essay began with a set of questions about the work of Frederick Jackson Turner, in its relation to the origins of an open society in America. The questions centered on the rival claims of the germ theory and the frontier thesis—the first stressing the importance of culture that was carried from Europe; the second emphasizing the American environment. Which was right?

In general the history of Virginia suggests that the contribution of the Turner thesis lies more in the spirit of its inquiry than the substance of its interpretation. The history of Virginia's westward movement does not support the frontier thesis. Neither, however, does it confirm the classic antithesis. Let us consider some of the major issues.

The Historical Problem: Continuity and Change

In the question of cultural continuity and change, Turner's frontier thesis holds that old European cultures broke down in the American environment, and that a new culture developed as an adaptation to material conditions in the New World.

Competing germ-theory models such as the *Altlandschaft* theory suggest, to the contrary, that the cultural values of "the first group able to effect a viable self-perpetuating society are of crucial significance for the later social and cultural geography of the area, no matter how tiny the initial band of settlers may have been."[1]

Our inquiry indicates that neither of these ideas is correct. A third model is necessary to mediate between them. As Virginians went west, they sang a song called "Shenandoah": "Away, I'm bound away." In a cultural sense they were indeed "bound away." We find repeated evidence of strong patterns of cultural persistence in frontier environments. Migrants to Ohio's Virginia Military District preserved Virginia's distinctive systems of settlement and landholding, stratification and wealth distribution, political structure and legal institutions, vernacular architecture and cultural values. This retention happened despite the exclusion of slavery, which many materialist scholars in the twentieth century have regarded as the primary determinant of southern cultural distinctiveness. The breadth and strength of these patterns of cultural persistence tell us that a central tenet of the Turner thesis, which holds that old cultures were shattered on the frontier, is mistaken.

On the other hand, the evidence does not support the *Altlandschaft* model, or what a twentieth-century American disciple of that school calls the doctrine of "first effective settlement." In every American region the first permanent settlements did not define the culture that developed there. Jamestown in Virginia, Plymouth in Massachusetts, and the Finnish and Swedish settlements in the Delaware Valley were all overtaken by more powerful cultural groups that arrived later and established a hegemony by gathering power firmly in their own hands.

The founders and leaders of the major hegemonic cultures appeared long after the first permanent settlements—in Virginia, two generations afterward; in the Delaware Valley, nearly three. The "law of first effective settlement" cannot be salvaged by tautological readings of "first" or "effective." Its central assertion is simply mistaken.

These hegemonic cultures developed in different ways. Some formed around small privileged elites, as in Virginia and South Carolina. Others derived their power from small populations with transcendent spiritual purposes—Quakers in the Delaware Valley; Puritans in Massachusetts. A third pattern appeared in the southern highlands: the hegemony of British borderers in the backcountry was that of a larger population with a highly integrated culture that proved to be exceptionally well adapted to the environment of the southern frontier.

None of these hegemonic cultures had everything its own way. But all of them controlled access to material resources, regulated the immigration that came after them, defined the leading institutions of their regions, and shaped the future of their settlements as a conscious act of individual will and collective purpose.

These hegemonic cultures were dynamic, not static. Berkeley's cavalier elite became in the Revolutionary era a Whig elite and in the early nineteenth century a Jeffersonian Republican elite. In the mid–nineteenth century that group changed again, becoming an open, individuated elite that operated within democratic processes. Instead of a simple Turnerian story of dynamic New World cultures spontaneously generated by environmental conditions or a simple *Altlandschaft* pattern of static Old World cultures from the earliest settlements, we find evidence of persistent but dynamic hegemonic cultures formed mainly by processes of migration, dominated by elites, changing in response to historical events and conditions, and preserving their power and influence for many generations.

The Environmental Problem: Free Land

A similar pattern appears in regard to free land, the prime mover in the frontier thesis. Turner and other American historians believed that free land — that is, abundant land — created a nation of small independent farmers and supplied the material base for individualism, freedom, and democracy. Turner observed this process happening in his native Wisconsin and generalized it into a universal tendency on frontiers in general.

In Europe and Latin America scholars such as Kliuchevsky and Nieboer believed, to the contrary, that free land gave rise to serfdom and slavery. They observed in Russia and the Indies that landlords introduced systems of forced labor to hold their workforce in environments where land was abundant. Like Turner, they also generalized from regions they knew best to global conclusions. Which of these answers is correct? In specific settings, both; in general terms, neither. Quantitative tests have shown that Turner's thesis accurately described the northern frontier of the United States, where he was born and raised. When a population of yeoman farmers moved from New England to the Old Northwest, their polity became more democratic, the comity grew more individualist, the distribution of land became somewhat more equal in an economy of free labor.

In Virginia and the American South, the story was different. As in New Spain, eastern Europe, and other parts of the world, small elites took the lion's share of the land and introduced systems of unfree labor to work it for them. As Virginians moved west, the distribution of land became even less equal than it had been in the East. The regions differed in the pattern of change.

In short, free land operated in one way in some regions and in quite another elsewhere. The problem can be solved only if one adds another factor: a social switching mechanism that operated in every settlement, though not always in the same way. This switch was in the hands of those who controlled access to the land, regulated the flow of migration, and established a framework of laws that defined the status of labor and land in a new environment.

This idea of a social switching mechanism takes us back to the idea of hegemonic cultures. In the northern parts of the United States, a system of small freeholds was introduced as a cultural artifact. In Virginia large land grants were common from the Berkeley era. The switch was thrown one way in the northern colonies and another way in the South.

Turner was right about the Wisconsin frontier where he grew up. He was wrong about frontiers in general. Kliuchevsky and Nieboer were correct about eastern Europe and South America, but they also were mistaken when they generalized more broadly. All erred when they reached beyond the limits of their own experience.

Free land alone did not create free institutions or slavery. It supplied the resources for both systems to expand, depending on the hegemonic culture that organized systems of land and labor. What made the difference was a cultural switching mechanism within the institutions and values that regulated access to the land.

Environmental Determinants: Other Factors

Turner and his critics both tended to think of the frontier in materialist terms, particularly in regard to land. The history of westward expansion in Virginia tells us that other environmental factors were equally important in shaping processes of cultural change and continuity.

Climate and health had a major effect on cultural development, particularly in tidewater Virginia. The supply of water as well as land was another important determinant. Americans whose thinking has been shaped by the East take the water supply for granted. Most of the world, however, is not so lucky; it suffers from too much water or too little. These problems have put narrow constraints on free institutions. Only in the twentieth century have human beings found ways of reconciling large systems of social control with freedom and individual rights.

Another factor, as important as what Turner called free land, is security. Virginia's environment in its early years was highly insecure—much more so than that of eastern New England or the Delaware Valley. But it should also be noted that military security was relative to the culture that was carried there. When many of Virginia's gentlemen-at-arms lived by a warrior ethic, they found themselves frequently at war with their Indian neighbors. The experience of the Quakers in the Delaware Valley was different in that respect. In regard to Woodward's "free security," as to Turner's "free land," culture and environment interacted in highly specific ways.

A Cultural Problem: Unity or Diversity?

Turner believed that "the frontier promoted the formation of a composite nationality for the American people." He wrote that in "the crucible of the frontier the immigrants were Americanized, liberated and fused into a mixed race."[2]

Here again, the evidence of Virginia's westward movement indicates that he was mistaken. In the eighteenth century especially, the westward movement opened Virginia to cultures of increasing diversity as a growing variety of cultural groups maintained their different identities and also as regional diversity added another dimension of difference.

Something similar happened in migration out of Virginia. In this large process there were many reasons for moving, many different emigrant groups, and many places to go. In general, most of these migrants tried to preserve much of the culture they had known before, but they did so in different ways. The westward movement did not separate these people from their past, as Turner believed. It did not break down old institutions, as his model suggested, but allowed room for cultural diversity to flourish.

The westward movement from Virginia did not make everyone the same. It supplied the space for people to coexist while preserving their differences.

This growth of cultural diversity was largely a function of cultural persistence. It hinged on the ability of individual cultures to survive in a new environment—not without change but without losing their identity.

Turner, of course, was not entirely mistaken. Virginia's Huguenots quickly assimilated, intermarrying at a rapid rate with English Protestants who shared similar values. In time, German and English groups also intermixed. But separate ethnic identities and different folkways persisted, especially on the frontier. The diversity of old cultures in a new world created a new foundation for freedom in America.

A Problem of Immigration:
Another Variable

The history of Virginia's westward movement was different from both the Turner thesis and the germ theory in yet another way. The migration process was itself a causal factor as powerful as environmental determinants or cultural imperatives.

Early students of this subject looked for universal laws of migration that operated in all times and places. This approach was mistaken. The process of migration has been a historical variable, operating very differently through the full span of modern history. In some periods and places, it was mainly a voluntary process; in others it became a system of forced movement. Motives for migration were variable too. Some people moved to escape persecution; others migrated primarily for material advantage. Many moved in groups; others, as individuals. Composition of immigrant populations by age, class, gender, and ethnicity varied greatly from one migration stream to another. So also did the structure and resources of elites and their success in controlling the flow of people.

Migration was always a process of what might be called cultural filtration. It always screened out some people and institutions and cultural values and allowed others to move freely. This filtering process is constant. But its cultural consequences are highly variable. It has operated in different ways at different times. The migration process determined what sorts of people moved and how they behaved when they reached their destinations.

On the northern frontier that Turner knew best, migration tended to be more voluntaristic than elsewhere. On southern frontiers it was voluntary for many people, but for others it contained a larger element of coercion. This factor alone made a major difference in the cultures that developed first in tidewater Virginia and then spread to the West. Many other migration factors were operating at the same time.

A Problem of Emigration: The Safety Valve

Another question is about the effect of emigration on the places that people left behind, and in particular the Turnerian problem of the safety valve. In general we have found evidence that the westward movement preserved and stabilized cultures in the East, but it did so differently in various regions. In the northern states there is evidence that the frontier worked as a safety valve in something like the way that Turner's followers believed. The linkages were highly complex, more so than early models suggested, but still very strong.

In the southern states something different happened. The westward movement functioned as a safety valve for slavery and greatly strengthened the South's peculiar institution. In obvious economic linkages the westward movement strengthened the material base of slavery. It supported slave prices by creating a new sectional market for bound labor. It also enlarged the plantation system.

At the same time it reinforced the South's peculiar institution in more subtle ways. Just as immigration into the Old Dominion increased the diversity of Virginia's culture in the eighteenth century, so emigration from the state increased its homogeneity in the nineteenth. Aliens and dissenters, particularly in the question of slavery, tended to leave the state.

The net effect of these processes in both the North and South was to increase cultural unity within sections but to enlarge cultural diversity in the nation as a whole. That powerful tendency led directly to civil war and in time to a new growth of freedom for America.

An Open or a Closed Society?

When Turner framed his fundamental question, he assumed that America had been, to his own time at least, an open society, moving toward increasing democracy, liberty, equality, and individuality. He believed that the central problem of American history was to explain the origins and development of an open society. Most historians of his generation agreed with him on the question, even as they were of different minds about the answer.

In the late twentieth century, a small group of academic historians who came of age in the generation of Vietnam and Watergate rejected this fundamental problem. They believed that the central task of American history is not to explain why America is an open society but to explain why it is not more open. Some thought of it as a closed, or at least a closing, society.

On this great question the history of Virginia and the westward movement strongly shows that these academic historians were very much mistaken. Turner's conclusion was more nearly correct, although not for the reasons he thought. Through nearly four centuries there was indeed a strong opening process in the history of Virginia. It was not simple, straightforward, or linear but a complex tendency with many reversals and countermovements along the way.

In the seventeenth century Sir William Berkeley's Virginia was, like many other American colonies, a closed society. During the eighteenth century the colony became more open and pluralist. A diversity of Old World cultures in a new environment gave rise to new ideas of freedom.

That process repeated itself on a larger scale in the nineteenth and twentieth centuries. Here again, there were countermovements as the opening of the great West and emigration from Virginia caused a closing of cultural institutions in the Old Dominion and gave slavery a new strength. But the westward movement also enlarged the base of free institutions in America and promoted a new pluralism of regional and ethnic cultures. A growing diversity of immigrants, clinging strongly to their inherited identities, created a new cultural system in America that was more open and free than any of those ethnic cultures individually had been. This opening process has always been incomplete. The ideal of an opening society has continued to grow more rapidly than its reality. That tension, however, is itself a source of further growth.

In short, the Turner thesis was the wrong answer to the right question. The central problem in American history continues to be about the origin and development of an open society, just as Turner believed. But the solution to that problem cannot be found in the physical environment of the frontier, or in any other monistic material determinant. Long after Turner's frontier closed, the opening process continues with more momentum than ever before. It has always been driven mainly by cultural imperatives, operating on the acts and choices of millions of Americans. Today we are still a nation of seekers. And we are still "bound away" as our ancestors were before us.

Notes

Abbreviations

VMHB   *Virginia Magazine of History and Biography*
WMQ   *William and Mary Quarterly*

Introduction

1. Herbert Baxter Adams, "Report of Proceedings of Ninth Annual Meeting of the American Historical Association," *Annual Report of the American Historical Association for the Year 1893* (Washington, D.C., 1894), p. 6; The Johns Hopkins University, *Herbert Baxter Adams, Tributes of Friends . . . ,* The Johns Hopkins University Studies in Historical and Political Science, extra no. (Baltimore, 1902).

2. Frederick Jackson Turner, "The Significance of the Frontier in American History," *Annual Report of the American Historical Association for the Year 1893,* pp. 199–227 (quotation on p. 199); Ray Allen Billington, *Frederick Jackson Turner: Historian, Scholar, Teacher* (New York, 1973), pp. 124–29.

3. Turner, "Significance of the Frontier in American History," pp. 221–23. For Turner's debt to Loria, see ibid., p. 207, and Lee Benson, *Turner and Beard: American Historical Writing Reconsidered* (New York, 1960), pp. 21–23.

4. Turner, "Significance of the Frontier in American History," pp. 200–201, 215.

5. The eyewitness was Andrew C. McLaughlin. See Billington, *Turner,* p. 514. For another report of the session, see "The Auxiliary Congresses," *The Dial* 15 (Aug. 1, 1893): 60.

6. For other responses, see James D. Bennett, *Frederick Jackson Turner,* Twayne's United States Authors Series (Boston, 1975), pp. 35–37.

7. Theodore Roosevelt, quoted in Billington, *Turner,* p. 130; Woodrow Wilson, "The Proper Perspective of American History," *Forum* 19 (1895): 544–59; Woodrow Wilson, "The Making of the Nation," *Atlantic Monthly* 80 (1897): 1–14. Wilson's articles were the first extended discussions of the Turner thesis to appear in print.

8. For the literature on the Turner thesis, see the excellent bibliography in Ray Allen Billington and Martin Ridge, *Westward Expansion: A History of the American Frontier* (4th ed.; New York, 1974), pp. 661–805; the listing by year in Vernon E. Mattson and

William E. Marion, *Frederick Jackson Turner: A Reference Guide* (Boston, 1985); "A Centennial Symposium on the Significance of Frederick Jackson Turner," *Journal of the Early Republic* 13 (1993): 133–249; James R. Grossman, ed., *The Frontier in American Culture* (Berkeley, Calif., 1994).

9. Turner, "Significance of the Frontier in American History," p. 199.

10. See, for example, John Donald Barnhart, *Valley of Democracy: The Frontier versus the Plantation in the Ohio Valley, 1775–1818* (Bloomington, Ind., 1953).

11. Carlton J. H. Hayes, "The American Frontier—Frontier of What?" *American Historical Review* 51 (1945–46): 199–216. Hayes delivered his paper as his presidential address to the American Historical Association in December 1945.

12. Also in this tradition is the work of Hubert G. W. Wilhelm, who writes, "The *Altlandschaft* theory of human settlement is perhaps ideally illustrated in the United States." See Hubert G. W. Wilhelm, "Settlement and Selected Landscape Imprints in the Ohio Valley," in Robert L. Reid, ed., *Always a River: The Ohio River and the American Experience* (Bloomington, Ind., 1991), pp. 67–104 (quotation on p. 68). The first statement of this model is August Meitzen, *Das Deutsche Volk in Seinen Volkstümlichen Formen* (Berlin, 1882). The term *Altlandschaft* was coined by Otto Schluter in *Die Siedlungsräume Mitteleuropas in Frühgeschichtlicher Zeit,* vol. 1, *Einführung in die Altlandschaftsforschung* (Remagen, 1952). This approach has heavily influenced the work of American geographers. It has been developed by Wilbur Zelinsky into what he calls the "doctrine of first effective settlement," the idea that "the specific characteristics of the first group able to effect a viable self-perpetuating society are of crucial significance for the later social and cultural geography of the area, no matter how tiny the initial band of settlers may have been." See Wilbur Zelinsky, *The Cultural Geography of the United States* (1973; rept. Englewood Cliffs, N.J., 1992), pp. 13–14.

13. Turner, "Significance of the Frontier in American History," p. 227. An essay by Martin Ridge suggests that the Turner thesis was similar to the *Altlandschaft* theory in its assertion that "the first settlers in a region could impose on it lasting cultural characteristics." This is true in one (and only one) respect. Turner argued that "each frontier leaves its traces behind it, and when it becomes a settled area the region still partakes of its frontier characteristics." In other respects the two models are fundamentally opposed. The frontier thesis is a predominantly materialist model that stresses change, environmental determinants, and the periphery as the critical area. The *Altlandschaft* theory tends to be an idealist model that emphasizes continuity, cultural values, and the core. In between there is a mediating model of *Albion's Seed:* a multiplicity of hegemonic cultures that maintain communications between the core and periphery and preserve their separate identities by adapting old folkways to a new environment. See Martin Ridge, "Turner the Historian: A Long Shadow," *Journal of the Early Republic* 13 (1993): 140; David Hackett Fischer, *Albion's Seed: Four British Folkways in America* (New York, 1989).

14. David Potter, *People of Plenty: Economic Abundance and the American Character,* Charles R. Walgreen Foundation Lectures (Chicago, 1954), p. 22.

15. H. J. Nieboer, *Slavery as an Industrial System: Ethnological Researches* (1910; rept. New York, 1971).

16. Evsey Domar, "The Causes of Slavery or Serfdom: A Hypothesis," *Journal of Economic History* 30 (1970): 18–32. For other discussions, see Orlando Patterson, "The Structural Origin of Slavery: A Critique of the Nieboer-Domar Hypothesis from a Comparative Perspective," in Vera D. Rubin and Arthur Tuden, eds., *Comparative Perspectives on Slavery in New World Plantation Societies*, in *Annals of the New York Academy of Sciences* 292 (1977): 15–25. A recent work in this tradition is Peter Kolchin, *Unfree Labor: American Slavery and Russian Serfdom* (Cambridge, Mass., 1987).

17. George W. Pierson, *The Moving American* (New York, 1973), pp. 229–58; Edward Kopf, "Untarnishing the Dream: Mobility, Opportunity, and Order in Modern America," *Journal of Social History* 11 (1977): 206–27.

18. For a survey of the literature, see Norman J. Simler, "The Safety-Valve Doctrine Re-evaluated," *Agricultural History* 32 (1958): 250–57.

19. For various shades of the new western history, see Patricia Nelson Limerick, *The Legacy of Conquest: The Unbroken Past of the American West* (New York, 1987); William Cronon, George Miles, and Jay Gitlin, eds., *Rethinking America's Western Past* (New York, 1991); Richard White, *It's Your Misfortune and None of My Own* (Norman, Okla., 1991); for the frontier as "f-word," see Patricia Limerick, "The Adventures of the Frontier in the Twentieth Century," in Grossman, *The Frontier in American Culture*, 72; James R. Grossman, *The Frontier in American Culture* (Chicago and Berkeley, Calif., 1994); Clyde A. Milner, ed., *A New Significance: Re-envisioning the History of the American West* (New York, 1966); William E. Reibsame, ed., *Atlas of the New West: Portrait of a Changing Region* (New York, 1997).

20. An introduction to the literature is Gerald D. Nash, *Creating the West: Historical Interpretations, 1890–1990* (Albuquerque, N.M., 1991).

1. Migration to Virginia

1. The same pattern has been found in five counties of southern England: Kent and Sussex (1580–1649), 77 percent; Suffolk and Norfolk (c. 1603–25), 82 percent. See H. Hanley, "Population Mobility in Buckinghamshire, 1573–83," *Local Population Studies* 15 (1975): 33–39; Peter Clark and David Souden, eds., *Migration and Society in Early Modern England* (London, 1987), p. 29.

2. Paul Slack, "Vagrants and Vagrancy in England, 1598–1664," *Economic History Review*, 2d ser., 27 (1974): 360–79.

3. Clark and Souden, *Migration and Society in Early Modern England*, p. 30; David G. Hey, *An English Rural Community: Myddle under the Tudors and Stuarts* (Leicester, Eng., 1974), p. 10.

4. John Patten, *English Towns, 1500–1700* (Folkestone, Eng., 1978), p. 133.

5. Clark and Souden, *Migration and Society in Early Modern England*, pp. 25–28.

6. A list of thirty English settlements planted before 1625 appears in Fischer, *Albion's Seed*, p. 784. For contrasting views of the immigration process, see Bernard Bailyn, *The Peopling of British North America: An Introduction* (New York, 1986), and *Voyagers to the West: A Passage in the Peopling of America on the Eve of the Revolution* (New York, 1986); Ian K. Steele, *The English Atlantic, 1675–1740: An Exploration of Communications and Community* (New York, 1986).

7. Jordan D. Fiore, ed., *Mourt's Relation: A Journal of the Pilgrims of Plymouth* (Plymouth, Mass., 1985), p. 23.

8. George Percy, "Observations by Master George Percy, 1607," in Lyon Gardiner Tyler, ed., *Narratives of Early Virginia, 1606–1625,* Original Narratives of Early American History (New York, 1907), p. 17.

9. "A Letter of Sir Humfrey Gilbert, Knight, sent to his Brother, Sir John Gilbert . . . ," in David Beers Quinn, ed., *The Voyages and Colonising Enterprises of Sir Humphrey Gilbert,* Works issued by the Hakluyt Society, 2d ser., vols. 83, 84 (London, 1940), 1:134.

10. "Introduction," ibid., 1:89. Sir Thomas More wrote in his *Utopia:* "He that hathe no grave is covered with the skye: and, the way to heaven out of all places is of like length and distance."

11. David Beers Quinn, ed., *The Roanoke Voyages, 1584–1590: Documents to Illustrate the English Voyages to North America . . . ,* Works issued by the Hakluyt Society, 2d ser., vols. 104, 105 (London, 1955), 1:90, 174.

12. Ibid., 1:19–22, 174, 2:514–15.

13. Percy, "Observations," p. 15; James Axtell, *After Columbus: Essays in the Ethnohistory of Colonial North America* (New York, 1988).

14. The *Susan Constant* was reported to carry 71 settlers; the *Godspeed,* 52; and the pinnace *Discovery,* 21, or 144 in all. The number that remained at Jamestown was variously estimated at 105 in John Smith's *Proceedings,* 100 in Smith's *Generall Historie,* and 104 in George Percy's "Observations." Two incomplete lists of names are given by Captain John Smith in *The Proceedings of the English Colony in Virginia* (Oxford, 1612) and his *Generall Historie of Virginia, New England, and the Summer Isles . . .* (London, 1624). Cf. Richard L. Morton, *Colonial Virginia* (2 vols.; Chapel Hill, N.C., 1960), 1:8; Percy, "Observations," p. 20; Philip L. Barbour, ed., *The Complete Works of Captain John Smith (1580–1631)* (3 vols.; Chapel Hill, N.C., and London, 1986), 1:207–9, 222–23, 240–42, 2:140–41, 160–61, 190–91.

15. Of colonists in the founding voyage that arrived in 1607, the first supply in early 1608, and the second supply in the fall of 1608, social origins of settlers are shown in table 1.

16. John Smith, "A True Relation . . . ," in Tyler, *Narratives of Early Virginia,* p. 37; Percy, "Observations," pp. 21–22.

17. J. A. Leo Lemay, *The American Dream of Captain John Smith* (Charlottesville, Va., and London, 1991), pp. 84–88, 197–220; Kevin J. Hayes, "Defining the Ideal Colonist: Captain John Smith's Revisions from *A True Relation* to the *Proceedings* to the Third Book of the *Generall Historie,*" *VMHB* 99 (1991): 123–44.

Table 1. Social origins of Virginia colonists, 1607–8

Status	1st planters		1st supply		2d supply	
	#	%	#	%	#	%
Gentlemen	51	(61)	31	(44)	28	(51)
Professions & skilled occupations	17	(20)	18	(25)	14	(25)
Unskilled	16	(19)	22	(31)	13	(24)
Total, known status	84	(100)	71	(100)	55	(100)
Unknown status	21		49		15	
Total	105		120		70	

Another twenty-two colonists are known to have arrived in this period but cannot be assigned to a particular voyage. Sources are lists of settlers in Philip L. Barbour, ed., *The Jamestown Voyages under the First Charter . . .* , Works issued by the Hakluyt Society, 2d ser., vols. 136, 137 (London, 1969), pp. xxv–xxviii; and Barbour, *The Complete Works of Captain John Smith* 1:207–9, 222–23.

18. Irene W. D. Hecht, "The Virginia Muster of 1624/5 as a Source for Demographic History," *William and Mary Quarterly,* 3d ser., 30 (1973): 74.

19. Edmund S. Morgan, *American Slavery, American Freedom: The Ordeal of Colonial Virginia* (New York, 1975), pp. 118–22.

20. Ibid., pp. 124–25, 128.

21. Ibid., pp. 116, 125.

22. David R. Ransome, "Wives for Virginia, 1621," *William and Mary Quarterly,* 3d ser., 48 (1991): 3–18.

23. Wesley Frank Craven, *The Southern Colonies in the Seventeenth Century, 1607–1689,* in Wendell Holmes Stephenson and E. Merton Coulter, eds., *A History of the South* 1 (Baton Rouge, La., 1949): 156.

24. J. Frederick Fausz, "Merging and Emerging Worlds: Anglo-Indian Interest Groups and the Development of the Seventeenth-Century Chesapeake," in Lois Green Carr, Philip D. Morgan, and Jean B. Russo, eds., *Colonial Chesapeake Society* (Chapel Hill, N.C., and London, 1988), p. 72.

25. J. Mills Thornton III, "The Thrusting Out of Governor Harvey: A Seventeenth-Century Rebellion," *VMHB* 76 (1968): 11–26.

26. H. P. R. Finberg, "Three Centuries in Family History: Berkeley of Berkeley," *Gloucester Studies* (Leicester, Eng., 1957), pp. 145–59; S. W. Bates-Harbin, *Members of Parliament from the County of Somerset* (Taunton, Eng., 1939); *Visitation of Somerset* (1623), s.v. "Berkeley"; MS 20/i, 137, Somerset Record Office; *A Walk Round St. Mary's, Bruton* (n.p., 1980); Fischer, *Albion's Seed,* pp. 207–12.

27. Sir William Berkeley to Henry Bennet, 1st earl of Arlington, June 5, 1667, in W. N. Sainsbury, ed., "Virginia in 1666–1667," *VMHB* 21 (1913): 43.

28. Sir William Berkeley, *A Discourse and View of Virginia* (1663; rept. London, 1914), p. 3.

29. Ibid., p. 3.

30. Thomas Ludwell to [Henry Bennet, 1st earl of Arlington?], Sept. 17, 1666, in Sainsbury, "Virginia in 1666–1667," p. 37.

31. Francis Moryson, ed., *The Lawes of Virginia Now in Force, Collected out of the Assembly Records, and Digested into One Volume . . .* (London, 1662).

32. Berkeley has been the victim of several strong trends in southern historiography. The first was the work of Thomas Jefferson Wertenbaker, Carl Bridenbaugh, and others who heaped ridicule on the so-called cavalier myth and argued that "the most significant feature of the Chesapeake aristocracy was its middle-class origin" (Carl Bridenbaugh, *Myths and Realities: Societies of the Colonial South* [Baton Rouge, La., 1952], p. 12; see also Thomas Jefferson Wertenbaker, *Torchbearer of the Revolution: The Story of Bacon's Rebellion and Its Leader* [Princeton, N.J., and London, 1940]). A second trend appeared in the work of the "Chesapeake group" of social historians, who were interested in market forces, demographic processes, and broad cultural tendencies, with little latitude for the agency of individuals. A third tendency has been a continuing interpretation of Bacon's Rebellion in ways unfavorable to Berkeley. To this day, liberal historians remember Berkeley as a failed reactionary and an alien presence in the American past. More sympathetic to Berkeley is Wilcomb E. Washburn, *The Governor and the Rebel: A History of Bacon's Rebellion in Virginia* (Chapel Hill, N.C., 1957). One of the few revisionist essays, Sister Joan de Lourdes Leonard, "Operation Checkmate: The Birth and Death of a Virginia Blueprint for Progress, 1660–1676," *WMQ*, 3d ser., 24 (1967): 44–74, argues that Berkeley was a failed progressive whose plans for economic development met with defeat. This assessment was true of specific projects such as the silk industry, but in other ways the southern colonies developed much as he intended in their labor system, class structure, and many of their folkways. There is no full-length published biography of Berkeley; but see Jane Dennison Carson, "Sir William Berkeley, Governor of Virginia: A Study in Colonial Policy" (Ph.D. diss., University of Virginia, 1951); and J. R. Pagan, "Notes on Sir William Berkeley," Gloucestershire Record Office. See also Warren M. Billings, "Sir William Berkeley—Portrait by Fischer: A Critique," and David Hackett Fischer's rejoinder, *WMQ*, 3d ser., 48 (1991): 598–611.

33. Edward Hyde, earl of Clarendon, *The History of the Rebellion and Civil Wars in England Begun in the Year 1641* (5 vols., 1706–7; rept. Oxford, 1888), 5:263.

34. Henry Cary, ed., *Memorials of the Great Civil War in England from 1646 to 1652* (2 vols.; London, 1842), 2:118; David Underdown, *Royalist Conspiracy in England, 1649–1660* (New Haven, 1960), p. 13; "Ingrams Proceedings," in "A Narrative of the Indian and Civil Wars in Virginia in the Years 1675 and 1676," in Peter Force, ed., *Tracts and Other Papers, Relating Principally to the Origin, Settlement, and Progress of the Colonies in North America . . .* (4 vols., 1836–46; rept. Gloucester, Mass., 1963), vol. 1, no. 11.

35. "Ingrams Proseedings," p. 34; Henry Norwood, "A Voyage to Virginia," in Force, *Tracts,* vol. 3, no. 10, p. 4; Henry J. Berkeley, "The Berkeley-Berkley Family and Their Kindred in the Colonization of Virginia and Maryland," *WMQ,* 2d ser., 3 (1923): 180–99.

36. Berkeley, *A Discourse and View of Virginia,* p. 9.

37. William Cabell Bruce, *John Randolph of Roanoke, 1773–1833* (2 vols.; New York, 1922), 1:10.

38. James LaVerne Anderson, "The Governors' Councils of Colonial America: A Study of Pennsylvania and Virginia, 1660–1776" (Ph.D. diss., University of Virginia, 1967); Leonard Woods Labaree, *Conservatism in Early American History* (New York and London, 1948), p. 7; Grace L. Chickering, "Founders of an Oligarchy: The Virginia Council, 1692–1722," in Bruce C. Daniels, ed., *Power and Status: Officeholding in Colonial America* (Middletown, Conn., 1986), pp. 255–77.

39. Fairfax Harrison, *Virginia Land Grants: A Study of Conveyancing in Relation to Colonial Politics* (Richmond, 1925).

40. Robert Quary to the Board of Trade, June 16, 1703, quoted in Chickering, "Founders of an Oligarchy," p. 262.

41. Kevin P. Kelly, "Economic and Social Development of Seventeenth-Century Surry County, Virginia" (Ph.D. diss., University of Washington, 1972), pp. 131, 135, 193.

42. "Narrative of George Fisher . . . [1750–55]," *WMQ,* 1st ser., 17 (1908–9): 123.

43. Hugh Jones, *The Present State of Virginia . . . ,* ed. Richard Lee Morton (Chapel Hill, N.C., 1956), p. 70; Philip Fithian to Enoch Green, Dec. 1, 1773, in Hunter Dickinson Farish, ed., *Journal and Letters of Philip Vickers Fithian, 1773–1774 . . .* (Williamsburg, Va., 1945), pp. 34–36.

44. Philip Alexander Bruce, *Social Life of Virginia in the Seventeenth Century* (Richmond, 1907), argued for the prevalence of a royalist or cavalier elite in early Virginia. Thomas Jefferson Wertenbaker and later the Chesapeake group of historians have ridiculed it without refuting it. In any case, small numbers are not the measure of influence or power. See John E. Manahan, "The Cavalier Remounted: A Study of the Origins of Virginia's Population, 1607–1770" (Ph.D. diss., University of Virginia, 1946).

45. Carl Bridenbaugh, *Vexed and Troubled Englishmen, 1590–1642* (New York, 1968), pp. 410, 432, 473; Richard S. Dunn, *Sugar and Slaves: The Rise of the Planter Class in the English West Indies, 1624–1713* (Chapel Hill, N.C., 1972), pp. 311–13; Russell R. Menard, "Population, Economy, and Society in Seventeenth Century Maryland," *Maryland Historical Magazine* 79 (1984): 71–92; Morgan, *American Slavery, American Freedom,* p. 404; Berkeley, *A Discourse and View of Virginia,* pp. 6–7; Wesley Frank Craven, *White, Red, and Black: The Seventeenth-Century Virginian* (Charlottesville, Va., 1971), p. 16; Russell R. Menard, "British Migration to the Chesapeake Colonies in the Seventeenth Century," in Carr, Morgan, and Russo, *Colonial Chesapeake Society,* pp. 99–132; James P. Horn, "Social and Economic Aspects of Local Society in England and the Chesapeake: A Comparative Study of the Vale of Berkeley, Gloucestershire, with the Lower Western Shore of Maryland, 1660–1700" (Ph.D. diss., University of Sussex, 1982), p. 6; W. W.

Hening, comp., *The Statutes at Large; Being a Collection of All the Laws of Virginia . . .* (13 vols.; Richmond, etc., 1809–23), 2:515.

46. Craven, *White, Red, and Black,* p. 5.

47. Abbot Emerson Smith, *Colonists in Bondage: White Servitude and Convict Labor in America, 1607–1776* (Chapel Hill, N.C., 1947), pp. 71, 308–9; David Galenson, *White Servitude in Colonial America: An Economic Analysis* (Cambridge, Mass., 1981), pp. 34–39; Edmund S. Morgan, "Headrights and Head Counts," *VMHB* 80 (1972): 361–71. See also James P. Horn, "Servant Emigration to the Chesapeake in the Seventeenth Century," in Thad W. Tate and David L. Ammerman, eds., *The Chesapeake in the Seventeenth Century: Essays on Anglo-American Society* (Chapel Hill, N.C., 1979), p. 92; Gary Nash, *The Urban Crucible* (Cambridge, Mass., 1979), p. 111; Menard, "British Migration to the Chesapeake Colonies in the Seventeenth Century," p. 109.

48. Horn, "Social and Economic Aspects of Local Society in England and the Chesapeake," p. 61.

49. Horn, "Servant Emigration to the Chesapeake in the Seventeenth Century," pp. 51–95. Similar findings appear in Anthony Salerno, "The Character of Emigration from Wiltshire to the American Colonies, 1630–1660" (Ph.D. diss., University of Virginia, 1977), p. 55; Galenson, *White Servitude in Colonial America,* pp. 34–64.

50. The sex ratio among Bristol servants (1654–86) was 308; among London servants it was 642. See Herbert Moller, "Sex Composition and Correlated Culture Patterns of Colonial America," *WMQ,* 3d ser., 2 (1945): 113–53.

51. "The Trappan'd Maiden: or, The Distressed Damsel," in C. H. Firth, ed., *An American Garland: Being a Collection of Ballads Relating to America, 1563–1759* (Oxford, 1915), pp. 51–53.

52. "A Net for a Night-Raven; or, A Trap for a Scold," ibid., pp. 54–59.

53. Peter Wilson Coldham, "The 'Spiriting' of London Children to Virginia, 1648–1685," *VMHB* 83 (1975): 280–87.

54. "The Lads of Virginia," in Firth, *An American Garland,* pp. 72–73.

55. William Edmundson, *A Journal of the Life, Travels, Sufferings, and Labour of Love in the Work of the Ministry . . .* (London, 1774), pp. 68–72; Stephen B. Weeks, *Southern Quakers and Slavery* (Baltimore, 1896), p. 36.

56. Morgan, *American Slavery, American Freedom,* p. 239.

57. William H. Cope, *A Glossary of Hampshire Words and Phrases* (London, 1883), p. vi.

58. "Enquiries to the Governor of Virginia . . . ," in Hening, *Statutes* 2:517.

59. Quoted in Fischer, *Albion's Seed,* p. 365.

60. Quoted ibid., p. 368.

61. Donald W. Meinig, *The Shaping of America: A Geographical Perspective of 500 Years of History,* vol. 1, *Atlantic America, 1492–1800* (New Haven, 1986), pp. 146, 149.

62. For an extended discussion and evidence, see Fischer, *Albion's Seed,* pp. 207–418.

63. Morton, *Colonial Virginia* 1:196.

64. Ibid., 1:197–98.

65. Philip Alexander Bruce, *Economic History of Virginia in the Seventeenth Century* (2 vols.; New York, 1895), 1:605–7.

66. Smith, *Colonists in Bondage,* p. 119.

67. Morton, *Colonial Virginia* 1:495; A. Roger Ekirch, *Bound for America: The Transportation of British Convicts to the Colonies, 1718–1775* (Oxford, 1987), p. 196; A. Roger Ekirch, "Bound for America: A Profile of British Convicts Transported to the Colonies, 1718–1775," *WMQ,* 3d ser., 42 (1985): 184–200. Smith reckoned 30,000, of which 20,000 came to the Chesapeake and perhaps 10,000 to Virginia. Ekirch, by adding 19,000 from Ireland, has raised these estimates to 50,000 overall. The heaviest flow of convict immigration came just before the American Revolution. Recent estimates increase the proportion sent to Maryland and Virginia. According to Marion Kaminknow and Jack Kaminknow, *Original Lists of Emigrants in Bondage from London to the American Colonies, 1719–1744* (Baltimore, 1967), of 7,010 criminals sent from London between 1718 and 1744, 97 percent came to the Chesapeake. See also Peter Wilson Coldham, *Bonded Passengers to America* (Baltimore, 1983). On vagrant children, see Robert C. Johnson, "The Transportation of Vagrant Children from London to Virginia, 1618–1622," in Howard S. Reinmuth, Jr., ed., *Early Stuart Studies* (Minneapolis, 1970), pp. 137–51; and James Curtis Ballagh, *White Servitude in the Colony of Virginia: A Study of the System of Indentured Labor in the American Colonies,* The Johns Hopkins University Studies in Historical and Political Science, ser. 13, nos. 6–7 (Baltimore, 1895).

68. Of 109 shiploads that sailed from Newgate and the Home Counties with known destinations in the period 1719–72, 47 were sent to Virginia.

69. Ekirch, "Bound for America," p. 196.

70. Quoted in Smith, *Colonists in Bondage,* pp. 129–30.

71. Morton, *Colonial Virginia* 2:541.

72. *The Interesting Narrative of the Life of Olaudah Equiano, or Gustavus Vassa, the African, Written by Himself* (2 vols.; London, 1789); G. I. Jones, "Olaudah Equiano of the Niger Ibo," in Philip D. Curtin, ed., *Africa Remembered: Narratives by West Africans from the Era of the Slave Trade* (Madison, Wis., 1968), pp. 60–98; Geraldine Murphy, "Olaudah Equiano, Accidental Tourist," *Eighteenth Century Studies* 27 (Summer 1994): 551–68.

73. Four studies find the pattern of African origins among Virginia slaves shown in table 2.

74. Orlando Patterson, *The Sociology of Slavery: An Analysis of the Origins, Development, and Structure of Negro Slave Society in Jamaica* (Rutherford, N.J., 1967), p. 143.

75. Ibid., p. 138.

76. *Practical Rules for the Management and Medical Treatment of Negroe Slaves, in the Sugar Colonies* (London, 1803), pt. 1, chap. 1.

77. Cecil Headlam, ed., *Calendar of State Papers, Colonial Series, . . . 1701* (London, 1910), pp. 720–21; Ulrich Bonnell Phillips, *American Negro Slavery* (1918; Baton Rouge, La., 1966), p. 43.

78. Henry Laurens to Devonsheir, Reeve, and Lloyd, May 22, 1755, in Philip M. Hamer et al., eds., *The Papers of Henry Laurens* (10 vols. to date; Columbia, S.C., 1968–), 1:252. Henry Laurens to Smith and Clifton, May 26, 1755: "The most certain article we can recommend . . . is a few fine Negro Men (not Callabars)" (ibid., 1:257). Henry

Table 2. African origins among Virginia slaves

Region	Virginia manifests 1710–69 (Curtin) %	Port York entries 1718–26 (Kulikoff) %	Port York entries 1728–39 %	Virginia runaways 1730–99 (Irwin et al.) %
Senegambia	14.9	4.0	10.0	8.7
Sierra Leone	5.3	1.0	0.0	0.0
Windward Coast	6.3	7.0	0.0	8.7
Gold Coast	16.0	13.0	5.0	8.7
Benin	0.0	0.0	0.0	0.0
Biafra	37.7	60.0	44.0	23.3
Angola & Congo	15.7	5.0	41.0	20.0
Madagascar	4.1	9.0	0.0	16.7
Unknown	0.0	0.0	0.0	0.0
Total	100.0	87.0	100.0	100.0
Number	(45,008)	(8,400)	(5,818)	(23)

Sources: Philip D. Curtin, *The Atlantic Slave Trade: A Census* (Madison, Wis., Milwaukee, and London, 1969), p. 157, based on primary data in Elizabeth Donnan, *Documents Illustrative of the History of the Slave Trade to America* (4 vols.; Washington, D.C., 1930–35), p. 127; Allan Kulikoff, *Tobacco and Slaves: The Development of Southern Cultures in the Chesapeake, 1680–1800* (Chapel Hill, N.C., and London, 1986), p. 322; unpublished research by Susan Irwin, Donna Bouvier, Mark Orlofsky, Andrea Katsenes, and David Hackett Fischer.

Laurens to Thomas Mears, June 27, 1755: "tall able people of any country but Callabars" (ibid., 1:275). Henry Laurens to Smith and Clifton, July 17, 1755: "There must not be a Callabar amongst them. Gold Coast or Gambias are best" (ibid., 1:295). Henry Laurens to Peter Furnell, Sept. 6, 1755: "Callabar which slaves are quite out of repute from numbers in every Cargo that have been sold with us destroying themselves" (ibid., 1:331).

79. Thomas Cable to John Maple, July 16, 1725, Cable Letterbook, MS no. 171, Maryland Historical Society, Baltimore.

80. L. Daniel Mouer, "Chesapeake Creoles: The Creation of Folk Culture in Colonial Virginia," in *The Archeology of Seventeenth Century Virginia*, special publication no. 30 of the Archeological Society of Virginia (Richmond, 1993), 149.

81. See Mechal Sobel, *The World They Made Together: Black and White Values in Eighteenth-Century Virginia* (Princeton, N.J., 1987); T. H. Breen and Stephen Innes,

Table 3. African origins of fugitive slaves in Virginia

Region	1730–39	1740–49	1750–59	1760–69	1770–79	1780–89	Total
Windward Coast							
Gambia		1					1
Mandingo	1			1	1		3
Bombarazo			1				1
Leeward Coast							
Gold Coast				2			2
Bight of Biafra							
Ibo, Ebo			1		5		6
Warrah	1						1
Congo-Angola							
Angola	2		3				5
East Africa							
Madagascar	2	2					4
Unidentified							
Guinea					1	2	3

Sources: Notes by G. W. Mullin and research by Susan Irwin, Donna Bouvier, Mark Orlofsky, Andrea Katsenes, and David Hackett Fischer.

"Myne Owne Ground": Race and Freedom on Virginia's Eastern Shore, 1640–1676 (New York and Oxford, 1980).

82. Research indicates the African origins of fugitive slaves in Virginia are as shown in table 3.

83. "Eighteenth-Century Maryland as Portrayed in the 'Itinerant Observations' of Edward Kimber," *Maryland Historical Magazine* 51 (1956): 327–28.

84. Charles Perdue, Jr., Thomas E. Barden, and Robert K. Phillips, eds., *Weevils in the Wheat: Interviews with Virginia Ex-Slaves* (Charlottesville, Va., 1976), pp. 129, 89.

85. Nicholas Creswell, *Journal . . . , 1774–1777* (New York, 1924), p. 30.

86. Thomas Jefferson, *Notes on the State of Virginia* (London, 1787), p. 233.

87. See Karen Linn, *That Half-Barbaric Twang: The Banjo in American Popular Culture* (Urbana and Chicago, 1991); Robert Winan, "The Banjo: From Africa to Virginia and Beyond," in Blue Ridge Institute, Ferrum College, *Blue Ridge Folk Instruments and Their Makers* (Ferrum, Va., 1992), pp. 10–25.

88. Karen Hess, "Historical Notes and Commentaries on the Virginia Housewife," in *Virginia Housewife*, by Mary Randolph (facsimile of 1824 edition, with additional material from 1825, 1828 editions, ed. Karen Hess; Columbia, S.C., 1984), pp. xxix–xxxii.

89. Keith Egloff and Deborah Woodward, *First People: The Early Indians of Virginia* (Richmond, 1992), p. 9.

90. The fullest account of the Powhatan tribe is Helen C. Rountree, *Pocahontas's People: The Powhatan Indians of Virginia through Four Centuries* (Norman, Okla., and London, 1990). On the Jesuit mission, see Clifford M. Lewis, S.J., and Albert J. Loomie, S.J., *The Spanish Jesuit Mission in Virginia, 1570–1572* (Chapel Hill, N.C., 1953).

91. For information in the preceding paragraphs, we are indebted to Don Gunter and Catherine Mishler for providing the label script for their exhibition "Tidewater to Trans-Allegheny: Virginia's Westward Expansion, 1607–1789" mounted at the Library of Virginia early in 1993.

92. Egloff and Woodward, *First People*, p. 42.

93. Gary B. Nash, *Red, White, and Black: The Peoples of Early America* (Englewood Cliffs, N.J., 1974), pp. 61–65.

94. Meinig, *The Shaping of America*, p. 145.

95. Todd L. Savitt, *Fevers, Agues, and Cures: Medical Life in Old Virginia* (Richmond, 1990), p. 16.

96. Egloff and Woodward, *First People*, p. 45.

97. Quoted from Mouer, "Chesapeake Creoles," 120.

98. Ibid., 116; W. Stitt Robinson, *The Southern Colonial Frontier, 1607–1763* (Albuquerque, N.M., 1979), 148, cited ibid., 105.

99. Mouer, "Chesapeake Creoles," 105–66.

2. Migration in Virginia

1. Social historians have found the rates of persistence and migration in seventeenth-century Virginia that are shown in table 4.

2. W. P. Palmer, ed., *Calendar of Virginia State Papers and Other Manuscripts, 1652–1781* (11 vols.; Richmond, 1875–93), 1:52.

3. Jones, *Present State of Virginia*, p. 73.

4. Peter M. Fontaine to John and Moses Fontaine, quoted in Jan Lewis, *The Pursuit of Happiness: Family and Values in Jefferson's Virginia* (Cambridge, 1983), pp. 12, 15.

5. Arthur Pierce Middleton, *Tobacco Coast: A Maritime History of Chesapeake Bay in the Colonial Era* (Newport News, Va., 1953), pp. 31, 34.

6. John Smith, "The Description of Virginia," in Tyler, *Narratives of Early Virginia*, p. 83.

7. Jones, *Present State of Virginia*, p. 73; Gregory A. Stiverson and Patrick H. Butler III, eds., "Virginia in 1732: The Travel Journal of William Hugh Grove," *VMHB* 85 (1977): 27–28.

8. Robert Beverley, *The History and Present State of Virginia*, ed. Louis B. Wright (1705; rept. Chapel Hill, N.C., 1947), p. 120.

Table 4. Persistence and migration in seventeenth-century Virginia

Place leaving	Population	Period	Staying %	Dying %	Moving %
Accomack Co., Va. (Perry)	landholders	1646–55	55		
Northampton Co., Va. (Morgan)	tithables	1664–74	45		
		1665–75	43		
		1666–76	46		
		1667–77	42		
Surry Co., Va. (Kelly)	tithables	1668–78	46		
		1678–88	47		
		1688–98	45		
Lancaster Co., Va. (Wheeler)		1669–79	39	35	26
		1678–88	43	31	26
		1688–98	45	27	28
		1700–10	47	28	25
Cogenhoe, Northamptonshire, Eng.	householders	1618–28	52	24	24

Sources: Morgan, *American Slavery, American Freedom,* p. 427; Kelly, "Economic and Social Development of Seventeenth-Century Surry County, Virginia," pp. 22–24; James R. Perry, *The Formation of a Society on Virginia's Eastern Shore, 1615–1655* (Chapel Hill, N.C., and London, 1990), p. 64; Robert A. Wheeler, "Lancaster County, Virginia, 1650–1750: The Evolution of a Southern Tidewater Community" (Ph.D. diss., Brown University, 1972), pp. 66, 82; James P. Horn, "Moving On in the New World: Migration and Out-Migration in the Seventeenth Century Chesapeake," in Clark and Souden, *Migration and Society in Early Modern England,* p. 185.

9. Johann David Schöpf, *Travels in the Confederation,* trans. and ed. Alfred J. Morrison (2 vols., 1788; rept. New York, 1968), 2:88.

10. Barbour, *Complete Works of Captain John Smith* 1:144.

11. Savitt, *Fevers, Agues, and Cures,* pp. 16–18.

12. Lorena S. Walsh, unpublished paper, quoted in Horn, "Moving On in the New World," p. 183.

13. Richard S. Dunn, "Black Society in the Chesapeake, 1776–1810," in Ira Berlin and Ronald Hoffman, eds., *Slavery and Freedom in the Age of the American Revolution* (Charlottesville, Va., 1983), maps the black population by county in 1755, 1782, and 1810.

14. Quoted in Morton, *Colonial Virginia* 1:153.

15. C. W. Alvord and Lee Bidgood, *The First Explorations of the Trans-Allegheny Region by the Virginians, 1650–1674* (Cleveland, 1912); William H. Gaines, Jr., "Abraham Wood and the Rivers of the West," *Virginia Cavalcade* 4 (Autumn 1954): 20–23; Alan Vance Briceland, *Westward from Virginia: The Exploration of the Virginia-Carolina Frontier, 1650–1710* (Charlottesville, Va., 1987), pp. 124–46.

16. Washburn, *The Governor and the Rebel*, p. vi.

17. Thomas Mathew, "The Beginning, Progress, and Conclusion of Bacon's Rebellion in Virginia in the Years 1675 and 1676," in Charles M. Andrews, ed., *Narratives of the Insurrections, 1675–1690*, Original Narratives of Early American History (New York, 1915), p. 40. For a discussion of this statement's authenticity, see Washburn, *The Governor and the Rebel*, pp. 229–30n.

18. Washburn, *The Governor and the Rebel*, p. vi; Wertenbaker, *Torchbearer of the Revolution*; Stephen Saunders Webb, *1676: The End of American Independence* (New York, 1984); Morgan, *American Slavery, American Freedom*, pp. 250–70; Morton, *Colonial Virginia* 1:240–96.

19. Morgan, *American Slavery, American Freedom*, pp. 226–27, 244–45, 418–20.

20. Louis B. Wright, ed., *Letters of Robert Carter, 1720–1727: The Commercial Interests of a Virginia Gentleman* (San Marino, Calif., 1940).

21. Nelson Addington Reed, *Family Papers* (St. Louis, 1990), pp. 168–69.

22. Quoted in William A. Hoge, ed., "The Proceedings . . . to Lay Out the Bounds of the Northern Neck of Virginia," *Northern Neck Historical Magazine* 15 (Dec. 1965): 1385.

23. Fairfax Harrison, *Landmarks of Old Prince William* (2 vols.; Richmond, 1924), 2:618–29. See also Lawrence Martin, "Warner's Map of the Rappahannock and Potomac Rivers," *WMQ*, 2d ser., 19 (1939): 82–83. E. M. Sanchez-Saavedra, *A Description of the Country: Virginia's Cartographers and Their Maps, 1607–1881* (Richmond, 1975), reproduces the Warner map on page 24 but misattributes it to William Mayo. Mayo's map is no. 60 in Earl G. Swem, *Maps Relating to Virginia* (1914; rept. Richmond, 1989).

24. Admittedly, some of this cordiality on the part of the General Assembly stemmed from the fact that Fairfax was old and had no children. Many assumed that on his death, his proprietary would pass to the state. Instead, Fairfax left his land to a nephew, who tried to collect both his inheritance and the Fairfax quitrents. For the resulting lawsuits, see F. Thornton Miller, "John Marshall versus Spencer Roane: A Reevaluation of *Martin* v. *Hunter's Lessee*," *VMHB* 96 (1988): 297–314.

25. Marshall was born in Uniontown, Pennsylvania, but he considered himself a Virginian. He was related to the Taliaferros, Pendletons, Randolphs, Catletts, and Carters, but his family roots were in the Northern Neck. His royalist ancestor Captain John Marshall arrived in Virginia in 1650 and settled in Westmoreland County, where his neighbors were Washingtons, Fitzhughs, and Lees. General Marshall attended Virginia Military Institute in Lexington, lived on the Northern Neck during World War II, and bought a farm, Dodona Manor, near Leesburg, to which he retired. See Marshall W. Fishwick, *Gentlemen of Virginia* (New York, 1961), pp. 271–72.

26. In 1929 Landon C. Bell asked five eminent Virginians to define the boundaries of Southside; he got five different answers. See Landon C. Bell, *Sunlight on the Southside: Lists of Tithes, Lunenburg County, Virginia, 1748–1783* (Philadelphia, 1931), pp. 9–12, quoted in Michael L. Nicholls, "Origins of the Virginia Southside, 1703–1753: A Social and Economic Study" (Ph.D. diss., College of William and Mary, 1972), p. 6.

27. William Byrd II, "The Secret History of the Line," in Louis B. Wright, ed., *The Prose Works of William Byrd of Westover* (Cambridge, Mass., 1966), p. 143.

28. Quoted in Kenneth A. Lockridge, *The Diary, and Life, of William Byrd II of Virginia, 1674–1744* (Chapel Hill, N.C., and London, 1987), p. 138.

29. Richmond C. Beatty and William J. Mulloy, eds., *William Byrd's Natural History of Virginia, or The Newly Discovered Eden* (Richmond, 1940), p. xxii.

30. See Michael L. Nicholls's study of tithables in Amelia, Lunenburg, Brunswick, and Prince George counties, 1737–50, in "Origins of the Virginia Southside, 1703–1753," p. 48. On the turnover of population, see Richard R. Beeman, *The Evolution of the Southern Backcountry: A Case Study of Lunenburg County, Virginia, 1746–1832* (Philadelphia, 1984), p. 29.

31. The history of the Skipwiths' American migrations and the royalist principles that set them in motion were summarized in Sir William Skipwith's gravestone:
"Sir William Skipwith, Baronet who deceased the 25th of February, 1764, aged 56 years. He descended from Sir Henry Skipwith of Prestwould in Leicestershire, created Baronet by King James the First—was honoured with King Charles the First's Commission for raising men against the usurping powers and proved loyal to the King, so that he was deprived of his estate by the usurper who occasioned his and his sons' deaths. Except Sir Grey Skipwith, grandfather of the abovesaid Sir William Skipwith, who was obliged to come to Virginia for refuge where the family hath since continued."

32. Susan McNeil Turner, "The Skipwiths of Prestwould Plantation," *Virginia Cavalcade* 10 (Summer 1960): 42–47.

33. Kelly, "Economic and Social Development of Seventeenth-Century Surry County, Virginia"; Fischer, *Albion's Seed,* p. 375.

34. Perry, *Formation of a Society on Virginia's Eastern Shore;* Breen and Innes, *"Myne Owne Ground."*

35. Robert McCrum, William Cran, and Robert MacNeil, *The Story of English* (New York, 1986), which draws on research by linguist David Shores, a resident of Tangier Island. See also Frances W. Dize, *Smith Island, Chesapeake Bay* (Centreville, Md., 1990).

36. Durand of Dauphine, *A Huguenot Exile in Virginia* (1689; New York, 1934), pp. 130, 174.

37. Thomas Perkins Abernethy, *Three Virginia Frontiers* (Baton Rouge, La., 1940), p. 45.

38. Walter Havighurst, *Alexander Spotswood, Portrait of a Governor* (Williamsburg, Va., 1967), pp. 4–5.

39. Two years after leaving the governor's office, Spotswood returned to England and married Anne Butler Brayne. The former governor and his wife returned to Virginia in 1730. After Spotswood's death, his widow married John Thompson, a minister in Culpeper County.

40. Mollie D. Somerville, "When the West Was East of the Appalachian Mountains," *Iron Worker* 28 (Autumn 1964): 4. The best summary of Spotswood's career is Bruce Lenman, "Alexander Spotswood and the Business of Empire," *Colonial Williamsburg* 13 (Autumn 1990): 49. A lengthier treatment is Leonidas Dodson, *Alexander Spotswood: Governor of Colonial Virginia, 1710–1722* (Philadelphia, 1932).

41. R. A. Brock, ed., *The Official Letters of Alexander Spotswood, Lieutenant-Governor of the Colony of Virginia, 1710–1722* . . . , Collections of the Virginia Historical Society, n.s., 1–2 (2 vols.; Richmond, 1882–85); Dodson, *Alexander Spotswood.* An argument that Spotswood may have engaged in deliberate fraud with his land grants is found in John Blankenbaker, "Col. Alexander Spotswood's 40,000 Acre Tract: A Study in Error and Fraud," *Beyond Germanna* 7 (May 1995): 382–84.

42. Philip D. Morgan, "Slave Life in Piedmont Virginia, 1720–1800," in Carr, Morgan, and Russo, *Colonial Chesapeake Society,* pp. 433–84; Sobel, *World They Made Together.* Evidence of the Africanization of the piedmont is found in the shift of Virginia's major slave port. The upper James received 50 percent of African slaves in 1734 and 62 percent in 1760–64, while the port of York withered away. Until the early 1770s most slave vessels bound for the upper James River docked at Bermuda Hundred, near Petersburg, which also supplied slaves to the rapidly growing Southside. See Allan Kulikoff, "The Origins of Afro-American Society in Tidewater Maryland and Virginia, 1700 to 1790," *WMQ,* 3d ser., 35 (1978): 245 n. 49.

43. Morton, *Colonial Virginia* 2:446.

44. "Journal of John Fontaine," in Ann Maury, comp., *Memoirs of a Huguenot Family: Translated and Compiled from the Original Autobiography of the Rev. James Fontaine* (New York, 1853), pp. 288–89.

45. Jones, *Present State of Virginia,* pp. 58, 166–67.

46. William Alexander Caruthers, *The Knights of the Horse-Shoe: A Traditionary Tale of the Cocked Hat Gentry in the Old Dominion* (Wetumpka, Ala., 1845); Rollin G. Osterweis, *Romanticism and Nationalism in the Old South* (New Haven, 1949), pp. 173, 179–81. We are grateful to Frederick Madison Smith of Marietta, Georgia, for the following communication: "Dr. William Alexander Caruthers was a native of Lexington, a graduate of Washington College (now Washington & Lee) and one of the first of what came to be known as 'professional southerners.' He was entirely of Scotch-Irish ancestry, deeply rooted in the culture of the Valley, not a native or resident of the Piedmont, lived in both Philadelphia and New York before returing to Lexington where he practiced medicine unsuccessfully and scribbled dilatorily. While living in Lexington he built a mock-Colonial Tidewater-style mansion where he lavishly entertained both his guests and his nostalgic predilection for a cavalier mystique foreign to the place and his own background. He subsequently moved to Savannah, the home of his wife, a descendant of one of Georgia's baronial landgrant colonial families, the Gibsons. Never a great man for business, Caruthers spent his time in Savannah promoting temperance and the Georgia Historical Society. Broken financially and in health, he died of tuberculosis in a sanitorium at the foot of Kennesaw Mountain near Marietta, Georgia, in 1846. For a de-

tailed discussion of his life and literary career, see Curtis Carroll Davis, *Chronicler of the Cavaliers;* and William Taylor, *Cavalier and Yankee."*

47. "Enquiries to the Governor of Virginia," in Hening, *Statutes* 2:517.

48. Philip Alexander Bruce, *Institutional History of Virginia in the Seventeenth Century* . . . (2 vols.; New York and London, 1910), 1:403.

49. There were exceptions—notably Rhode Island and Maryland. But these colonies were so wracked by internal strife that their example reinforced repressive tendencies in other colonies.

50. Lord Cornbury to the Lords of Trade, Oct. 14, 1706, in E. T. Corwin, ed., *Ecclesiastical Records of the State of New York* (7 vols.; Albany, 1901–16), 3:1670.

51. Sanford H. Cobb, *The Rise of Religious Liberty in America: A History* (New York, 1902), pp. 83–115 (quotation on p. 98).

52. Ibid., p. 106.

53. See James L. Bugg, Jr., "The French Huguenot Frontier Settlement of Manakin Town," *VMHB* 61 (1953): 359–64; Patricia Holbert Menk, "Notes on Some Early Huguenot Settlements in Virginia," ibid., 52 (1944): 194–96; R. A. Brock, ed., *Documents, Chiefly Unpublished, Relating to the Huguenot Emigration to Virginia* . . . , Collections of the Virginia Historical Society, n.s., 5 (Richmond, 1886); Jon Butler, *The Huguenots in America: A Refugee People in New World Society* (Cambridge, Mass., 1983); Edward Porter Alexander, ed., *The Journal of John Fontaine: An Irish Huguenot Son in Spain and Virginia, 1710–1719* (Williamsburg, Va., 1972).

54. Larry Dale Gragg, *Migration in Early America: The Virginia Quaker Experience,* Studies in American History and Culture, 13 (1978; rept. Ann Arbor, Mich., 1980), p. 4. Still very helpful is Weeks, *Southern Quakers and Slavery.*

55. Rufus M. Jones, *The Quakers in the American Colonies* (1911; rept. New York, 1966), p. xvi; Gragg, *Migration,* p. 15.

56. This average is derived from a sample of 1,231 Virginia Quaker immigrants, in Gragg, *Migration,* pp. 10, 22, 23, 35 (quotation).

57. Ibid., p. 12.

58. Ibid., pp. 48 (quotation), 51.

59. See map in Weeks, *Southern Quakers and Slavery,* endpaper.

60. Ibid., p. 96.

61. Quoted in Gragg, *Migration,* p. 43.

62. Ibid., p. 81.

63. "Journal of John Fontaine," p. 268.

64. Ibid.

65. Alexander, *The Journal of John Fontaine,* p. 88 (Nov. 21, 1715).

66. Marianne Wokeck, "Harnessing the Lure of the 'Best Poor Man's Country': The Dynamics of English Speaking Immigration to British North America, 1683–1783," in Ida Altman et al., eds., *"To Make America": European Emigration in the Early Modern Period* (Berkeley, Calif., 1991), pp. 228, 242.

67. Ibid., p. 212.

68. John Walter Wayland, *The German Element of the Shenandoah Valley of Virginia* (Harrisonburg, Va., 1989), pp. 52–53.

69. Samuel Kercheval, *A History of the Valley of Virginia* (1833; 3d rev. ed., Woodstock, Va., 1902), p. 46.

70. Wayland, *German Element of the Shenandoah Valley,* pp. 87–89, 92, 104–33.

71. We are grateful to Klaus Wust, historian of Virginia's Germans, for information about the location of German-speaking populations.

72. Edward A. Chappell, "Acculturation in the Shenandoah Valley: Rhenish Houses of the Massanutten Settlement," *Proceedings of the American Philosophical Society* 124 (1980): 55–89.

73. A. G. Roeber, "The Origin of Whatever Is Not English among Us," in Bernard Bailyn and Philip D. Morgan, eds., *Strangers within the Realm: Cultural Margins of the First British Empire* (Chapel Hill, N.C., and London, 1991), pp. 220–83 (quotation on p. 282).

74. Wayland, *German Element of the Shenandoah Valley,* pp. 153–76.

75. Ibid., pp. 20, 30 (quotation).

76. Ibid., pp. 21, 30.

77. Forrest McDonald and Ellen Shapiro McDonald, "The Ethnic Origins of the American People, 1790," *WMQ,* 3d ser., 37 (1980): 179–99; Thomas L. Purvis, "The European Ancestry of the United States Population, 1790," ibid., pp. 85–101; John B. Sanderlin, "Ethnic Origins of Early Kentucky Land Grantees," *Register of the Kentucky Historical Society* 85 (1987): 103–10.

78. Terry G. Jordan and Matti Kaups, *The American Backwoods Frontier: An Ethnic and Ecological Interpretation* (Baltimore, 1989).

79. Warren R. Hofstra, "The Opequon Inventories, Frederick County, Virginia, 1749–1796," *Ulster Folklife* 35 (1989): 51; Warren R. Hofstra, "Land, Ethnicity, and Community at the Opequon Settlement, Virginia, 1730–1800," *VMHB* 98 (1990): 423–48.

80. Fischer, *Albion's Seed,* pp. 747–53. The Gini ratio is a measurement of wealth concentration in which zero indicates perfect equality and 1.00 indicates extreme inequality.

81. Economic and material aspects of this process are discussed in Robert D. Mitchell, *Commercialism and Frontier: Perspectives on the Early Shenandoah Valley* (Charlottesville, Va., 1977), and Robert D. Mitchell, ed., *Appalachian Frontiers: Settlement, Society, and Development in the Preindustrial Era* (Lexington, Ky., 1991).

82. Suzanne Lebsock, *"A Share of Honour:" Virginia Women, 1600–1945* (Richmond, 1984), p. 35.

83. See Phyllis J. Nixon, "A Glossary of Virginia Words," *Publication of the American Dialect Society* 5 (1946): 3–43.

84. Beeman, *Southern Backcountry,* pp. 66–67; Turk McCleskey, "Rich Land, Poor Prospects: Real Estate and the Formation of a Social Elite in Augusta County, Virginia, 1738–1770," *VMHB* 98 (1990): 449–86; Turk McCleskey, "Across the First Divide: Frontiers of Settlement and Culture in Augusta County, Virginia, 1738–1770" (Ph.D. diss., College of William and Mary, 1990).

85. Albert H. Tillson, Jr., *Gentry and Common Folk: Political Culture on a Virginia Frontier, 1740–1789* (Lexington, Ky., 1991).

86. John Murray, 4th earl of Dunmore, to the earl of Dartmouth, May 1774, CO 5/1352, ff. 72–73, Public Record Office, Kew.

3. Migration beyond Virginia

1. J.-P. Brissot de Warville, *Nouveau voyage dans les Etats-Unis de l'Amérique* (1791), ed. Durand Echeverria (Cambridge, Mass., 1964), pp. 215–16, 340.

2. Isaac Weld, Jr., *Travels through the States of North America, and the Provinces of Upper and Lower Canada . . .* (2 vols.; London, 1799), 1:126.

3. Mitford M. Mathews, comp., *A Dictionary of Americanisms on Historical Principles* (1951; Chicago, 1956), s.v. "frontier."

4. Turner, "Significance of the Frontier in American History," p. 200.

5. John T. Juricek, "American Usage of the Word 'Frontier,' from Colonial Times to Frederick Jackson Turner," *Proceedings of the American Philosophical Society* 110 (1966): 10–34.

6. Mathews, *Dictionary of Americanisms*, s.v. "immigrant."

7. Henry Ruffner, *Address to the People of West Virginia* (Lexington, Va., 1847), p. 16.

8. *Biographical Directory of the American Congress, 1774–1989* (Washington, D.C., 1989), pp. 57–58.

9. A study by Phyllis Hunter, Virginia Historical Society, commissioned for this project, yielded the following results shown in table 5 for 3,575 Virginia Revolutionary War veterans who moved to another state and appeared on the pension rolls of 1835.

10. Quoted in Ormond Somerville, Jr., comp., *Dr. James Somerville, His Ancestors and Descendants* (Birmingham, Ala., 1983), p. 20.

11. Table 6 shows native Virginians living in other states and territories as they were counted in the censuses of 1850 and 1860.

12. W. P. Cumming, "The Earliest Permanent Settlement in Carolina: Nathaniel Batts and the Comberford Map," *American Historical Review* 45 (1939–40): 82–89. The Comberford Map (copies of which are in the New York Public Library and the National Maritime Museum, Greenwich, Eng.) shows the Batts House near Roanoke Sound.

13. Sir William Berkeley to the Council in Albemarle, Mar. 7, 1670, in William S. Powell, ed., *Ye Countie of Albemarle in Carolina: A Collection of Documents, 1664–1675* (Raleigh, N.C., 1958), pp. 37–38. Berkeley married Stephens's widow.

14. Betty Linney Waugh, "The Upper Yadkin in the American Revolution: Benjamin Cleveland, Symbol of Continuity" (Ph.D. diss., University of New Mexico, 1971), p. 80.

15. E. Merton Coulter, *Old Petersburg and the Broad River Valley of Georgia* (Athens, Ga., 1965), p. 9.

16. Charles Saggus, "Agrarian Arcadia: Anglo-Virginians in Georgia: The Greater Planters of Wilkes County, Georgia, in the 1850s," typescript kindly provided by Professor Saggus of Augusta College.

Table 5. Virginia Revolutionary War pensioners in other states

State	Virginia pensioners
Kentucky	1,538
Tennessee	460
Ohio	459
Indiana	335
North Carolina	216
District of Columbia	112
South Carolina	104
Missouri	96
Illinois	91
Alabama	89
Other states	75
Total	3,575

From a different perspective—that of the percentage of Virginians among a state's Revolutionary War veterans—55 percent of Missouri veterans had served with Virginia units, 42 percent of Tennesseans, and 31 percent of Georgians and Louisianans, 19 percent of those from Ohio and the District of Columbia, 17 percent of South Carolinians, 13 percent of North Carolinians, and only 5 percent of Marylanders.

17. Lucy Josephine Cunyus, *The History of Bartow County (formerly Cass) [Georgia]* (1933; rept. Easley, S.C., 1976), p. 101. We are indebted to Frederick Madison Smith of Marietta, Georgia, for drawing our attention to this information.

18. The document appears as Appendix 1 in Max Dixon, *The Wataugans* (Nashville, 1976), pp. 73–75.

19. John Murray, 4th earl of Dunmore, to the earl of Dartmouth, CO 5/1352, ff. 72–73, Public Record Office, Kew.

20. *Dictionary of American Biography*, s.v. "Sevier, John." Basic sources on Sevier are Carl Driver, *John Sevier, Pioneer of the Old Southwest* (Chapel Hill, N.C., 1932); Lynette B. Wrenn, "John Sevier," in Charles W. Crawford, ed., *The Governors of Tennessee*, vol. 1, *1790–1835* (Memphis, 1979), pp. 31–62; Robert M. McBride and Dan Robison, eds., *Biographical Directory of the Tennessee General Assembly*, vol. 1, *1796–1861* (Nashville, 1975), pp. 659–60.

21. John Donelson, "Journal of a Voyage intended by God's permission, in the good boat Adventure," Tennessee Historical Society Collection, Tennessee State Library and Archives.

Table 6. Native Virginians living in other states, 1850 and 1860

	1850 Census			1860 Census		
	No. of Virginians	Total population*	%	No. of Virginians	Total population	%
Alabama	10,387	420,032	2	7,598	516,769	—
Arkansas	4,737	160,345	3	6,484	320,594	2
California	3,407	69,610	5	5,157	233,466	2
Connecticut	228	332,525	—	302	379,541	—
Delaware	139	438,916	—	171	101,253	—
Florida	643	45,320	1	654	73,370	1
Georgia	7,331	518,079	1	5,275	583,417	1
Illinois	24,697	736,931	3	32,978	1,387,308	2
Indiana	41,819	931,392	4	36,848	1,232,244	3
Iowa	7,861	191,881	4	17,944	568,832	3
Kansas	—	—	—	3,487	94,513	4
Kentucky	54,694	740,881	7	45,310	870,402	5
Louisiana	3,216	205,921	2	2,986	295,247	1
Maine	94	551,129	—	116	590,826	—
Maryland	7,030	438,916	2	7,560	522,324	1
Massachusetts	796	830,066	—	1,391	970,952	—
Michigan	1,504	341,591	—	2,176	600,020	—
Minnesota	59	4,007	1	849	113,295	1
Mississippi	8,357	291,114	3	6,897	346,116	2
Missouri	40,777	520,826	8	53,957	906,540	6
New Hampshire	48	304,227	—	71	304,135	—
New Jersey	628	430,444	—	880	549,227	—
New York	3,347	2,439,296	—	3,650	2,882,095	—
North Carolina	10,838	577,750	2	9,899	658,264	2
Ohio	85,762	1,757,556	4	75,874	2,011,257	4
Oregon	469	11,992	—	1,273	47,343	3
Pennsylvania	10,410	2,014,619	1	11,062	2,475,710	—
Rhode Island	191	124,299	—	138	137,266	—
South Carolina	1,621	274,813	1	1,117	291,316	—
Tennessee	46,631	755,655	6	36,647	812,856	5
Texas	3,580	137,053	3	9,081	378,227	2
Vermont	21	280,966	—	30	282,355	—
Virginia	872,923	926,154	94	1,001,710	1,070,395	99
Wisconsin	1,611	197,912	1	1,983	498,954	—
D.C.	4,950	42,956	12	—	—	—

*Population figures are ambiguous in both cases. These figures should include whites and free blacks, but not slaves. Nativities are not given for slaves.

22. Nicholas Perkins Hardeman, *Wilderness Calling: The Hardeman Family in the American Westward Movement, 1750–1900* (Knoxville, Tenn., 1977), p. 8.

23. This and the preceding paragraphs are drawn from ibid.

24. Within the present boundaries of Alabama, the heaviest concentration of Revolutionary veterans from Virginia (25 percent of the total for the state) was in Madison County, clustered around the town of Huntsville (research by Phyllis Hunter from the U.S. Pension Rolls, 1835).

25. A rich file of correspondence on the migration from Virginia to Alabama appears in the Hooe-Harrison letters, 1832–36, University of Virginia Library, Charlottesville.

26. Quoted in Charles Gano Talbert, *Benjamin Logan, Kentucky Frontiersman* (Lexington, Ky., 1962), p. 140.

27. Quoted in Patricia Watlington, *The Partisan Spirit: Kentucky Politics, 1779–1792* (New York, 1972), pp. 7, 18; Thomas D. Clark, *A History of Kentucky* (New York, 1937), p. 105.

28. L. Scott Philyaw, "Views West: The Virginia Elite and the Trans-Appalachian West, 1750–1800," p. 4, paper read at the annual meeting of the Southern Historical Association in Atlanta, Nov. 6, 1992.

29. Quoted in Watlington, *Partisan Spirit*, p. 24.

30. Gail S. Terry, "Family Empires: A Frontier Elite in Virginia and Kentucky, 1740–1815" (Ph.D. diss., College of William and Mary, 1992), p. 315 n. 2.

31. Fischer, *Albion's Seed*, pp. 220–21.

32. See Hazel Dicken-Garcia, *To Western Woods: The Breckinridge Family Moves to Kentucky in 1793* (Rutherford, N.J., London, and Toronto, 1991).

33. Quoted in Bayrd Still, "The Westward Migration of a Planter Pioneer in 1796," *WMQ*, 2d ser., 21 (1941): 318–19 n. 2.

34. Mary Cronan Oppel, "Paradise Lost: The Story of Chaumière des Prairies," *Filson Club History Quarterly* 56 (Apr. 1982): 201–3.

35. Quoted in Harold B. Gill, Jr., and George M. Curtis III, eds., "A Virginian's First Views of Kentucky: David Meade to Joseph Prentis, August 14, 1796," *Register of the Kentucky Historical Society* 90 (1992): 122.

36. David Meade to Ann Randolph, Sept. 1, 1796, quoted in Still, "Planter Pioneer," pp. 321, 338, 342.

37. Ibid., pp. 340–42.

38. Quoted in Oppel, "Paradise Lost," pp. 203–4.

39. Quoted ibid., p. 209.

40. Quoted ibid., p. 207.

41. Marion Nelson Winship, "The Portable Planter: Virginia Gentry Travel across the Appalachians, 1790–1810," p. 1, paper read at the annual meeting of the Southern Historical Association in Atlanta, Nov. 6, 1992.

42. John Mack Faragher, "But a Common Man," *American History Illustrated* 27 (Nov.–Dec. 1992): 68, 70.

43. Ibid., pp. 70, 73; Fischer, *Albion's Seed*, pp. 747–53.

44. Reed, *Family Papers*, p. 184; Don Gunter and Catherine Mishler, *Tidewater to Trans-Allegheny: Virginia's Western Expansion, 1607–1789* (Richmond, 1993), n.p.

45. John Lee McElroy, "Notes from the Curator," *VMHB* 56 (1948): 66–69. A full account is given in A. A. Lambing, ed., "Céleron's Journal," *Ohio Archaeological and Historical Quarterly* 29 (1920): 335–96.

46. O. H. Marshall, "Céleron's Exposition to the Ohio in 1749," *Ohio Archaeological and Historical Quarterly* 29 (1920): 426–27.

47. Richard M. Ketchum, *The World of George Washington* (New York, 1974), pp. 30–32.

48. For an account of the reluctance of the gentry to mobilize the militia and widespread indifference among the poorer and middling sorts to distant squabbles over territory in the Ohio Valley, see James Titus, *The Old Dominion at War* (Columbia, S.C., 1991), pp. 25, 36, 41–45, 77–78, 144–45.

49. Quoted in Ketchum, *George Washington,* p. 34.

50. Quoted in John H. Rhodehamel, "George Washington's Bounty Lands," Mount Vernon Ladies' Association *Annual Report, 1984* (Mount Vernon, Va., 1985), p. 32.

51. Donald Jackson and Dorothy Twohig, *The Diaries of George Washington* (6 vols.; Charlottesville, Va., 1976–79), 2:277 (Oct. 5, 1770).

52. Quoted in Ketchum, *George Washington,* p. 67.

53. Other sources concerning Washington are: W. W. Abbot, "George Washington, the West, and the Union," *Indiana Magazine of History* 24 (Mar. 1988): 3–14; George B. Atlin, "George Washington Looks Westward," *Michigan History Magazine* 16 (1932): 127–42; John W. Wayland, "Washington West of the Blue Ridge," *VMHB* 48 (1940): 193–201; Charles H. Ambler, *George Washington and the West* (Chapel Hill, N.C., 1936); Roy Bird Cook, *George Washington's Western Lands* (Strasburg, Va., 1930); Ada Hope Hixon, "George Washington, Land Speculator," *Journal of the Illinois State Historical Society* 11 (1919): 566–75.

54. George Rogers Clark to Patrick Henry, Feb. 3, 1779, in "George Rogers Clark Papers, 1771–1781," *Illinois State Historical Society Collections* 8 (1912): 97–100. Major sources on Clark are John E. Bakeless, *Background to Glory: The Life of George Rogers Clark* (Philadelphia, 1951), and Hugh F. Rankin, *George Rogers Clark and the Winning of the West* (Richmond, 1976).

55. Dumas Malone, *Jefferson the Virginian* (Boston, 1948), p. 308.

56. William T. Utter, "Chillicothe Junto," *American Heritage* 4 (Spring 1953): 38–39, 70–71.

57. *Dictionary of American Biography,* s.v. "Worthington, Thomas."

58. Beverley W. Bond, Jr., *The Civilization of the Old Northwest: A Study of Political, Social, and Economic Development, 1788–1812* (New York, 1934), pp. 13–15, 99–118; see also Andrew R. L. Clayton, "Land, Power, and Reputation: The Cultural Dimensions of Politics in the Ohio Country," *WMQ,* 3d ser., 47 (1990): 266–86.

59. Adlai E. Stevenson, *Major Campaign Speeches of Adlai E. Stevenson, 1952* (New York, 1952), p. xv.

60. Quoted in *Dictionary of American Biography,* s.v. "Lewis, Meriwether."

61. Ibid.

62. Gerald S. Snyder, "First across the Continent," *Iron Worker* 36 (Spring–Summer 1972): 7–8.

63. James A. Robertson, ed., *Louisiana under the Rule of Spain, France, and the United States, 1785–1807* (2 vols.; Cleveland, 1911), 2:125–26.

64. Albert K. Weinberg, *Manifest Destiny: A Study of Nationalist Expansionism in American History* (Baltimore, 1935), p. 34.

65. Paul C. Nagel, *Missouri, a History* (Lawrence, Kans., 1988), p. 31.

66. Ibid., pp. 36, 55.

67. Marie George Windell, ed., "The Road West in 1818: The Diary of Henry Vest Bingham," *Missouri Historical Review* 40 (1945–46): 21–33.

68. E. Maurice Bloch, *The Paintings of George Caleb Bingham: A Catalogue Raisonné* (Columbia, Mo., 1986), pp. 132, 134, 142, 148, 151, 159, 183, 185, 188, 214, 252–53, 256.

69. Floyd Calvin Shoemaker, *Missouri's Hall of Fame* (Columbia, Mo., 1921), pp. 132, 177–79, 216; biographical notes kindly supplied by John Neal Hoover, St. Louis Mercantile Library Association.

70. William E. Parrish, ed., *A History of Missouri* (5 vols.; Columbia, Mo., 1971–), 2:37–38.

71. Mary B. Kegley, *Wythe County, Virginia: A Bicentennial History* (Wytheville, Va., 1989), pp. 332–33.

72. Ibid., pp. 333–35.

73. Walter Prescott Webb, ed., *The Handbook of Texas* (3 vols.; Austin, Tex., 1952–76), 1:344, 739, 2:1124; Randolph B. Campbell, *An Empire for Slavery: The Peculiar Institution in Texas, 1821–1865* (Baton Rouge, La., and London, 1989).

74. Stephen F. Austin to Nicholas Biddle, April 9, 1836, Texas Memorial Museum, Austin.

75. Louis Wiltz Kemp, *The Signers of the Texas Declaration of Independence* (Houston, Tex., 1944). The other Virginia signers were John Fisher of Richmond; James Gaines of Culpeper; Benjamin Briggs Goodrich of Brunswick County; Sam Houston of Rockbridge County; William Demetris Lacey, who had lived in Kentucky and Tennessee before coming to Texas in 1831; Junius William Mottley; Martin Palmer, who came to Texas from Tennessee; John S. Roberts; William Bennett Scoates of Halifax County; Elijah Stapp, who arrived in Texas from Missouri; and Edwin Waller of Spotsylvania County.

76. Webb, *Handbook of Texas* 1:141, 406, 2:856; "A Virginian 'Ranger' of Texas [William A. A. Wallace]," *Virginia Cavalcade* 5 (Summer 1955): 40–43; Saul Viener, "Surgeon Moses Albert Levy: Letters of a Texas Patriot," *Publications of the American Jewish Historical Society* 46 (Dec. 1956): 101–13.

77. The seventeen Virginians were Robert Allen, John J. Baugh, William R. Carey, William Garnett, John C. Goodrich, Patrick Henry Herndon, James Kenny, William Irvine Lewis, William J. Lightfoot, Byrd Lockhart, George Washington Main, Edward F. Mitchasson, Robert B. Moore (Martinsburg), James Northcross, William Sanders Oury (Abingdon), John William Smith, and John Sutherland (Danville). Thirteen were killed; four left as couriers before the final assault.

78. *Dictionary of American Biography,* s.v. "Houston, Samuel, Jr.." Biographies of
Houston include Marquis James, *The Raven: A Biography of Sam Houston* (Garden City,
N.J., 1929); Marion K. Wisehart, *Sam Houston, American Giant* (Washington, D.C.,
1962); Donald Braides, *Solitary Star* (New York, 1974); John Hoyt Williams, *Sam Houston: A Biography of the Father of Texas* (New York, 1993); and Marshall DeBruhl, *Sword
of San Jacinto: A Life of Sam Houston* (New York, 1993).

79. Webb, *Handbook of Texas* 1:224, 596, 260.

80. W. L. Moody to James H. Moody, May 23, 1861, Moody Mansion and Museum,
Galveston, Texas.

81. W. L. Moody & Co., *Three Quarters of a Century of Progress: W. L. Moody & Company, Bankers* (Galveston, Tex., 1941).

82. Merrill J. Mattes, *Platte River Road Narratives* (Urbana and Chicago, 1988), item
678, p. 224.

83. Joel P. Walker, *A Pioneer of Pioneers: Narrative of Adventures thro' Alabama,
Florida, New Mexico, Oregon, California, &c.* (Los Angeles, 1953).

84. Information courtesy of Valerie Verzuh, Oakland Museum; for travel accounts of
Virginians on the Oregon Trail, see Mattes, *Platte River Road Narratives,* entries 89, 405,
448, 451, 495, 545, 678, 1131, 1162, 1820, 1978.

85. Ibid.; J. Max Bland, "The Negro in Los Angeles" (M.A. thesis, University of
Southern California, 1936), p. 154.

86. Hubert Howe Bancroft, *History of California,* vol. 6, *1848–59,* in *Works of Hubert
Howe Bancroft* 23 (Santa Barbara, Calif., 1980): 34 n. 19, 77, 96 n. 22; Georgia Willis
Read and Ruth Gaines, eds., *Gold Rush: The Journals, Drawings, and Other Papers of J.
Goldsborough Bruff* (New York, 1944), p. 469; *San Joaquin Republican,* Dec. 13, 1853, p. 2,
Dec. 22, 1853, p. 2; *San Andreas Independent,* July 17, 1858, p. 2.

87. Doris Muscatine, *Old San Francisco: A Biography of a City from Early Days to the
Earthquake* (New York, 1975), pp. 55, 125, 362–63.

88. Alton Brooks Parker Barnes, *Gold Fever and a Virginia Doctor* (Onley, Va., 1989),
pp. 18–20. The George C. Tyler letters, on which this account is based, are in the collection of the Virginia Historical Society.

89. Quoted in Bernard J. Henley, "A Richmonder in Search of Gold: The 1849 California Gold Rush," *Richmond Quarterly* 3 (Winter 1980): 47.

90. Mattes, *Platte River Road Narratives,* entry 354.

91. T. K. Cartmell, *An Historic Sketch of the Two Fairfax Families in Virginia* (New
York, 1913); Florence Donnelly, "The Lord and His Lady," San Rafael *Independent Journal,* Sept. 17, 1966, M6–M8; Barbara Brebner, "No Land without a Lord: A Brief Look
at California's Only Political Peer" (seminar paper, University of San Francisco, 1988),
courtesy Fairfax Historical Society. The description of the house at Bird's Nest Glen
appears in "Our Only Baronial Estate," *San Francisco Examiner,* Jan. 1, 1893.

92. Florence Donnelly, "San Rafael's Pioneer Physician," San Rafael *Independent
Journal,* Mar. 13, 1965, pp. M6–M9.

93. Bancroft, *History of California* 6:657 n. 29, 679 n. 2.

94. Richard Dale Batman, "The California Political Frontier: Democratic or Bureaucratic," *Journal of the West* 7 (1968): 461–70; R. A. Burchell, "The Character and Function of a Pioneer Elite: Rural California, 1848–1880," *Journal of American Studies* 15 (1981): 377–89.

95. Dictated by James P. Beckwourth to T. D. Bonner, *The Life and Adventures of James P. Beckwourth, Mountaineer, Scout, and Pioneer, and Chief of the Crow Nation of Indians* (New York, 1856).

96. *Dictionary of American Biography*, s.v. "Bridger, Jim"; *Story of the Great American West* (Pleasantville, N.Y., and Montreal, 1977), p. 90. Biographies of Bridger include Stanley Vestal, *Jim Bridger, Mountain Man* (New York, 1946), and J. C. Alter, *James Bridger: Trapper, Frontiersman, Scout, and Guide* (Salt Lake City, 1925).

97. Helen S. Carlson, *Nevada Place Names: A Geographical Dictionary* (Reno, Nev., 1974), pp. 239–40.

98. Louis Morton, *Robert Carter of Nomini Hall: A Virginia Tobacco Planter of the Eighteenth Century* (1941; rept. Williamsburg, Va., 1964). Carter's grandson Thomas Jones had different beliefs. He was one of the "portable planters" who took eighteen slaves to Kentucky in 1810.

99. Charles Royster, *Light-Horse Harry Lee and the Legacy of the American Revolution* (New York, 1982), p. 164.

4. Problems of Cause and Consequence

1. Quoted in Joan E. Cashin, *A Family Venture: Men and Women on the Southern Frontier* (New York and Oxford, 1992), pp. 33–34.

2. Quoted in Roger G. Kennedy, "Introduction" to *The Smithsonian Guide to Historic America: Virginia and the Capital Region* (New York, 1989), p. 16.

3. Quoted in Virginius Dabney, *Virginia: The New Dominion* (Garden City, N.Y., 1971), p. 277.

4. Quoted in Kennedy, "Introduction" to *Smithsonian Guide*, p. 13; Robert P. Sutton, "Nostalgia, Pessimism, and Malaise: The Doomed Aristocrat in Late-Jeffersonian Virginia," *VMHB* 76 (1968): 41–42.

5. Elizabeth Trist to Nicholas P. Trist, Jan. 21, 1823, Trist Papers, Southern Historical Collection, University of North Carolina, Chapel Hill.

6. Kennedy, "Introduction" to *Smithsonian Guide*, p. 16.

7. Michael Tadman, *Speculators and Slaves: Masters, Traders, and Slaves in the Old South* (Madison, Wis., 1989), p. 45.

8. Quoted in Dabney, *Virginia*, p. 279.

9. Branch T. Archer to Frances Archer and Jane Segar Archer, Dec. 19, 1848, Archer Family Papers, Virginia Historical Society.

10. J.-P. Mayer, ed., *De la démocratie en Amérique* (2 vols.; Paris, 1961), 1:397–98, nn. 73–74, cited in Pierre Marambaud, *William Byrd of Westover (1674–1744)* (Charlottesville, Va., 1971), p. 268; John Randolph of Roanoke quoted in Hugh A. Garland, *The Life of John Randolph of Roanoke* (2 vols.; New York and Philadelphia, 1850), 2:15.

11. John Randolph to John R. Randolph, Apr. 7, 1830, quoted in Marambaud, *William Byrd of Westover,* p. 264.

12. Quoted in Sutton, "Nostalgia, Pessimism, and Malaise," p. 46.

13. John Hartwell Cocke to Philip Cocke, Dec. 3, 1835, quoted ibid., p. 43.

14. James Mercer Garnett to John Randolph, Oct. 16, 1827, quoted in Marambaud, *William Byrd of Westover,* p. 264.

15. Francis Eppes to Nicholas P. Trist, Mar. 2, 1828, Trist Papers.

16. William M. Bridges to William Price Palmer, Nov. 16, 1856, Palmer Family Papers, Virginia Historical Society.

17. Sutton, "Nostalgia, Pessimism, and Malaise," p. 43; Nathaniel Beverley Tucker, *George Balcombe: A Novel* (2 vols.; New York, 1836).

18. George Tucker, *The Valley of Shenandoah, or, Memoirs of the Graysons* (2 vols.; New York, 1824), 2:31, quoted in Marambaud, *William Byrd of Westover,* p. 265.

19. Kennedy, "Introduction" to *Smithsonian Guide,* p. 13.

20. Quoted in Dabney, *Virginia,* p. 277.

21. John Pendleton Kennedy, *Swallow Barn* (Philadelphia, 1860), p. 164, quoted in Marambaud, *William Byrd of Westover,* p. 265. See Charles H. Bohner, "Swallow Barn: John P. Kennedy's Chronicle of Virginia Society," *VMHB* 68 (1960): 317–30.

22. *Proceedings and Debates of the Virginia State Convention of 1829–1830* (Richmond, 1830), cited in Marambaud, *William Byrd of Westover,* p. 265.

23. Sutton, "Nostalgia, Pessimism, and Malaise," p. 47.

24. James Mercer Garnett to John Randolph, Oct. 16, 1827, quoted in Marambaud, *William Byrd of Westover,* p. 264.

25. Francis Eppes to Nicholas P. Trist, Nov. 7, 1826, Trist Papers.

26. Robert E. Shalhope, *The Roots of Democracy: American Thought and Culture, 1760–1800* (Boston, 1990), p. 168.

27. Gordon S. Wood, *The Radicalism of the American Revolution* (New York, 1992), pp. 367–68.

28. Miles Mark Fisher, *Negro Slave Songs in the United States* (Ithaca, N.Y., 1953), pp. 111, 114–15, 117.

29. Ibid., pp. 84–85, 110, 115–16. For Gabriel's and Nat Turner's revolts, see Philip J. Schwarz, "Gabriel's Challenge: Slaves and Crime in Late Eighteenth-Century Virginia," *VMHB* 90 (1982): 283–309; Douglas R. Egerton, *Gabriel's Rebellion: The Virginia Slave Conspiracies of 1800 and 1802* (Chapel Hill, N.C., and London, 1993); John Duff and Peter Mitchell, eds., *The Nat Turner Rebellion: The Historical Event and the Modern Controversy* (New York, 1971); Nicholas Halasz, *The Rattling Chains: Slave Unrest and Revolt in the Antebellum South* (New York, 1966), p. 158; Edgar Toppin, *A Biographical History of Blacks in America since 1528* (New York, 1969), pp. 91, 431–33; Herbert Aptheker, *American Negro Slave Revolts* (New York, 1963), pp. 293–306; Joseph Carroll, *Slave Insurrections in the United States, 1800–1865* (Boston, 1938), pp. 48–50, 129.

30. Quoted in Alison Goodyear Freehling, *Drift toward Dissolution: The Virginia Slavery Debate of 1831–1832* (Baton Rouge, La., 1982), p. 84.

31. Clement Eaton, *The Mind of the Old South* (Baton Rouge, La., 1967), p. 8. See also Joseph Clarke Robert, *The Road from Monticello: A Study of the Virginia Slavery Debate of 1832,* Historical Papers of the Trinity College Historical Society 24 (Durham, N.C., 1941).

32. Quoted in Eaton, *The Mind of the Old South,* p. 5.

33. Jesse Burton Harrison, *Review of the Slave Question,* Extracted from *The American Quarterly Review,* Dec. 1832 . . . (Richmond, 1833), p. 47.

34. Ruffner, *Address to the People of West Virginia,* p. 17.

35. Ibid., p. 16; for a discussion of this pamphlet, see William Gleason Bean, "The Ruffner Pamphlet of 1847: An Antislavery Aspect of Virginia Sectionalism," *VMHB* 61 (1953): 260–82.

36. Joseph Glover Baldwin, *The Flush Times of Alabama and Mississippi* (1854; rept. New York, 1957), pp. 47, 238.

37. Somerville, *Dr. James Somerville.*

38. Quoted in Cashin, *Family Venture,* p. 56.

39. George P. Garrison, "'A Memorandum of M. Austin's Journey from the Lead Mines in the County of Wythe in the State of Virginia to the Lead Mines in the Province of Louisiana West of the Mississippi,' 1796–1797," *American Historical Review* 5 (1899–1900): 525–26.

40. Richard Douglas Spence, "John Donelson and the Opening of the Old Southwest," *Tennessee Historical Quarterly* 50 (Fall 1991): 163.

41. John Filson, *The Discovery, Settlement, and Present State of Kentucky* (1784; New York, 1962), pp. vii, 20–21.

42. Marion Tinling and Godfrey Davies, eds., *The Western Country in 1793: Reports on Kentucky and Virginia* (San Marino, Calif., 1948), p. 59, quoted in Gragg, *Migration,* p. 129.

43. Quoted in Terry, "Disruption and Reunion," p. 3.

44. National Society of the Colonial Dames of America in the Commonwealth of Kentucky, *Liberty Hall, Orlando Brown House* (Lexington, Ky., 1989), p. 4.

45. Branch T. Archer to Frances Archer and Jane Segar Archer, Dec. 19, 1848, Archer Family Papers; "Sallie F." to unidentified cousin, Jan. 25, 1859, Virginia Historical Society; Eugenia T. Bumpass, ed., "Diary Kept by Sarah Ann Quarles Chandler on Her Trip from Virginia to Missouri," *Louisa County Historical Magazine* 20 (Spring 1989): 44; Cashin, *Family Venture,* pp. 46, 97.

46. Francis Eppes to Nicholas P. Trist, Nov. 7, 1826, Trist Papers.

47. M. E. R. Eppes to Virginia Trist, c. Mar. 18, 1828, ibid.

48. Cashin, *Family Venture,* pp. 54, 93, 106.

49. Quoted in Fredrika J. Teute, "Anne Henry Christian, a Frontier Woman," Virginia Historical Society, *An Occasional Bulletin,* no. 44 (1982): 10.

50. Cashin, *Family Venture,* pp. 41–42, 47.

51. Terry, "Disruption and Reunion," p. 4.

52. Edward D. Jervey and James E. Moss, eds., "From Virginia to Missouri in 1846: The Journal of Elizabeth Ann Cooley," *Missouri Historical Review* 60 (1965–66): 162–206 (quotations on pp. 170, 172–73, 181, 183, 186, 189, 195, 206).

53. Cashin, *Family Venture,* pp. 616–20, 64, 89, 106–7.

54. Lacy K. Ford, Jr., "Frontier Democracy: The Turner Thesis Revisited," *Journal of the Early Republic* 13 (1993): 152.

55. Jervey and Moss, "From Virginia to Missouri in 1846," p. 174; Bumpass, "Diary Kept by Sarah Ann Quarles Chandler," p. 38.

56. Weeks, *Southern Quakers and Slavery,* p. 247.

57. Ibid.

58. Quoted in Teute, "Anne Henry Christian," p. 10.

59. Bumpass, "Diary Kept by Sarah Ann Quarles Chandler," p. 40.

60. Levi Coffin, *Reminiscences,* p. 34, quoted in Weeks, *Southern Quakers and Slavery,* p. 246.

61. Weeks, *Southern Quakers and Slavery,* p. 247.

62. Quoted ibid., p. 247.

63. Marquis James, *The Raven: A Biography of Sam Houston* (Indianapolis, 1929), pp. 12–13.

64. Quoted in Still, " Planter Pioneer," p. 319.

65. Ibid., pp. 320, 327 (quotation).

66. Winship, "Portable Planter," pp. 7–13.

67. James Somerville to Helen Glassell Wallace Somerville, Oct. 30, 1835, Special Collections, University of Alabama Library.

68. Francis Eppes to Nicholas P. Trist, Nov. 6, 1828, Trist Papers.

69. Quoted in Gerald W. McFarland, *A Scattered People: An American Family Moves West* (Amherst, Mass., 1985), pp. 46–47.

70. Quoted in Elizabeth A. Perkins, "The Consumer Frontier: Household Consumption in Early Kentucky," *Journal of American History* 78 (1991–92): 489.

71. Winship, "Portable Planter," p. 4.

72. Estill Curtis Pennington, *William Edward West, 1788–1857: Kentucky Painter* (Washington, D.C., 1985), p. 48.

73. Jones Family Papers, Library of Congress, reel 576. We are indebted to Marion Nelson Winship for drawing our attention to this document.

5. African-American Migration

1. Frederic Bancroft, *Slave-Trading in the Old South* (Baltimore, 1931), p. 386; Tadman, *Speculators and Slaves,* p. 12.

2. Kulikoff, *Tobacco and Slaves,* p. 394.

3. Bancroft, *Slave-Trading,* p. 291.

4. Perdue, Barden, and Phillips, *Weevils in the Wheat,* p. 153.

5. This is a low estimate of Virginia's share, because it compares a net emigration from Virginia with gross emigration throughout the country. See Tadman, *Speculators and Slaves,* p. 12.

6. Estimates by Michael Tadman (ibid.) of net interregional slave emigration in the United States are shown in table 7.

7. Quoted in Willie Lee Rose, ed., *A Documentary History of Slavery in North America* (New York, London, and Toronto, 1976), p. 157.

8. Ibid., p. 158. On protest through song, see Lawrence W. Levine, *Black Culture and Black Consciousness: Afro-American Folk Thought from Slavery to Freedom* (New York, 1977).

9. Tadman, *Speculators and Slaves,* pp. 296–302.

10. Jonathan W. McCalley to William J. McCalley, Jan. 7, 1849, Virginia Historical Society.

11. Cashin, *Family Venture,* p. 51.

12. Mrs. Fannie Berry (b. 1841) of Petersburg, quoted in Perdue, Barden, and Phillips, *Weevils in the Wheat,* pp. 32–33.

13. Samuel Chilton, quoted ibid., p. 71.

14. Tadman, *Speculators and Slaves,* p. 247.

15. Dicken-Garcia, *To Western Woods,* pp. 180, 187.

16. Terry, "Disruption and Reunion," p. 10.

17. Mrs. Fannie Berry, quoted ibid., p. 33.

18. Cashin, *Family Venture,* p. 72.

19. Quoted in Rose, *A Documentary History of Slavery in North America,* p. 161.

20. Luther Porter Jackson, *Free Negro Labor and Property Holding in Virginia, 1830–1860* (1942; rept. New York, 1969), p. 51.

21. W. L. Moody to James H. Moody, June 1853, Moody Mansion and Museum, Galveston, Texas.

22. William Macon Waller to Sarah Armistead Garland Waller, Oct. 4, 1847, William Macon Waller Papers, Virginia Historical Society.

23. Ralph L. Ketcham, "The Dictates of Conscience: Edward Coles and Slavery," *Virginia Quarterly Review* 36 (Winter 1960): 47.

24. Ibid., pp. 58–59.

25. Ibid., p. 60.

26. Ibid., p. 93; Elizabeth Langhorne, "Edward Coles, Thomas Jefferson, and the Rights of Man," *Virginia Cavalcade* 23 (Summer 1973): 30–37.

27. Frank F. Mathias, "John Randolph's Freedmen: The Thwarting of a Will," *Journal of Southern History* 39 (1973): 263–72.

28. Ibid.

29. Ibid.; *The History of the John Randolph Freed Slaves of Roanoke, Virginia* (Piqua, Ohio, n.d.), n.p.; *Richmond Times-Dispatch,* Feb. 21, 1993, p. C8.

30. James Wesley Smith, *Sojourners in Search of Freedom: The Settlement of Liberia by Black Americans* (Lanham, Md., New York, and London, 1987). We are grateful to Lauranett L. Lee for this information.

Table 7. Net interregional slave emigration in the United States

State	1790–99	1800–09	1810–19	1820–29	1830–39	1840–49	1850–59
Va.	-22,767	-41,097	-75,562	-76,157	-118,474	-88,918	-82,573
Md.	-22,221	-19,960	-33,070	-32,795	-33,753	-21,348	-21,777
Del.	-4,523	-3,204	-817	-2,270	-1,314	-912	-920
D.C.		-1,123	-576	-1,944	-2,575	-2,030	-1,222
N.C.		-407	-13,361	-20,113	-52,044	-22,481	-22,390
S.C.				-20,517	-56,683	-28,947	-65,053
Ky.				-916	-19,907	-19,266	-31,215
Tenn.							-17,702
Georgia							-7,876
Total	-49,511	-65,791	-123,386	-154,712	284,750	-183,902	-250,728

31. W. E. B. Du Bois, *Dictionary of American Biography,* s.v. "Roberts, Joseph Jenkins."

32. Randall M. Miller, ed., *"Dear Master": Letters of a Slave Family* (Ithaca, N.Y., 1978), pp. 27–34 (quotation on p. 34).

33. Ibid., pp. 47, 142–51. Other letters from Liberia are printed in Bell I. Wiley, ed., *Slaves No More: Letters from Liberia, 1833–1869* (Lexington, Ky., 1980), and Marie Tyler-McGraw, ed., "'The Prize I Mean Is the Prize of Liberty': A Loudoun County Family in Liberia," *VMHB* 97 (1989): 355–74.

34. John Gunther, *Inside Africa* (New York, 1955), pp. 859–60.

35. Miller, *"Dear Master,"* p. 47.

36. *Niles' Weekly Register* 21 (Sept. 29, 1821): 71.

37. John W. Blassingame, ed., *Slave Testimony: Two Centuries of Letters, Speeches, Interviews, and Autobiographies* (Baton Rouge, La., 1977), p. 609.

38. *Milwaukee Journal,* Jan. 31, 1993, p. G3.

39. Edna Greene Medford, "'It Was a Very Comfortable Place for Poor Folks': Subsistence in a Rural Antebellum Free Black Community," *Locus* 5 (1993): 131–44; Petition of Patty Barrett, Charles City Co., Legislative Petition A-3960–61 (1827), Petition of Ephraim and Betsy Cary, Charles City Co., Legislation Petition A-3967 (1835), Petition of Judith Hope, Richmond City, Legislative Petitions A-9298 (1819), A 9304 (1820), Library of Virginia, Richmond. We are grateful to Lauranett L. Lee for acquainting us with this material.

40. W. B. Hartgrove, "The Story of Maria Louise Moore and Fannie M. Richards," *Journal of Negro History* 1 (1916): 23–33.

41. Ibid.

42. John N. Grant, "Chesapeake Blacks Who Immigrated to New Brunswick, 1815," *National Genealogical Society Quarterly* 60 (Sept. 1972): 194–98.

43. Blassingame, *Slave Testimony,* pp. 217–25.

44. Rochester, New York, was named for Colonel Nathaniel Rochester (1752–1831), a native of Westmoreland County, Virginia. See George Harrison Sanford King, *Marriages of Richmond County, Virginia, 1668–1853* (Fredericksburg, Va., 1964), p. 172.

45. Austin Steward, *Twenty-Two Years a Slave, and Forty Years a Freeman . . .* (Rochester, N.Y., 1859).

46. John E. Vacha, "The Case of Sara Lucy Bagby: A Late Gesture," *Ohio History* 76 (Autumn 1967): 222–33 (quotation on p. 225).

47. Ibid., pp. 226, 228.

48. Ibid., p. 229.

49. Ibid., pp. 222–31.

50. Quoted in Virginia Hamilton, *The Defeat and Triumph of a Fugitive Slave* (New York, 1988), p. 48.

51. Anthony Burns to Richard H. Dana, Jr., Aug. 23, 1854, Massachusetts Historical Society.

52. Other sources on Burns are Blassingame, *Slave Testimony,* p. 109 and n. 63; Charles Emery Stevens, *Anthony Burns, A History* (Boston, 1856); and Lerone Bennett, Jr., *Before the Mayflower: A History of Black America* (New York, 1984).

53. "'May God Spare You from Enduring What I Then Endured': A Daring Escape from Slavery (1848)," in Maurice Duke and Daniel P. Jordan, eds., *A Richmond Reader, 1733–1983* (Chapel Hill, N.C., and London, 1983), pp. 92–99.

54. Philip J. Schwarz, "Escape from Slavery: The Newby Family of Virginia and Ohio," paper read at the annual meeting of the American Historical Association in Washington, D.C., Dec. 29, 1992.

55. Quoted in Edgar Toppin, *A Biographical History of Blacks in America since 1528* (New York, 1971), p. 114.

56. Don E. Fehrenbacher, *The Dred Scott Case: Its Significance in American Law and Politics* (New York, 1978), p. 580.

6. The Cultural Legacy

1. Wilhelm, "Settlement and Selected Landscape Imprints," pp. 67–104.

2. Howe, *Historical Collections of Ohio,* p. 560.

3. Wilhelm, "Settlement and Selected Landscape Imprints," p. 85.

4. *Oxford English Dictionary,* s.v. "Virginia fence."

5. Wilhelm, "Settlement and Selected Landscape Imprints," p. 89, citing Norman J. W. Thrower, *Original Survey and Land Subdivision: A Comparative Study of the Form and Effect of Contrasting Cadastral Surveys,* Association of American Geographers Monograph Series, 4 (Chicago, Ill., 1966), p. 5.

6. Wilhelm, "Settlement and Selected Landscape Imprints," p. 91.

7. We are much indebted to William M. S. Rasmussen for his manuscript, "Architecture from 'Old Virginia': A Legacy of the Westward Movement," for the section that follows.

8. Donald A. Hutslar, *The Architecture of Migration: Log Construction in the Ohio Country, 1750–1850* (Athens, Ohio, 1986); Fred B. Kniffen and Henry Glassie, "Building in Wood in the Eastern United States: A Time Place Perspective," *Geographical Review* 54 (1966): 40–66; Fred B. Kniffen, "Folk Housing: Key to Diffusion," *Annals of the Association of American Geographers* 55 (1965): 549–77.

9. The Dandridge dynasty in Virginia was established in 1715 with the arrival from England of William Dandridge of Elsing Green, King William County, and John Dandridge of New Kent County, whose daughter Martha married George Washington. The genealogy of the Dandridges, both in England and Virginia, is too incomplete, however, to trace the descent of Robert Dandridge of Alabama or to identify his tidewater place of birth (Wilson Miles Cary, "The Dandridges of Virginia," *WMQ*, 1st ser., 5 [1896]: 30–37; Mary Selden Kennedy, *Seldens of Virginia and Allied Families* [New York, 1911], pp. 2, 13–55).

10. Information about Daniel Wade courtesy of Robert Gamble of the Alabama Historical Commission; see also Robert Gamble, "Endangered Aristocrats," *Alabama Heritage* 23 (Winter 1992): 22–30, for a survey of this group. Some examples from the group have been lost, and some survivors are threatened.

11. The term *I-house* was coined in the 1930s by a Louisiana State University professor studying Louisiana folk houses of the type. Fred Kniffen traced their prototype to three states whose names begin with the letter *I*—Illinois, Indiana, and Iowa—and so named the "I-house." Extracted from Kniffen's context as it now is, the term is a misnomer that denies the widespread popularity of the type.

12. Features of the Virginia I-house cited here have been identified in Ohio examples by Hubert Wilhelm of Ohio University in his videotape *Log Cabins and Castles: Virginia Settlers in Ohio* (Copyright Ohio Landscape Productions, Athens, Ohio, 1991).

13. Examples are pictured in Mills Lane, *Architecture of the Old South: Virginia* (Savannah, Ga., 1987), pp. 132–38; and Mills Lane, *Architecture of the Old South: North Carolina* (Savannah, Ga., 1985), pp. 111–25.

14. An upper-floor staircase at Sportsman's Hill with boards of a cutout design is clear evidence of the transmission of Germanic motifs by settlers of Germanic origin, for the type is found in Pennsylvania in buildings erected by German settlers (see Clay Lancaster, *Antebellum Architecture of Kentucky* [Lexington, Ky., 1991], pp. 68–70).

15. Ibid.

16. There is no evidence to prove whether the Carter mansion was built by John Carter or his son Landon Carter (Roger Kennedy, *Architecture, Men, Women, and Money in America, 1600–1860* [New York, 1985], pp. 292–305; *Dictionary of American Biography*, s.v. "Carter, Landon").

17. National Register of Historic Places nomination form for Grouseland, courtesy of Patrick R. Ralston, director of the Indiana Department of Natural Resources.

18. Lorethea Hamke, *All about William Henry Harrison* (Vincennes, Ind., 1985), pt. 2, pp. 1–11.

19. The large and well-known Georgian plantation house in Charles City County, Virginia, known today as Weyanoke was not a Minge property but was built in 1798 by Fielding Lewis, a nephew of the better-known Fielding Lewis of Kenmore in Fredericksburg.

20. "Minge Family Register," *WMQ*, 1st ser., 21 (1912): 31–33; "Historical and Genealogical Notes," ibid., 15 (1907): 280–82.

21. National Register of Historic Places nomination form for Belle Mont, courtesy of Robert Gamble of the Alabama Historical Commission.

22. Charles E. Brownell, Calder Loth, William M. S. Rasmussen, and Richard Guy Wilson, *The Making of Virginia Architecture* (Richmond, 1992), p. 220; Lancaster, *Antebellum Architecture of Kentucky*, pp. 158–60. Ampthill in Cumberland County, Virginia, designed by Jefferson for Randolph Harrison, and Folly in Augusta County, Virginia, built by owner Joseph Smith apparently without the aid of Jefferson, illustrate the influence of the second Monticello (see Calder Loth, ed., *The Virginia Landmarks Register* [3d ed.; Charlottesville, Va., 1987], pp. 115, 44).

23. Oppel, "Paradise Lost: The Story of Chaumière des Prairies," p. 206.

24. Howe, *Historical Collections of Ohio*, p. 401.

25. Cyrus McCormick, *The Century of the Reaper* (New York, 1931); Herbert N. Casson, *Cyrus Hall McCormick: His Life and Work* (Chicago, 1989); Herbert N. Casson, *The Romance of the Reaper* (New York, 1908); Stewart Holbrook, *The Age of the Moguls* (Garden City, N.Y., 1953).

26. Merle Curti, *The Making of an American Community: A Case Study of Democracy in a Frontier County* (Stanford, Calif., 1959).

27. A recent study of western Pennsylvania, settled mainly by British borderers, also finds that in the early years of the westward movement, there were vast social and economic disparities in that frontier region. An elite emerged, became dominant, filled political and judicial offices, and apportioned the best lands among themselves. R. Eugene Harper has tried to explain this pattern in terms of broad materialist determinants that operated throughout the westward movement. See R. Eugene Harper, *The Transformation of Western Pennsylvania, 1770–1800* (Pittsburgh, 1991), p. 139.

28. H. James Henderson, "Taxation and Political Culture: Massachusetts and Virginia, 1760–1800," *WMQ*, 3d ser., 47 (1990): 114.

29. Baldwin, *Flush Times of Alabama and Mississippi*, p. 78.

30. These expatriates came from fifty-one counties and fourteen towns in present-day Virginia and nine counties of modern West Virginia. Forty-two representatives and sixteen senators from Kentucky were Virginians. Twenty-two representatives and five senators of Tennessee were natives of the Old Dominion, as were nineteen congressmen and ten senators from Georgia. There were seventeen Virginia representatives and four senators from Ohio. Orange County native Zachary Taylor, who did not serve in Congress, became president after moving West. See Richard Beale Davis, "The Jeffersonian Virginia Expatriate in the Building of the Nation," *VMHB* 70 (1962): 51–54.

31. Donnelly, "San Rafael's Pioneer Physician"; W. L. Moody to James H. Moody, Feb. 1848, Moody Mansion and Museum, Galveston, Tex.

32. James Rives Childs, *Reliques of the Rives* (Lynchburg, Va., 1929), p. 274.

33. Joan Wells Coward, *Kentucky in the New Republic: The Process of Constitution Making* (Lexington, Ky., 1979), pp. 12–47, 124–61.

34. Benjamin F. Wright, "Democracy and the Frontier," *Yale Review* 20 (1930–31): 349–65; Benjamin F. Wright, "Political Institutions and the Frontier," in Dixon Ryan Fox, ed., *Sources of Culture in the Middle West: Backgrounds versus Frontier* (1934; rept. New York, 1964), pp. 15–38.

35. New York invented yet another solution that was copied by Vermont. South Carolina went its own way with wording that was followed by the Southwest Territory, Tennessee, Alabama, and Mississippi. The Delaware Valley solution was also borrowed by Georgia and Rhode Island, the only exceptions to these close regional patterns. The study was confined to enactments before 1837. See Elizabeth G. Brown, *British Statutes in American Law, 1776–1836* (Ann Arbor, Mich., 1964), p. 25.

36. Chilton Williamson, *American Suffrage: From Property to Democracy, 1760–1860* (Princeton, N.J., 1960), p. 208.

37. Ibid., p. 209. Williamson's findings have been replicated by David Urbach, a research assistant working for David Hackett Fischer at Brandeis University; see also Lewis Cecil Gray, *History of Agriculture in the Southern United States to 1860* (2 vols.; 1941; rept. Gloucester, Mass., 1958), 2:619–21.

38. Bertram Wyatt-Brown, *Southern Honor* (New York and Oxford, 1982), p. 82.

39. Bruce, *The Social Life of Virginia*, pp. 246–47.

40. Donnelly, "The Lord and His Lady," p. M8; Linda Leazer, "Randolph of Roanoke on the Field of Honor," Virginia Historical Society, *An Occasional Bulletin*, no. 53 (1986): 6–8.

41. Cashin, *Family Venture*, pp. 104, 106.

42. Quoted in Reed, *Family Papers*, pp. 22, 283.

43. "Sallie F." to unidentified cousin, Jan. 25, 1859, Virginia Historical Society; Bumpass, "Diary Kept by Sarah Ann Quarles Chandler," p. 44; Samuel Townes, quoted in Cashin, *Family Venture*, p. 97.

44. David R. Goldfield, *Urban Growth in the Age of Sectionalism: Virginia, 1847–1861* (Baton Rouge, La., and London, 1977), p. 12.

45. D. H. Wright to W. L. Moody, June 29, 1852, Moody Mansion and Museum, Galveston, Tex.

46. Robert V. Remini, *Henry Clay, Statesman for the Union* (New York and London, 1991), pp. 1–14.

47. Quoted ibid., p. 786.

48. Quoted ibid., p. xxix.

49. Abraham Lincoln to John M. Clay, Aug. 9, 1862, quoted ibid., p. 786.

50. Henry Adams, *History of the United States of America* (9 vols.; New York, 1889–90), 3:157.

51. Quoted in Remini, *Clay*, p. 295.

52. *Dictionary of American Biography,* s.v. "Randolph, John."

53. Bruce, *Randolph of Roanoke* 2:203.

54. Weeks, *Southern Quakers and Slavery,* p. 249.

55. Ibid., p. 248.

56. Ibid., p. 249.

57. Ibid., pp. 95, 98. Stanton was a North Carolina Quaker.

58. Branch T. Archer to Frances Archer and Jane Segar Archer, Dec. 19, 1848, Archer Family Papers.

59. Quoted in Parke Rouse, Jr., *Below the James Lies Dixie: Smithfield and Southside Virginia* (1968; rept. Richmond, 1972), p. 30.

60. Quoted in Clement Eaton, *Freedom of Thought Struggle in the Old South* (1940; rept. New York, 1964), p. 238. For other examples of hostility to northerners, see Richard H. Abbott, "Yankee Farmers in Northern Virginia, 1840–1860" *VMHB* 76 (1968): 56–63.

61. Eaton, *Freedom of Thought,* p. 239.

Conclusion

1. Zelinsky, *Cultural Geography of the United States,* pp. 13–14.

2. Frederick Jackson Turner, *Frontier and Section: Selected Essays,* Classics in History Series (Englewood Cliffs, N.J., 1961), p. 51.

Acknowledgments

The exhibition and catalog from which this book derived were underwritten by an exceptionally generous grant from the National Endowment for the Humanities.

For many good suggestions in the early stages of the project we are grateful to Lonnie G. Bunch III, curator at the National Museum of American History and a specialist on African Americans in the West; Warren R. Hofstra of Shenandoah University, an expert on migration within Virginia; geographer Donald W. Meinig of Syracuse University; Robert D. Mitchell, geographer at the University of Maryland; and Dell Upton of the University of California at Berkeley, a specialist in material culture and architecture.

We are grateful to Don Gunter and Catherine Mishler of the Library of Virginia for sharing the label script for their exhibition "Tidewater to Trans-Allegheny: Virginia's Western Expansion, 1607–1789." Charles Saggus generously shared his manuscript concerning Virginia planters in Wilkes County, Georgia. Likewise, we thank Gregory H. Nobles, L. Scott Philyaw, Philip J. Schwarz, Gail S. Terry, and Marion Nelson Winship for allowing us to see copies of papers read at scholarly meetings.

At the Virginia Historical Society, invaluable aid was rendered by research assistants Lauranett L. Lee, whose minority internship was underwritten by Philip Morris USA, and Rachel Teagle, an exceptionally talented graduate student from the College of William and Mary. At an early stage the project benefited from the research of Phyllis Hunter, a doctoral candidate at William and Mary, who studied Revolutionary War pension records to trace the migration of Virginians. Elizabeth Arnold and Jacqueline Jeruss at Brandeis University also assisted with quantitative research. Simon Finger helped with the preparation of the index.

Acknowledgments

Among those who directed us to sources are William Watson of the Oregon-California Trail Association; Mrs. Dorothy Hardin; Ancella Bickley, Charleston, West Virginia; Nelson Reed, author of *Family Papers;* Betty DeBusk, Brooksville, Florida; Professor Wade Hall, Bellarmine College, Louisville; Professor Joan E. Cashin, Ohio State University; Beth Hager, Harrisburg, Pennsylvania; Bill J. Dunfee, Huntington, West Virginia; John Lundstrom, Milwaukee Public Museum; and Dr. David Nelson, a descendant of Dr. James Somerville, who was "bound away" to Alabama.

Foremost in our thanks is Charles F. Bryan, Jr., our colleague, friend, and director of the Virginia Historical Society. He supported this project steadfastly through ten years, since he first thought of it one hot August evening on his back porch.

Illustration Credits

30. National Park Service, Colonial National Historical Park
35. Courtesy, American Antiquarian Society, Worcester, Mass.
40. Prestwould Foundation
43. Colonial Williamsburg Foundation
45. Virginia Department of Historic Resources, Richmond
46. The Mercer Museum of the Bucks County Historical Society, Doylestown, Pa.
47. Collection of the Museum of Early Southern Decorative Arts, Winston-Salem, N.C., Mrs. Bahnson Gray Purchase Fund
48. Roddy and Sally Moore
49. Corbin family on loan to the Colonial Williamsburg Foundation
50. Reprinted from David Hackett Fischer, *Albion's Seed: Four British Folkways in America* (New York: Oxford Univ. Press, 1989)
51–52. Frontier Culture Museum of Virginia, Staunton
54. Rockbridge Historical Society, Lexington, Va.
58. William H. Guthman Collection
59. Tennessee State Museum, Nashville, Tennessee Historical Society Collection
60. Tennessee State Museum Collection, Nashville
61. On permanent loan to the Tennessee State Museum from John Donelson III, William Donelson, Sarah M. Williams, Mary Williams Wolf, Elizabeth Williams Butler, and James Williams IV
62. Reprinted by permission of Ada Mae Hardeman from Nicholas Perkins Hardeman, *Wilderness Calling: The Hardeman Family in the American Westward Movement, 1750–1900* (Knoxville, 1977)
64–65. Cincinnati Historical Society
66–67. Colonial Williamsburg Foundation
68. Copyright © 1991, from *Antebellum Architecture in Kentucky*, by Clay Lancaster. Reprinted with permission of The University Press of Kentucky.
70. The Filson Club Historical Society, Louisville, Ky.
71. Hubert Wilhelm and Ohio Landscape Productions
72–73. Missouri Historical Society, St. Louis
75–76. The Center for American History, The University of Texas at Austin
77. Tennessee State Museum, Nashville, Tennessee Historical Society Collection
78. Fairfax Historical Society, Fairfax, Calif.
79. Marin County Historical Society, San Rafael, Calif.
80. Nevada Historical Society, Reno
81. Used by permission, Utah State Historical Society, all rights reserved
90. Courtesy, American Antiquarian Society, Worcester, Mass.
91. Abby Aldrich Rockefeller Folk Art Center, Williamsburg, Va.
92. Courtesy, Colorado Historical Society, Denver
93. Illinois State Historical Society
94. Milwaukee Public Museum, Wis.
95. The Western Reserve Historical Society, Cleveland, Ohio

97. The Library Company of Philadelphia
98. Missouri Historical Society, St. Louis
99. Ohio Historical Society
100. Virginia Department of Historic Resources, Richmond
101. Photograph by Lee Phillips, courtesy of Alabama Historical Commission, Montgomery
102–103. Ohio Landscape Productions
104. Kentucky Heritage Council, Frankfort
105–106. Ohio Landscape Productions
108. Herb Roberts, Tennessee Department of Conservation, Division of Parks and Recreation, Sycamore Shoals State Historic Area
110. Francis Vigo Chapter, DAR
112. Birmingham Public Library, Department of Archives and Manuscripts
113. Coolidge Collection of Thomas Jefferson Manuscripts, N-48, Massachusetts Historical Society, Boston
114. Mark Dauber
116. Kentucky Heritage Council, Frankfort
117. James D. Schwartz
119. Tennessee State Museum Collection, Nashville

Index

Italized page numbers indicate illustrations.

Index

Susan Constant (ship), 20, 308
Susquehannock Indians, 82–83
Sussex County (Del.), 92
Sutherland, John, 328
Suttle, Charles, 247
Swallow Barn (Kennedy), 206
Swedenborgianism, 199
Sweeney, Joel Walker, 66
Swiss, 88, 111, 130
Sydney, Algernon, 39

Talbot, John Williston, 143
Taliaferro, Alfred, 192, 193, 194, 221, 281
Taliaferro, James, 235
Tallahassee, 218
Taney, Roger, 252
Tangier, 94
Tappahannock (Va.), 188, 285
Tayloe, Henry, 221
Taylor, Zachary, 121, 338
Tennessee, migration to, 108, 140, 141,
    144–46, 149, 150, 152, 221, 254, 279, 295
Tennessee Valley, 79
Texas: migration to, 140, 152, 181–82,
    184–86, 188, 216, 218, 220–21, 281, 282,
    295; Declaration of Independence, 328
Thames River, 76
Thayer, Eli, 292
Thornton, Mildred, 152
Thrower, Norman, 256
tidewater, 94; settlement of, 75–77; and bi-
    ological environment, 78; evolution of,
    129–32; as cradle of Virginia, 293
Tiffin, Edward, 171, 172
Tilden, Daniel, 245
Tillson, Albert, 131
Timber Ridge (Va.), 184
Tipton family, 147
tithables, 75, 95, 319
tobacco: first planting of, 18; growth of, 28,
    178, 274; glutting of European markets
    by, 31; as a cause of European-Indian
    wars, 70; trade in, 95; replacement by di-

versified agriculture, 130, 234–35, 275; as
    cause of piedmont migration, 144; as
    cause of economic depression, 205–6;
    nomenclature, 225. See also agriculture
Tocqueville, Alexis de, 204, 222
toleration, 129, 132, 177, 294
Toleration Act, 46, 104–5, 107
Toryism, 93, 143
Toulmin, Harry, 215
Townes, Samuel, 281
towns, planning of, 256
Townsend, John, 189
Transylvania University, 281
Trappan'd Maiden, The (song), 44
Travers, Raleigh, 85
Treaty of Greenville, 171
Treaty of Lancaster, 165
Trist, Elizabeth, 203
Trist, Nicholas, 216, 218
Trist, Randolph, 218
Tuckahoe (Va.), 263, 264
Tucker, George, 205
Tucker, William, 27
Tucker, William Beverley, 205
Tugaloo Valley (S.C.), 143
Turkey Island Creek, 95
Turner, Frederick Jackson: and the
    Columbian Exposition, 1, 2, 3; as social
    historian, 11; failure to acknowledge biol-
    ogy, 78; and oceans, 93; and log cabins,
    122; conception of "frontier," 136. See
    also frontier thesis
Turner, Nat, 134, 208, 209
Tustin, William Isaac, 188
Twain, Mark, 180
Tyler, George Colbert, 189

University of Virginia, 186
Utopia (More), 16

Valador (ship), 239
Valley of Shenandoah (Tucker), 205
Vasquez, Rafael, 186

JUN 2000